I0793172

IMAGES
of America

PLEASANT GARDEN

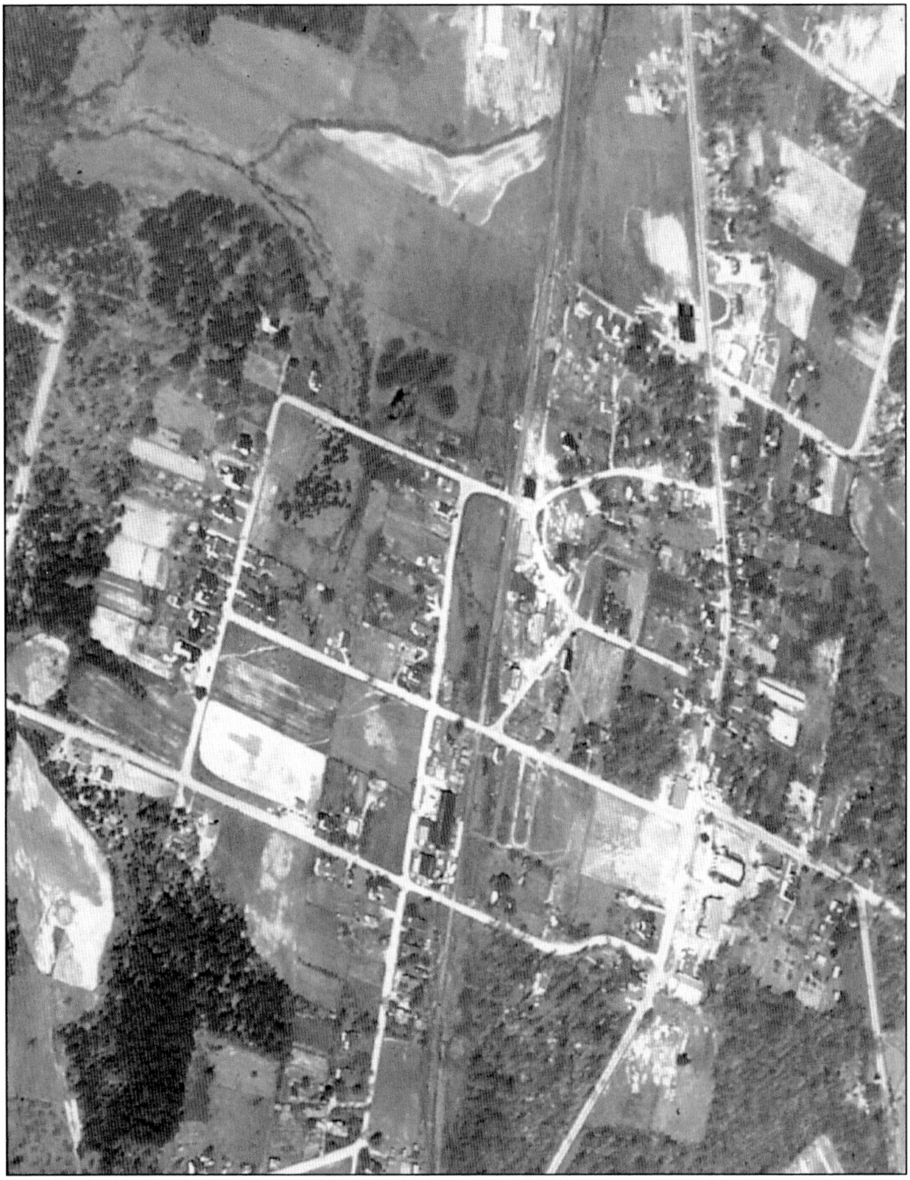

N.B. Cheek Jr. enlisted Jack Reddick to fly over familiar territory so Cheek could capture this view of Pleasant Garden as it existed in 1948. At the top of the photograph is the newly opened Boren Brick Plant. As Pleasant Garden Road winds to the south, it is intersected by Forest Acres Circle, Laurel Knoll, Briarcrest, Thrower, Neelley, and Sheraton Park Roads. Two roads in this image no longer exist because Founders Furniture and Pleasant Garden Dry Kiln expanded their operations. The red-clay baseball field across the road from the school awaits the season opener. (Author's collection.)

On the Cover: Principal Eugene D. Idol is right of center on the second row amidst the 1921 student body of Pleasant Garden High School. He served as principal from 1919 to 1925 and 1932 to 1942. The family returned to the village permanently in 1945, when Idol was named Guilford County superintendent of schools. (Author's collection.)

IMAGES
of America

PLEASANT GARDEN

Nancy Jo Smith

ARCADIA
PUBLISHING

ISBN 978-1-4671-3383-8

Published by Arcadia Publishing
Charleston, South Carolina

Printed in the United States of America

Library of Congress Control Number: 2015932704

For all general information, please contact Arcadia Publishing:
Telephone 843-853-2070
Fax 843-853-0044
E-mail sales@arcadiapublishing.com
For customer service and orders:
Toll-Free 1-888-313-2665

Visit us on the Internet at www.arcadiapublishing.com

With humble appreciation and deep affection for my family and friends

Contents

ACKNOWLEDGMENTS

Although I have lived in Pleasant Garden nearly all of my life, I realize that I still know only bits and pieces of its story. Approximately 15 years ago, I began spending Sunday afternoons scanning the *Greensboro Patriot* microfiche collection in the Greensboro Public Library, where I discovered entries from early 20th-century correspondents who regularly reported Pleasant Garden happenings. Armed with this new information, I shared the details with the late Mary Clapp, then listened to her version. The late Bill Shore provided more details about life in the 1930s and 1940s.

Invaluable professional assistance came from Les Eger, Guilford County planner; Chandra Burch in the North Carolina Preservation Office; and Elise Allison, archivist with the Greensboro Historical Museum. William Heroy, owner of Old Photo Specialist, made high-resolution copies of large faded photographs.

It has been a pleasure to renew friendships and make new ones in the process of gathering materials for this book. Phillip Way gave me access to his vintage photographs. Ruth Ann Marley Jones was especially helpful by her family archives and proofreading the manuscript. Ellen Osborne found old yearbooks that fleshed out the 1930s. Martha Boren and JoAnne Davis loaned photographs from the 1960s. Many others are noted throughout the book. There were also those who recognized faces from the past and shared memories. Thank you all.

Some images in this volume appear courtesy of Carol W. Martin/Greensboro Historical Museum Collection (CWM) or North Carolina Historic Preservation Office (NCHPO); unless otherwise noted, the rest of the images are from the author's personal collection.

Introduction

As the population grew in Pennsylvania, land became more scarce and more expensive. Those who lived near the cities expected newcomers to live on the frontier and serve as buffer or protection from the Native Americans they were displacing. The opportunity to buy land at an affordable price set the stage for a mass exodus of Scots Irish and German immigrants to make their way south down the Great Wagon Road through the Shenandoah Valley to the backwoods of North Carolina beginning around 1750.

The differences in language and religion caused the groups who entered piedmont North Carolina to settle among those of similar backgrounds. As a rule, Germans were farmers; Scots Irish were herders. Their differences were minimal when compared to those that separated yeoman farmers from the planters living in the tidewater. That area enjoyed its association the Church of England. The backwoodsmen were Presbyterians, Lutherans, Quakers, and Baptists.

It was nearly impossible to get a patent (title) because ownership was entangled, a situation that remained until after the Revolutionary War. The buyer was expected to travel to the county seat to record a deed. For future Pleasant Gardeners, that would have been Hillsborough or Salisbury, since Guilford County was created from portions of Orange and Rowan Counties. When the tax collector arrived and unrealistically demanded to be paid in silver, unable to comply, the settlers were left to move again. Tensions grew between the yeomen farmers and the royal government, culminating in May 1771 at the Battle of Alamance. Governor Tryon personally commanded the militia to fire upon protesters. The short confrontation sent the Regulators into hiding; many packed up and left.

While the fight was with England, in reality it was neighbor against neighbor in this region. Among Regulators from this area who were captured after the Battle of Alamance were several members of the William Field family. They were paroled on the condition that they swore allegiance to the Crown. By honoring that pledge, they became Tories and suffered defeat again.

One of the important battles in the Revolutionary War, the Battle of Guilford Courthouse occurred approximately 15 miles from this sparsely populated region. Troops from both sides would march through as they left the field of battle on March 15, 1781. After North Carolina ceased to be a British colony, it did not take long for the local officials to confiscate the property of those they determined to be Tories, or representing the Crown. According to some sources, the process was to their benefit.

Large family groups left the landlocked Eastern Shore of Maryland because there was not enough land to support the ever-increasing population and the practice of primogeniture, the eldest male inheriting the family property. It is likely the Kirkmans, Sullivans, Sherwoods, Hendrixes, Hacketts, and others who moved from Dorchester, Caroline, and Cecil Counties were the younger children. Some of them stayed in the area, but within 20 years, others were on their way to settle another frontier.

The Marylanders were aligned with the Wesleyan movement within the Anglican Church known as Methodism. They settled between two of the oldest congregations in the county, Alamance Presbyterian and Centre Friends. The rationale of the name Pleasant Garden is not known, but that Methodist Episcopal church established between 1788 and 1792 became the name source for the settlement, the village, and then the town. Within the next 20 years, other Methodist churches formed within five miles, as the population spread across the land.

In the 1830s, economic conditions were bleak, and there was unrest over the issue of slavery; as debts mounted, farm families moved out to Indiana and Ohio. That migration became opportunity for men like Fisher B. Taylor, Frederick Fentress, and William Dickey Ross, who acquired enough land that upon reaching adulthood, each of their children had a sizable farm.

Fisher B. Taylor owned land that stretched from the center of the village to Ritters Lake Road and beyond. He even bought a mill near New Salem. A newcomer from Delaware, he and North Carolina–born Jane Craft married in 1815 and reared nine children. The Taylors were members of the Methodist church. Fisher participated in the life of the community by serving when called for jury duty, maintaining roads, and laying off estates. He died within two months of the beginning of the Civil War. Documents exist that tell of the hardships Jane endured at the end of the war, with troops foraging her cattle and fences.

Most of the land Frederick Fentress accrued was south of the village. Of the three men, he was the most politically active and enterprising. In 1842, Fentress Post Office was established at his home, and he was appointed justice for his militia/tax district. The 18 districts in Guilford County became townships in 1868. In recognition of his years of leadership, Fentress Township was named for him.

William Dickey Ross bought land early in his married life that became the heart of the village of Pleasant Garden. The land he and Elizabeth Hendrix Ross made available for Pleasant Garden Academy in 1868 would play a major role in the development of the village.

The 1880 US Census enumerator J.M. Fentriss listed on a single page a total of 15 persons living in five residences in the vilage [*sic*] of Pleasant Garden. The heads of household were Esther Ross, keeper of a boardinghouse; G.L. Stalker, shoe and bootmaker; Geo. W. Ross, physician; P.L. Groome, minister of the Gospel; and F.M. Watson, farmer. Fentriss also noted that there was a church, seminary (or academy), parsonage, and post office.

Two big events took place during 1883 and 1884 that proved to be pivotal for the little village. Dr. George W. Ross sold his farm to John and Rebecca Kearns Riley, and their son and daughter-in-law, Peter Manley and Clarinda Johnson Riley. Perhaps more important was the arrival of the Atlantic and Yadkin Railway. Two decades later after the death of John Riley, William C. Tucker, Edgar R. Tucker, and Luke W. White bought the 89-acre Riley farm. Then, William H. Ragan joined with the Tucker cousins to found the Pleasant Garden Company. Thus begins the 20th-century story Pleasant Garden.

One

The Early Years

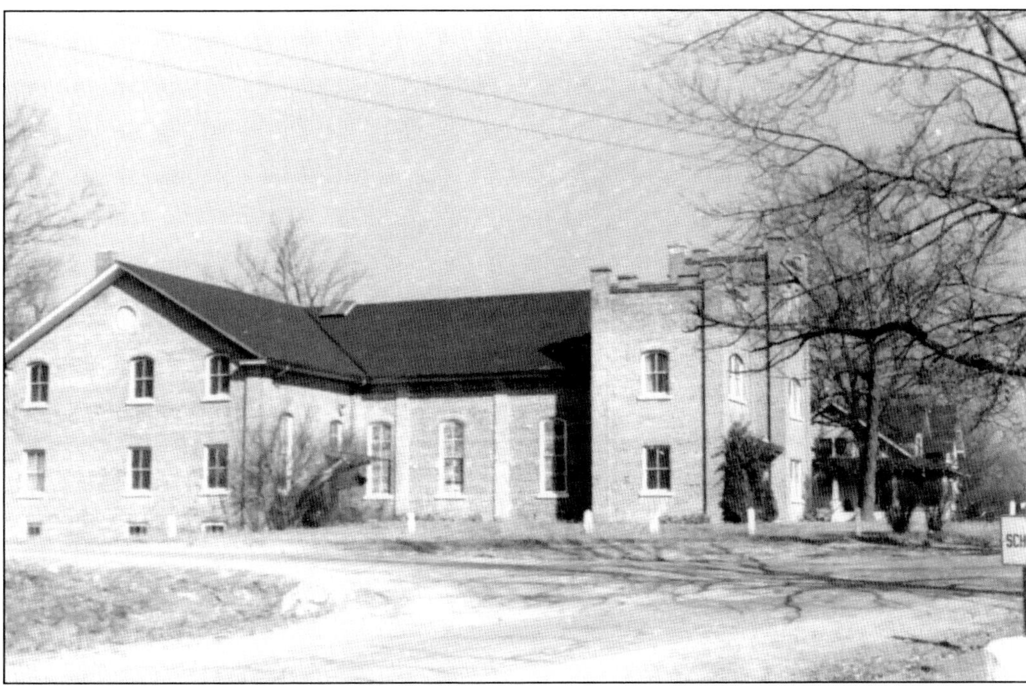

Pleasant Garden Methodist Episcopal Church, established in 1792, is the name source of the town. This 1947 photograph shows the third and fourth church buildings. The center portion is the sanctuary constructed in 1892 of locally made bricks during the pastorate of the Reverend Moses Jackson Hunt. His son William Baker Hunt, a contractor, led the expansion and remodeling effort that began in 1921. It included the front towers and large classroom addition. (Courtesy of Phillip Way.)

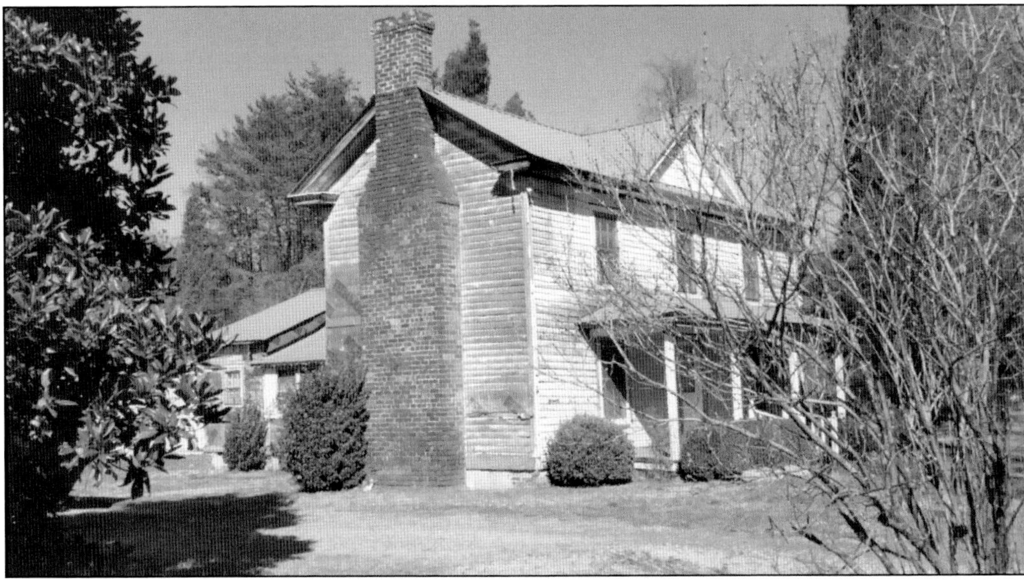

Photographed in 2006, the William Dickey and Elizabeth Hendrix Ross house most likely dates to 1856, when he bought a 573-acre farm that was sold to settle Vincent Russom's debts after Russom moved west. Pleasant Garden Academy and Pleasant Garden Methodist Church received deeds out of this tract for token payments. As the three Ross sons came of age, they were given land. Annie Virginia Ross received her share upon her father's death in 1905; a portion of this became Westdale Acres. The Julius Ross land faced Steeple Chase Road, once called Ross Road; John Frank Ross's land was on Sheraton Park Road. Dr. George Washington Ross and his wife, Frances Erwin, lived within the village of Pleasant Garden, as noted in the 1880 census. Shortly before the Atlantic and Yadkin Railway came through his farm in 1884, they moved to Randolph County, where he practiced medicine in Randleman. Widowed within a year, Frances Erwin Ross entered the business world as a single mother of two sons. Both sons became physicians; one, Dr. Floyd Ross, established North Carolina's first public-health department, in Guilford County.

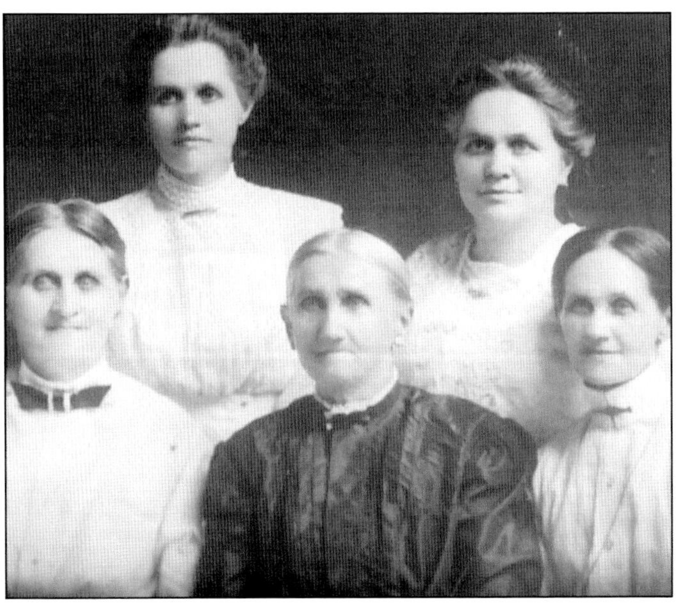

Nancy Letitia Hendrix Ross (1836–1923) would have known her pioneer grandparents Henry and Mary Kirkman Hendrix. They were among the first members of Pleasant Garden Methodist Episcopal Church. Ross and her elder sister attended Greensboro College and married brothers: Elizabeth, William Dickey; and Letitia, Addison Sheppard Ross. She is shown in the center of four of their 12 children around 1900. Counterclockwise from lower left are Julia Hodgin, Letitia, Mary Hunt, Lalah Perkins, and Bette Landreth. (Courtesy of Phal Hodgin.)

William Charles and Georgia Greeson Kirkman are pictured here around the time of their 1895 marriage. An ancestor, George Kirkman, migrated to Guilford County from the Eastern Shore of Maryland and was among the trustees who received the deed for Pleasant Garden Methodist Episcopal Church in 1792. Most of the elder Kirkman's descendants moved to Kentucky and Illinois. (Courtesy of Jane Kimel.)

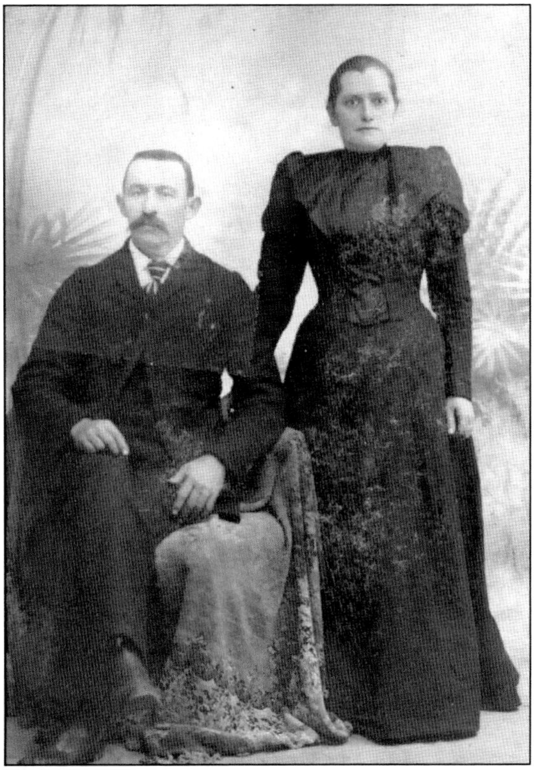

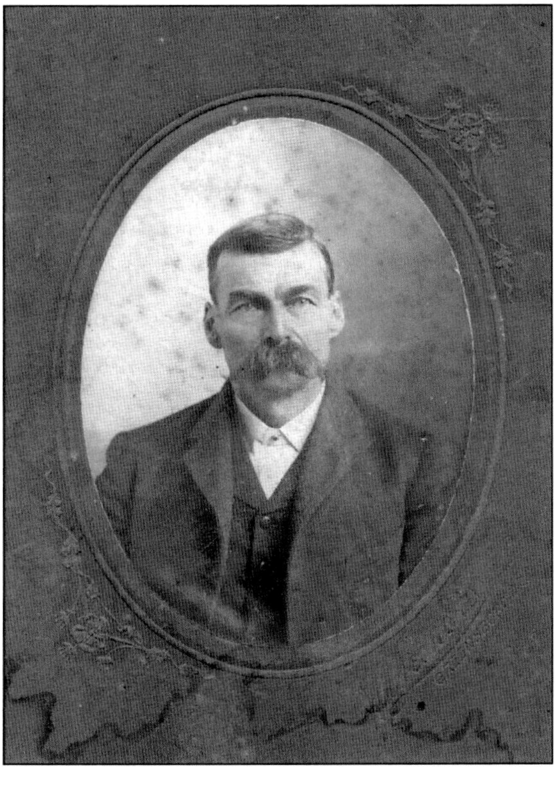

John L. Riley and his son Peter Manley Riley (pictured) and their respective wives, Rebecca Kearns and Clarinda Johnson, from Randolph County bought an 89-acre tract from George Washington Ross in 1885. After the elder Riley's death, William Council Tucker, Edgar Rankin Tucker, and Luke Wellesby White bought the entire farm in 1907. That land formed the heart of the village of Pleasant Garden. (Courtesy of Martha Oakes.)

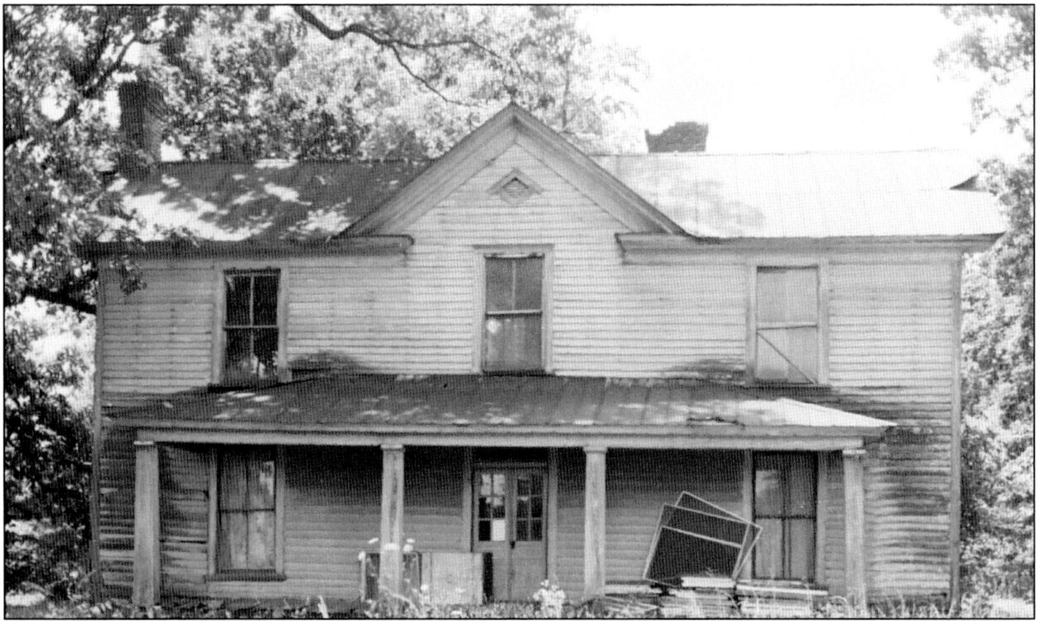

Adger and Maud Hodgin Kirkman built this 3,000-square-foot farmhouse around 1900. It was unique for the era, consisting of a pair of two-story I-shaped buildings that intersected to form a T. According to the family, it was designed to house Pleasant Garden Academy boarding students. (Courtesy of NCHPO.)

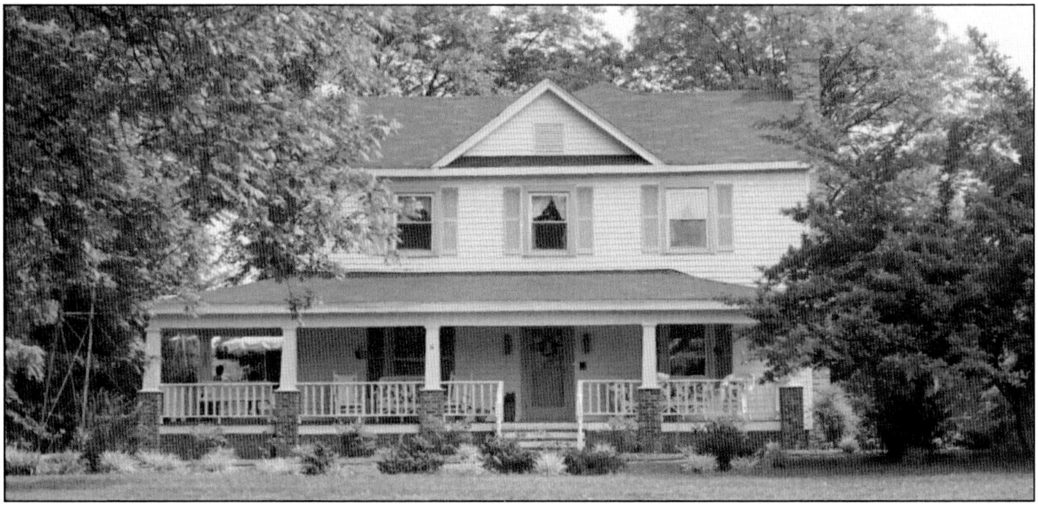

Frederick Fentress built this home around 1857. He married Sarah Macy in 1840; she was the daughter of a Nantucket Quaker, John Macy, to whom Fentress was bound as a child. They had eight children. After Sarah's death, Fentress married Mariah Ross. They also had eight children. An enterprising businessman, Frederick acquired more than 8,000 acres of land, sold commodities, and became a stockholder of the Bank of North Carolina. For many years, he was a Guilford County justice of the peace; the district he represented was named Fentress Township in 1868 when the North Carolina Constitution established townships in each county. A post office established at his home in 1842, where he served as its postmaster for 25 years, also bore his name. His daughters Callie and Rachel were the last Fentress postmasters before the Pleasant Garden Post Office was established in 1876. (Courtesy of NCHPO.)

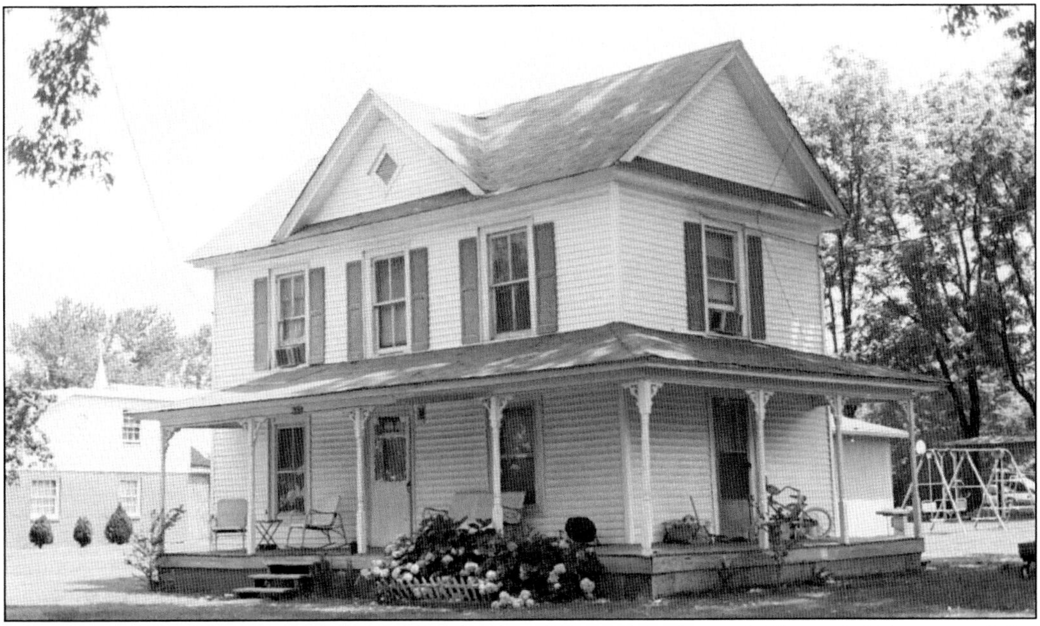

In 1911, Victor and Hattie Riley Rockfield, a daughter of Manley and Clarinda Riley, raised the roof of their one-story cottage. She was Pleasant Garden postmaster from 1905 to 1912, using a room in their home with a southern entrance. Golden and Grace Washburn bought it in the 1940s. The house in the background was remodeled and used as a church, Pleasant Garden Friends; it later became Lighthouse Baptist. (Courtesy of NCHPO.)

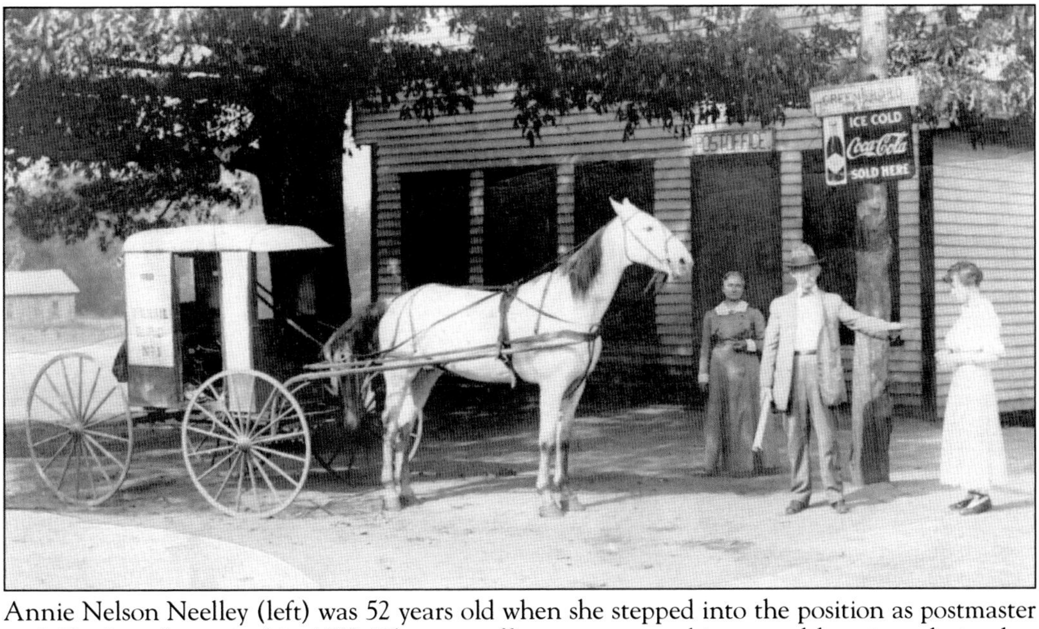

Annie Nelson Neelley (left) was 52 years old when she stepped into the position as postmaster and 65 when she retired in 1927. The post office was operated in several locations during her tenure. Dr. Robert Fentress (center) became the first Pleasant Garden rural mail carrier in 1905. Agnes Neelley is the young lady on the right in this photograph from about 1915. Annie Hanner Causey was employed as a mail messenger; she carried the mail to the post office from the depot. (Courtesy of Phillip Way.)

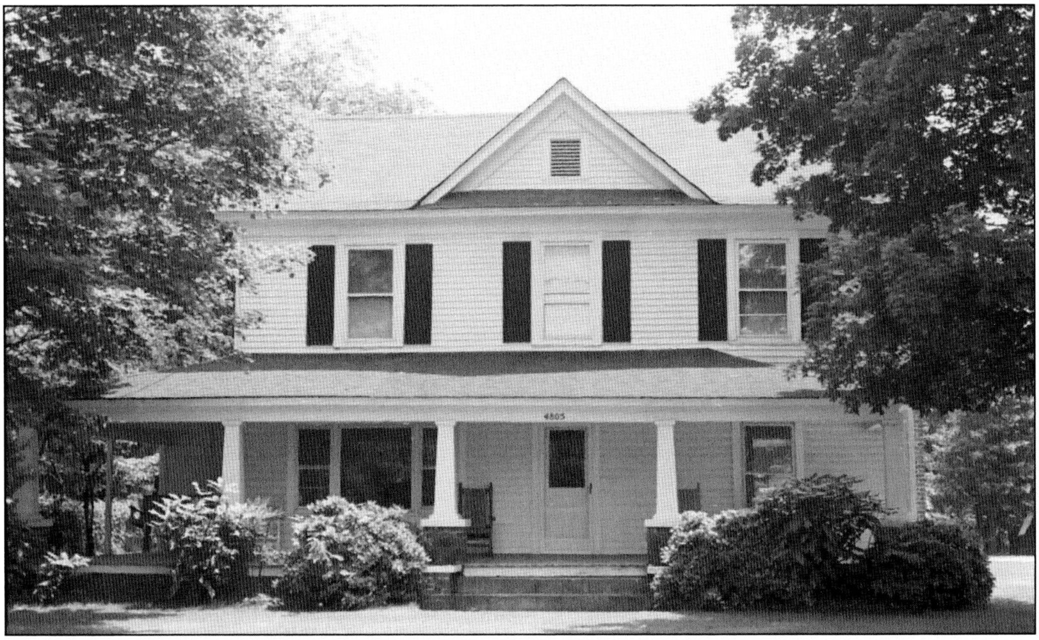

Jonathan Brooks and Sarah Brown Watlington's arrival in Pleasant Garden with their young son, Paul, direct from Manchester hunting preserve, was announced by the *Greensboro Patriot* in the fall of 1911. He was to supervise a new dormitory, which may have been this house. (Courtesy of NCHPO.)

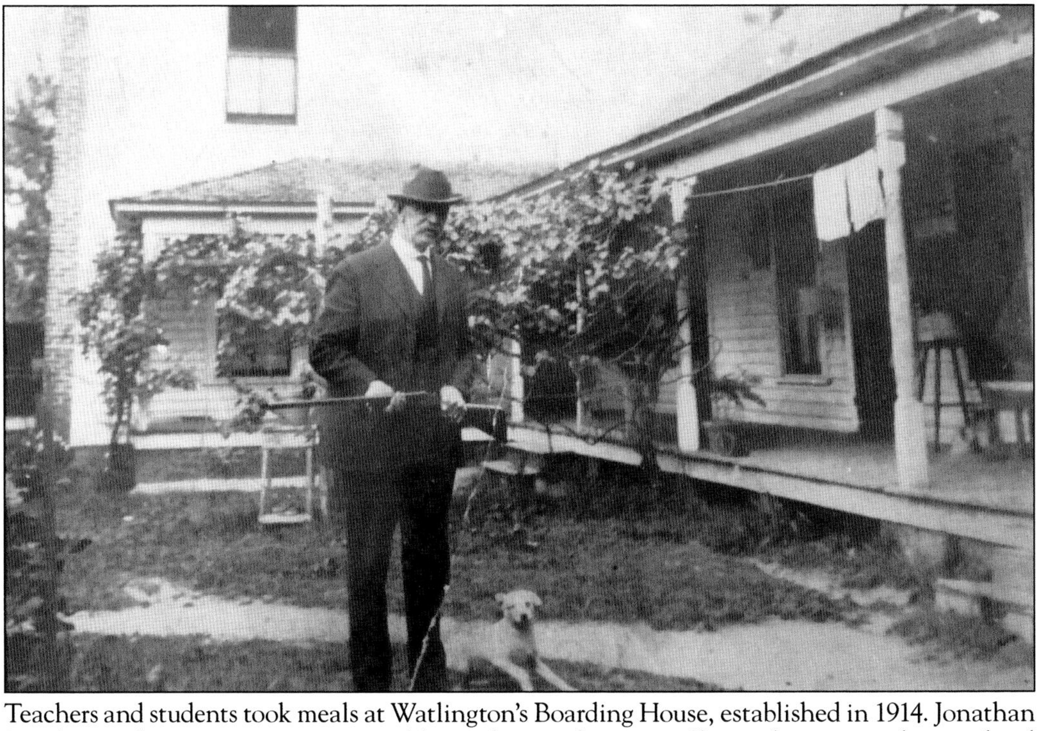

Teachers and students took meals at Watlington's Boarding House, established in 1914. Jonathan Brooks Watlington was a notary public and named truant officer when compulsory school attendance became the law. (Courtesy of Phillip Way.)

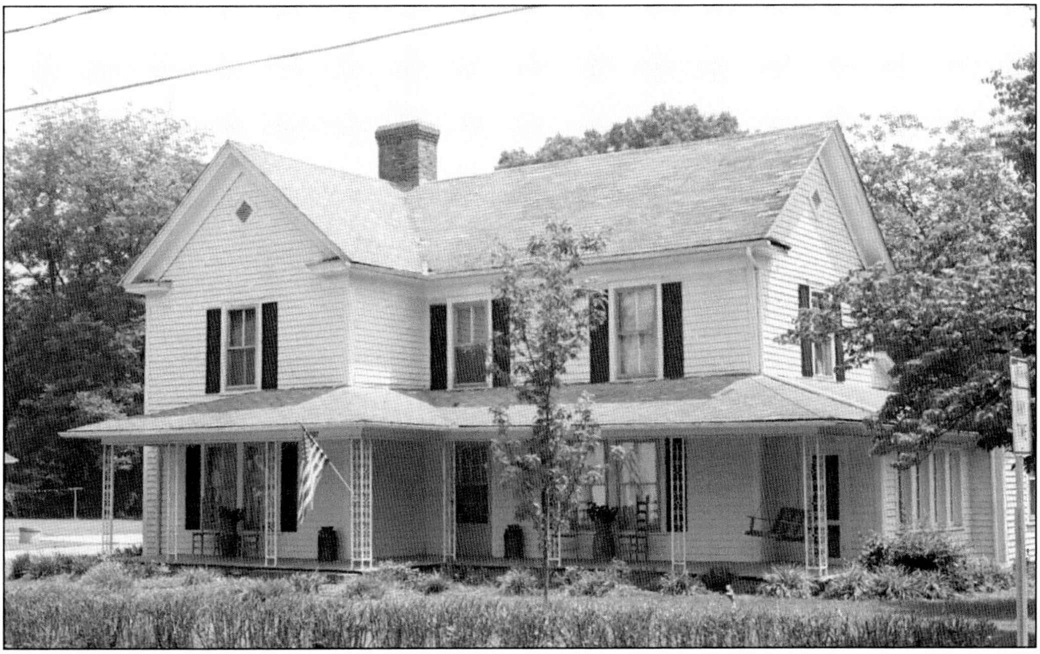

John B. Hockett may have built the house Thomas Hicks sold to E.R. Tucker in 1924. Hicks was the miller for Pleasant Garden Company and later superintendent of the Guilford County Home. Edgar Rankin and Margaret Coble Tucker, graduates of Pleasant Garden Academy, were married in 1894. They enjoyed a wide circle of friends who were pleased that the Tuckers and their young family returned to the village from Greensboro, where he was co-owner of Tucker-Erwin Grocery on South Elm Street until their move in 1907. (Courtesy of NCHPO.)

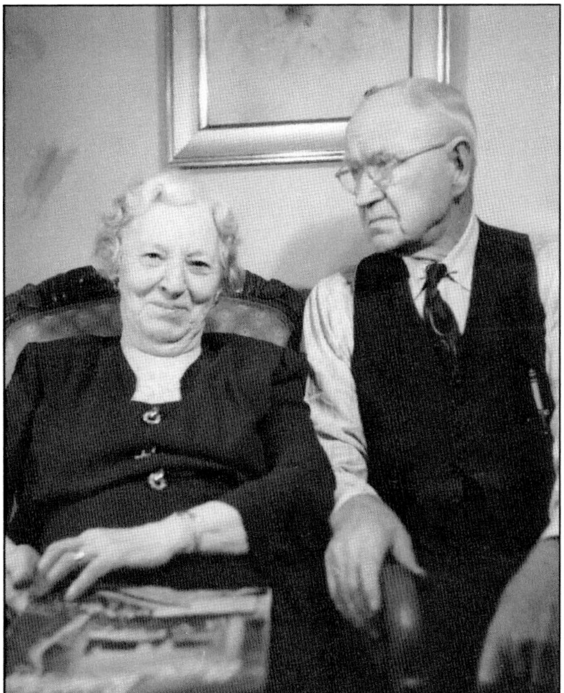

This photograph was made at the time of the E.R. Tuckers' 50th wedding anniversary. Tucker was renowned as a dapper dresser. He developed real estate, sold insurance, and operated a grocery store. Margaret Coble Tucker began playing the organ for church at the age of five, before her feet reached the pedals. Later, she directed the choir and led a youth group, the Epworth League.

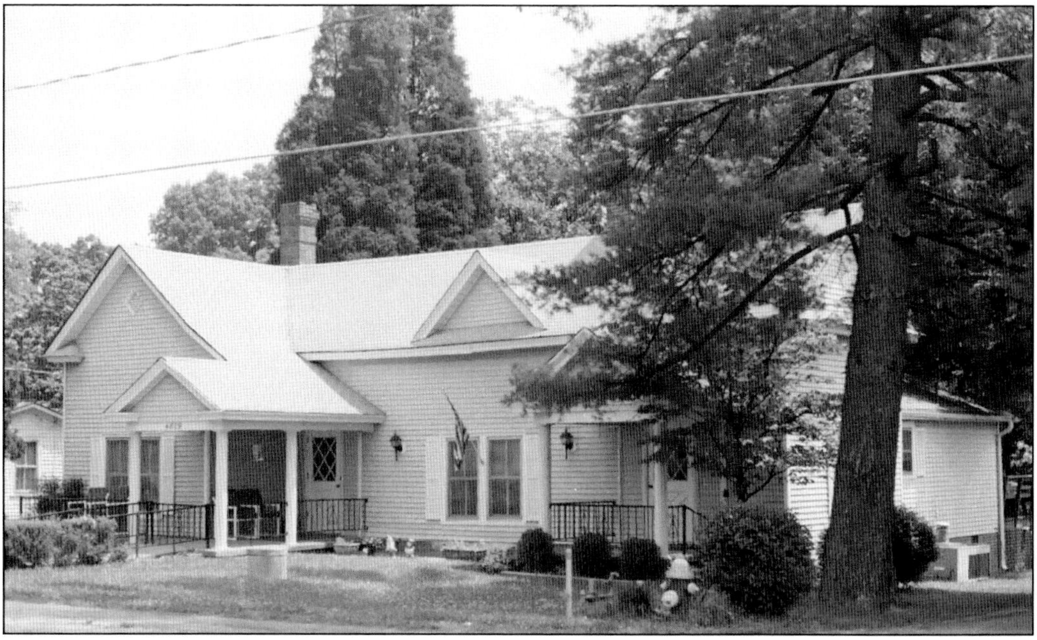

Arthur Lee Teachey came to Pleasant Garden in 1915 to teach agriculture. He rose through the ranks to became state supervisor of vocational agriculture for North Carolina. He and Lacy Dickens were married in 1918, shortly after her high school graduation. Lacy's father, C.E. Dickens, was superintendent of the ill-fated Fentress Mine. After his death, she inherited this house in 1928 and other properties he owned. (Courtesy of NCHPO.)

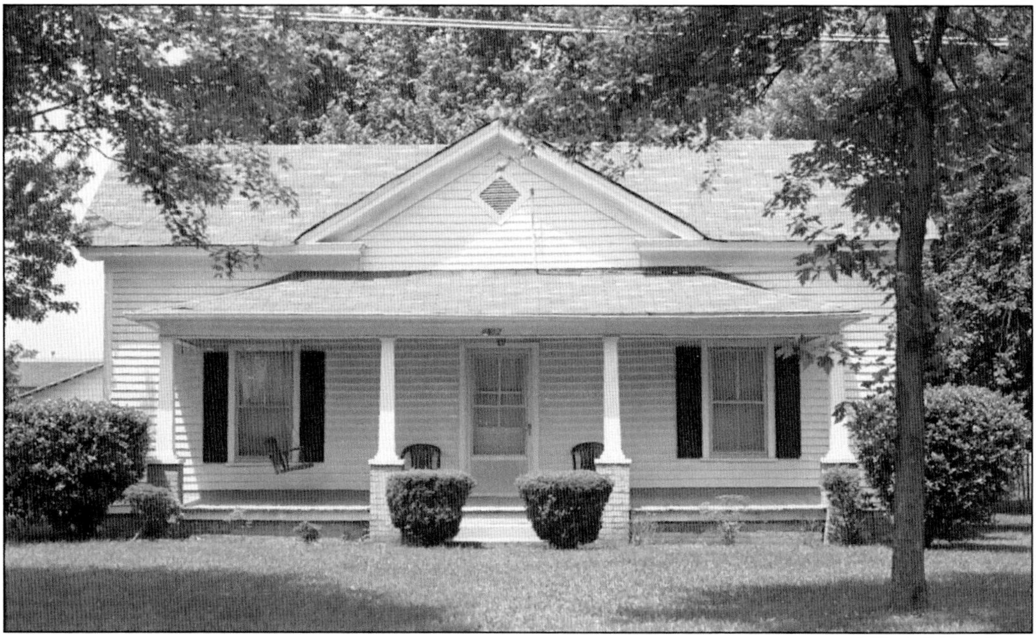

Dr. Robert Fentress, a widower and father of two, gave up dentistry and moved into the village when his house burned. He joined daughter Lena and her husband, Marvin Murrow, when they moved to Bonlee in Chatham County to open a hunting lodge. Arthur Lee and Lacy Dickens Teachey were the first of many to live in this house after Fentress. (Courtesy of NCHPO.)

Mary Mendenhall and Daniel Gillespie Neelley, shown here in a late 19th-century portrait, lived in a house on the crest of a hill overlooking the road that bears their family name. He was the only child of Elizabeth Gillespie and James Neelley, who built the house as early as the 1840's. The Neelley, Gillespie, and Mendenhall families were living in Guilford County prior to the Revolutionary War. The first two were Presbyterians; the latter, Quaker. (Courtesy of Stanley Cichowicz.)

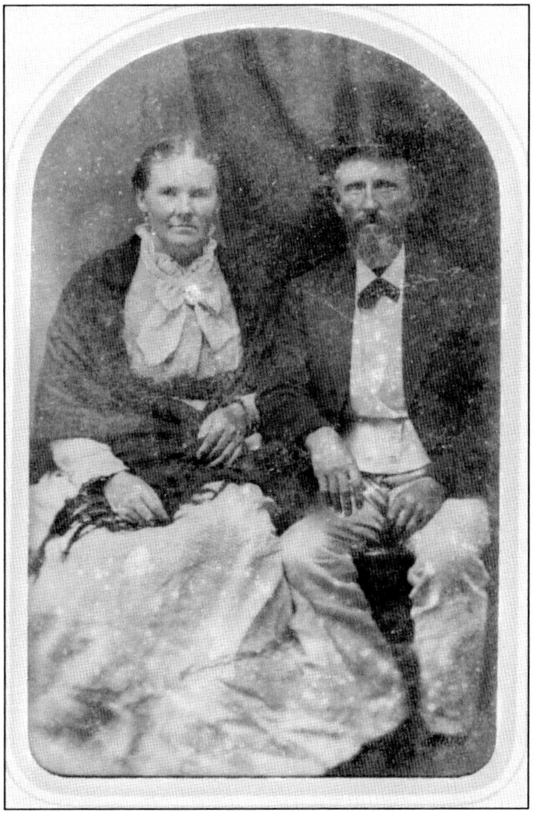

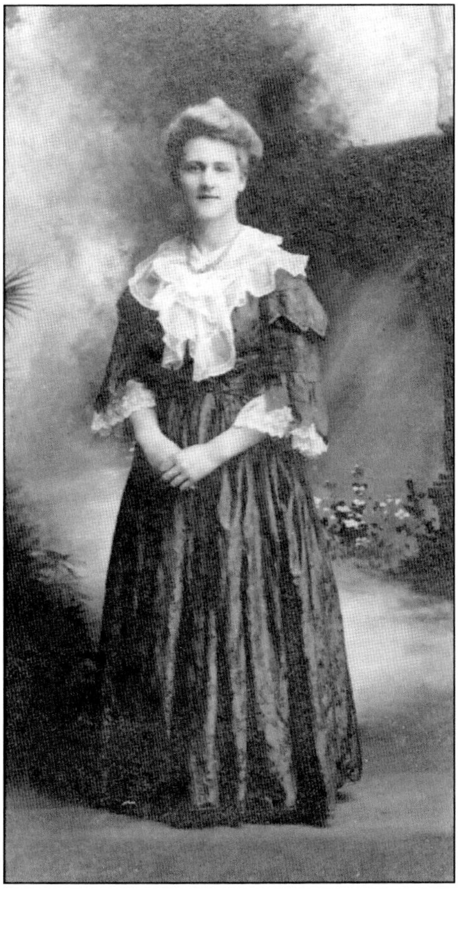

The second child of Annie and Julius Neelley, Mary Frances Neelley was an early graduate of Pleasant Garden High School. She received a scholarship to study at the State Normal and Industrial College, now the University of North Carolina at Greensboro. Tragically, Mary Frances contracted tuberculosis and died in 1912, at the age of 21. She was among a dozen or so young adults who lived in the heart of the village who succumbed to this disease in the early 1900s. (Courtesy of Stanley Cichowicz.)

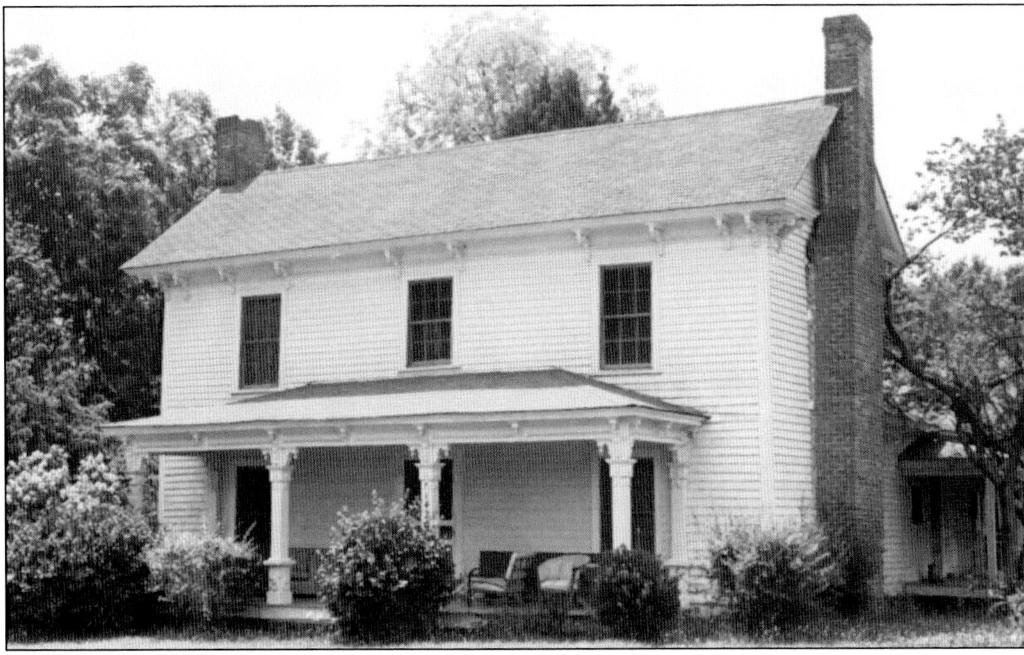

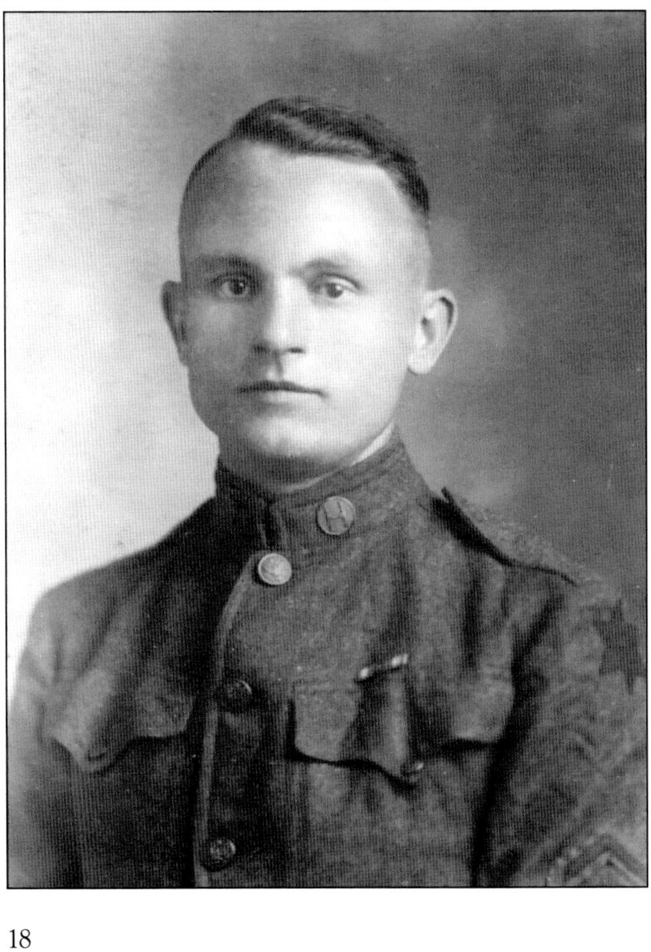

The eldest son of D.G. and Mary M. Neelley, Julius Neelley completed this house in 1887 shortly before he married Annie Nelson. He was a farmer. After rearing five children, she held a variety of jobs—postmaster, depot agent, and recording birth and death certificates when serving as registrar of vital statistics for Fentress Township. (Courtesy of NCHPO.)

Annie and Julius Neelley were the parents of five children. Beatrix and Mary died young, and Ione never married. Placcida and Elmo Michael had five children. Their only son, Noel Gillespie Neelley, was a flagman for the Atlantic Coast Line Railroad when he was shipped overseas to fight in World War I. Upon returning, he promptly returned to Wilmington and resumed his former occupation. He retired as a railroad conductor, living to be 92 years old. (Courtesy of Stanley Cichowicz.)

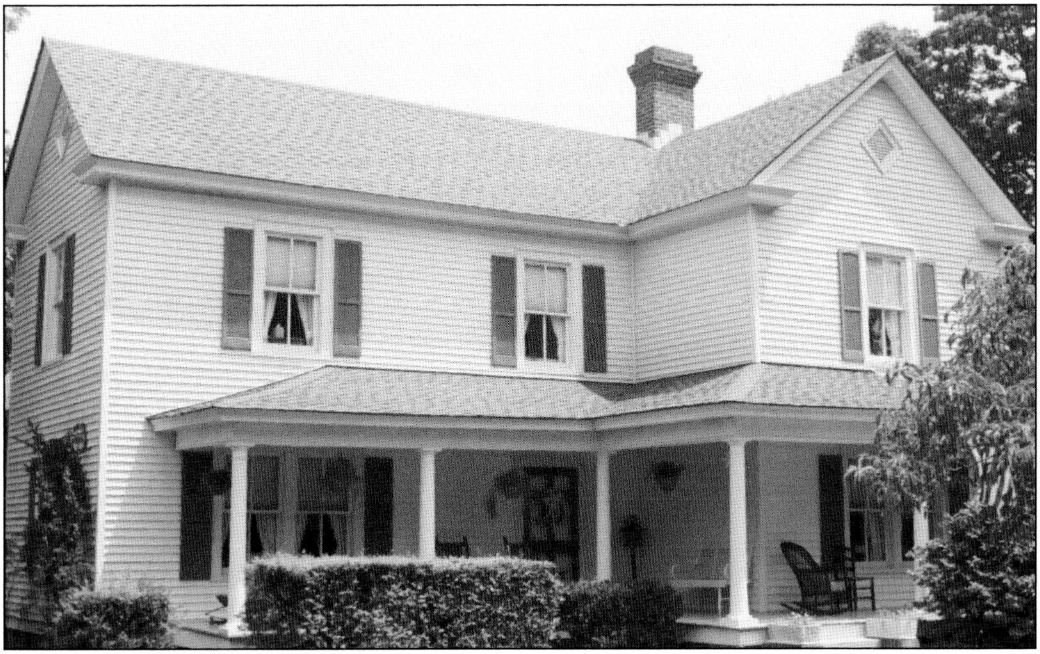

Charles Francis and Emma Stanley Neelley lived in Greensboro during the early years of their marriage. He worked in law enforcement; at one time, he was chief of police in Greensboro and Madison. After they built this house around 1910, Emma usually stayed in Pleasant Garden with the children. When he served as constable for Badin, North Carolina, the family moved there and rented out to newcomers. (Courtesy of NCHPO.)

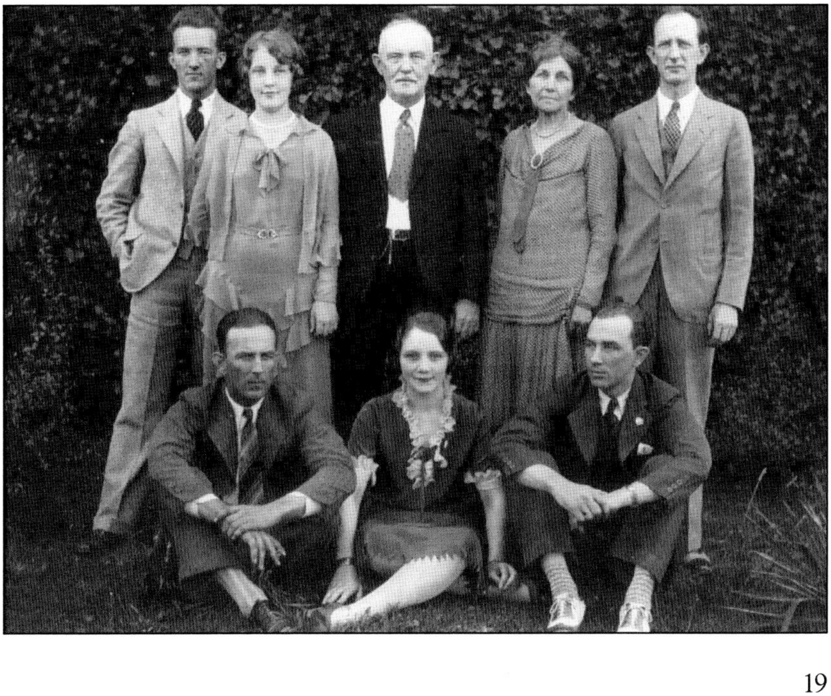

The Charles F. Neelley family poses for this photograph in the 1920s. They are, from left to right, (first row) Ralph, Doris, and Charles; (second row) Worth, Mildred, Charles F., Emma, and Harry. Charles and Ralph lived in Pleasant Garden; the others, nearby. (Courtesy of Rosa Nesbitt.)

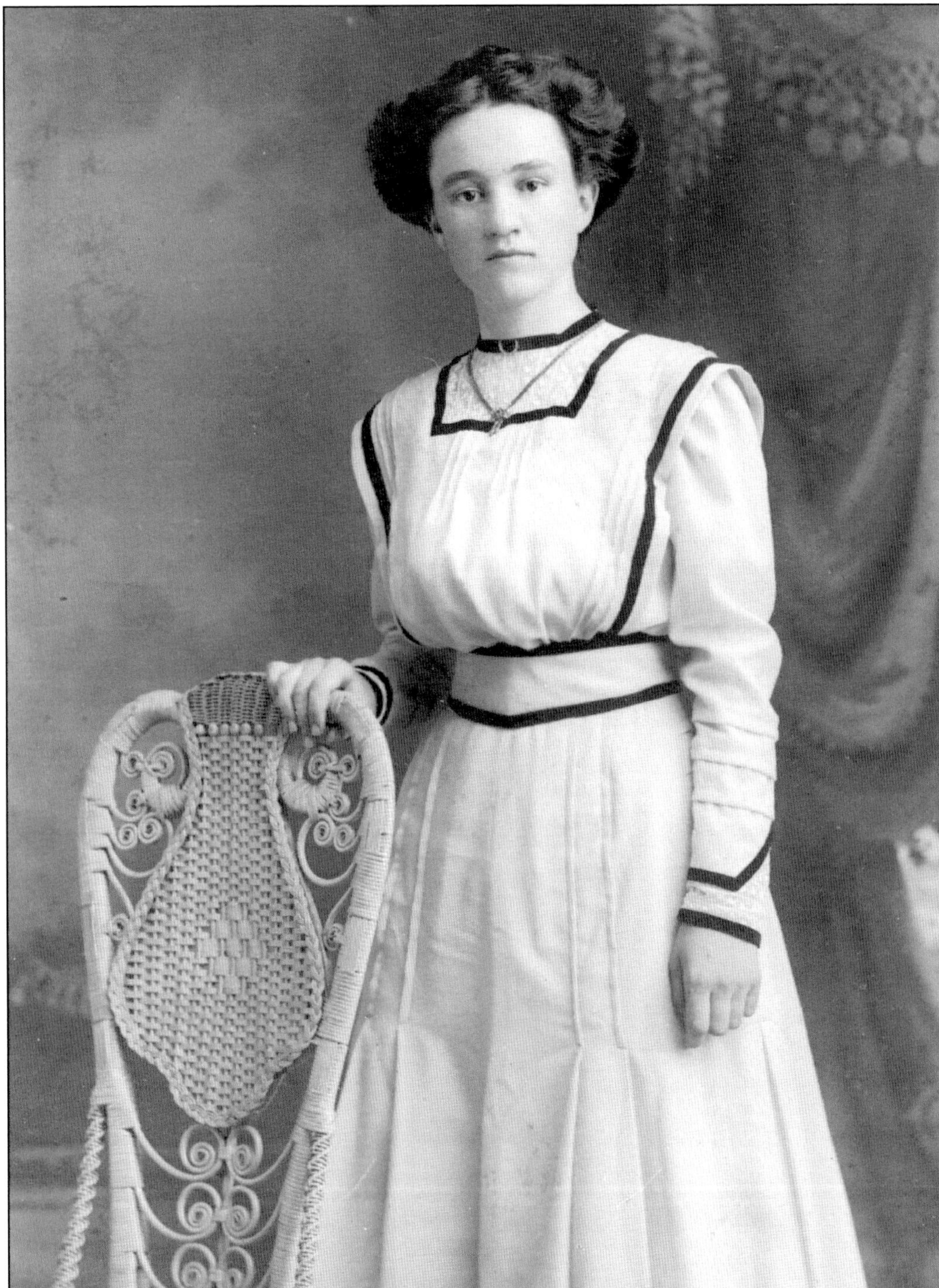

Placcida Neelley and her neighbor/suitor Elmo Michael attempted to elope twice; each attempt was foiled by her father, Julius Neelley, who told her that she could not get married before she was 18. The Michaels were married two days after her 18th birthday, in 1911. (Courtesy of Stanley Cichowicz.)

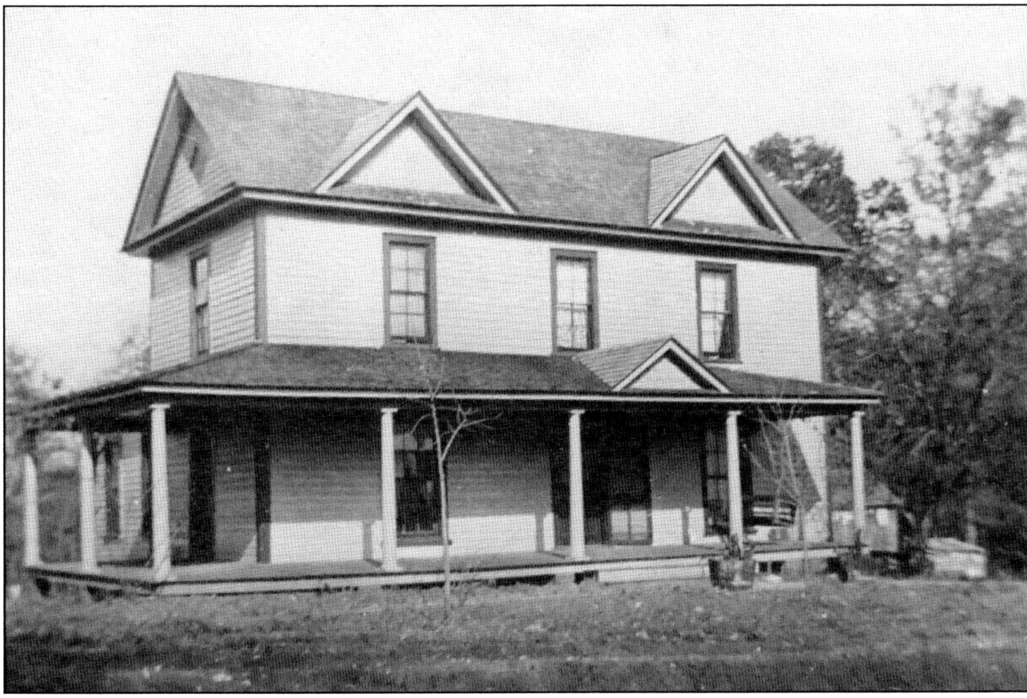

The parsonage of Pleasant Garden Methodist Episcopal Church was home to itinerant clergy from 1883 until 1909, when Ada Michael, a math and Latin teacher at the new high school became the owner. Single and a 1900 graduate of Elon College, she became the de facto head of her family. When Michael left the village in 1917, Emma Nora Smith bought the house. (Courtesy of Stanley Cichowicz.)

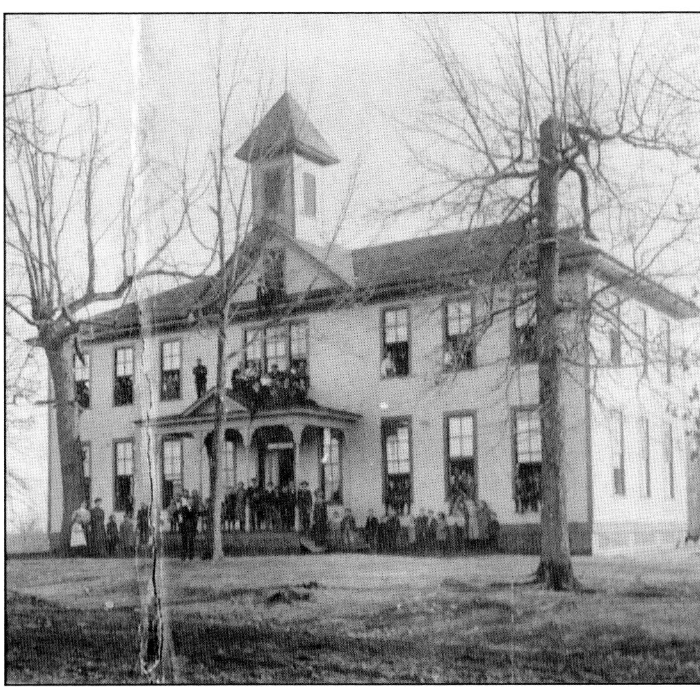

In 1903, Fentress Township was one of the first in North Carolina to vote a special tax to fund public schools. The issue passed 93-20. The school was centrally located in Pleasant Garden and opened in 1905, housing first through tenth grades. The high school was tuition-free to all township students above the seventh grade. Rugby School closed because it was nearby. The corner schools—Cedar Hill, Tucker, Piney Grove, and Fields—received new buildings and patent desks and continued to educate children near their homes through the seventh grade. (Courtesy of Phillip Way.)

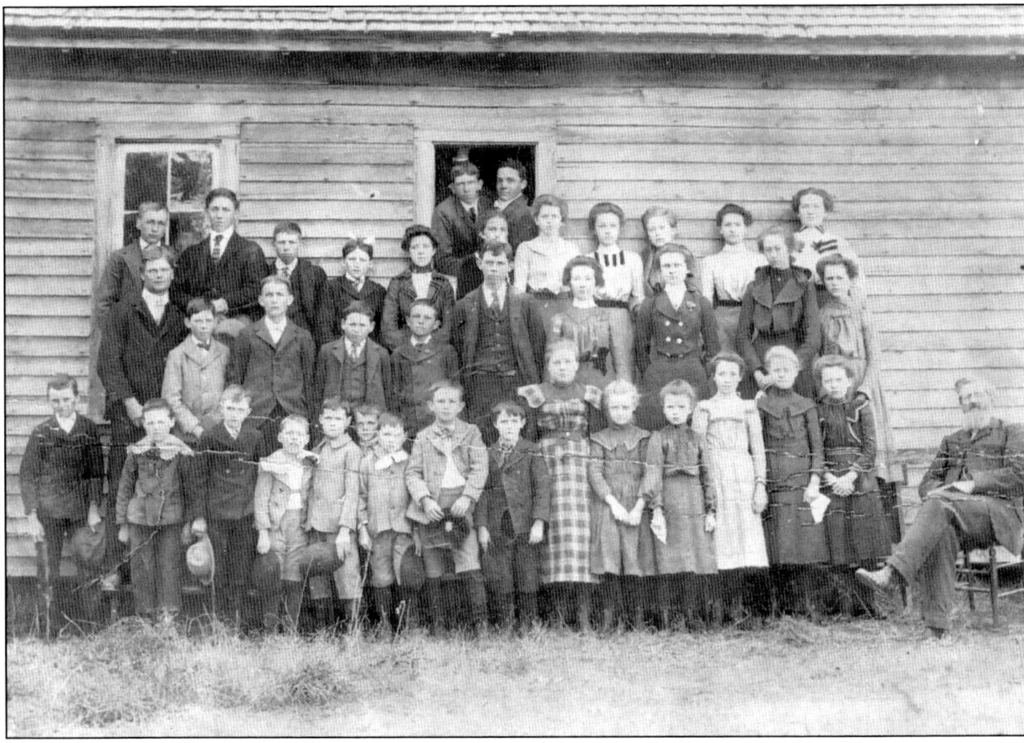

Cedar Hill School was a two-room schoolhouse located in the northern section of Fentress Township known as Vandalia. It is pictured here around 1905, when Prof. Will Rankin conducted the school. When the school merged with Pleasant Garden in 1923, D.W. Tucker bought the 1.25 acres of land and building for $175. (Courtesy of David N. Kirkman.)

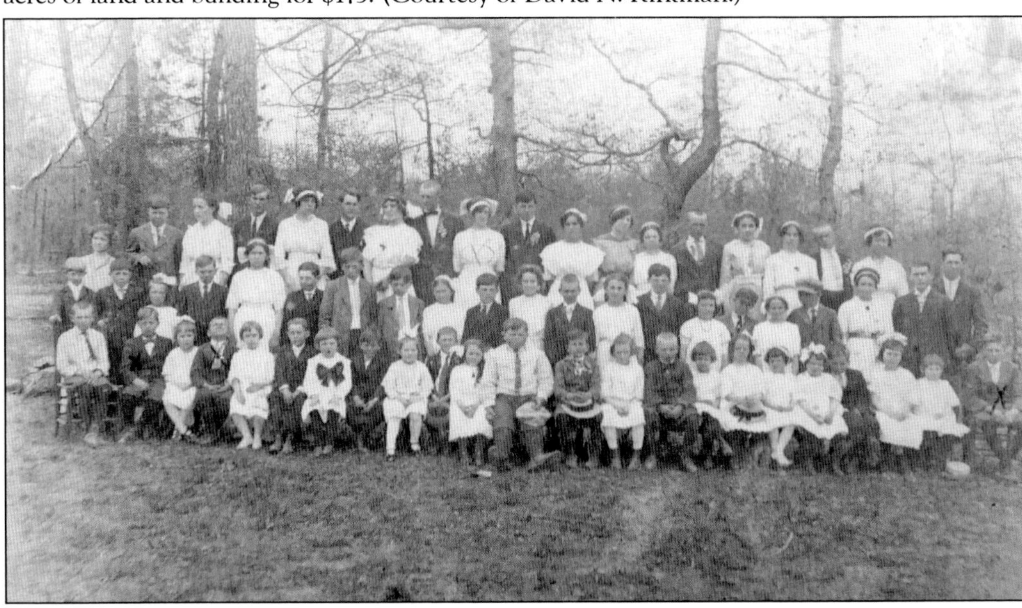

Oak Hill School, once known as Fields School, was near Bethlehem Church. It was in existence until 1925. This photograph was made during year-end exercises around 1915. (Courtesy of Ruth Ann Jones.)

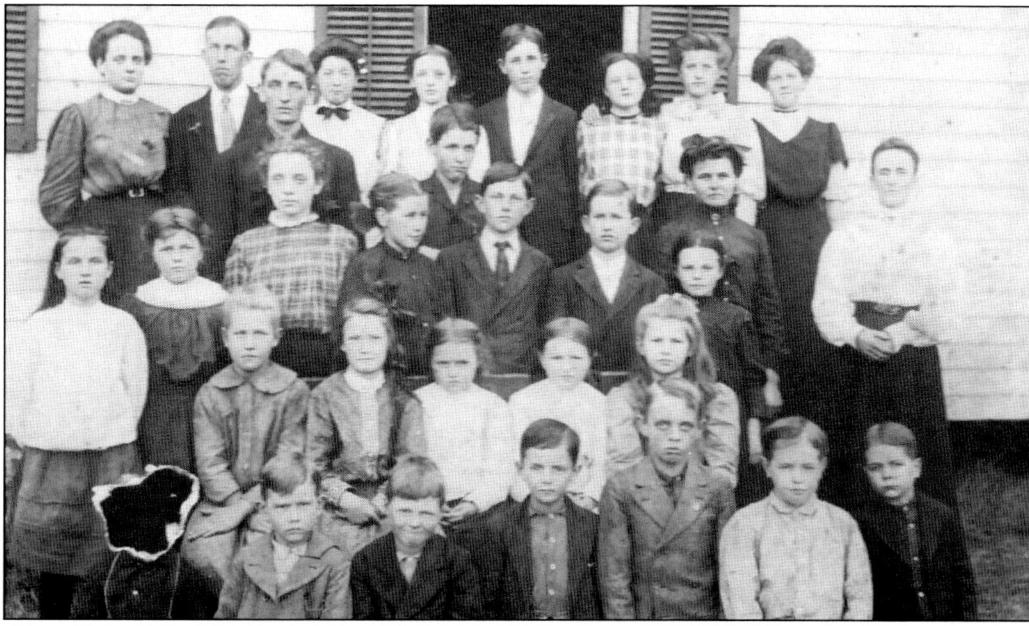

Piney Grove School served students living in the southern part of Fentress Township. It is likely that this was a subscription school, a school open only to students whose parents paid a teacher's salary to teach after the four-month-term regular school ended. Pictured are, from left to right, (first row) Joe Marley, Henry Marley, Jim Marley, Earl Johnson, Stacy Hockett, Phal Hodgin, and Luther Breedlove; (second row) Ida Voncannon, Ellen Marley, Ivetus Marley, Cornie Marley, Furlie Marley, and Esther Marley; (third row) Blanch Marley, Eula Hockett, Tela Hodgin, Charles Voncannon, Earl Marley, and Tassie Johnson; (fourth row) Wilbur Hockett, D. Hodgin, Mary Hart, and Mrs. Laubacker, teacher; (fifth row) Lura Hockett, Arthur Marley, Lelia Elliott, unidentified, Cecil Marley, Carrie Voncannon, Tula Fentress, and Flora Marley. After his father made the remark that he "looked like a biscuit," young Joe Marley scratched out his image. (Courtesy of Ruth Ann Jones.)

Although Tabernacle School was in Clay township, many of the students from this two-room school eventually attended Pleasant Garden High School. Isla Causey (wearing a plaid dress, fourth from the right on the second row) was one of the teachers when this photograph was made around 1913. (Courtesy of Craig Emerson.)

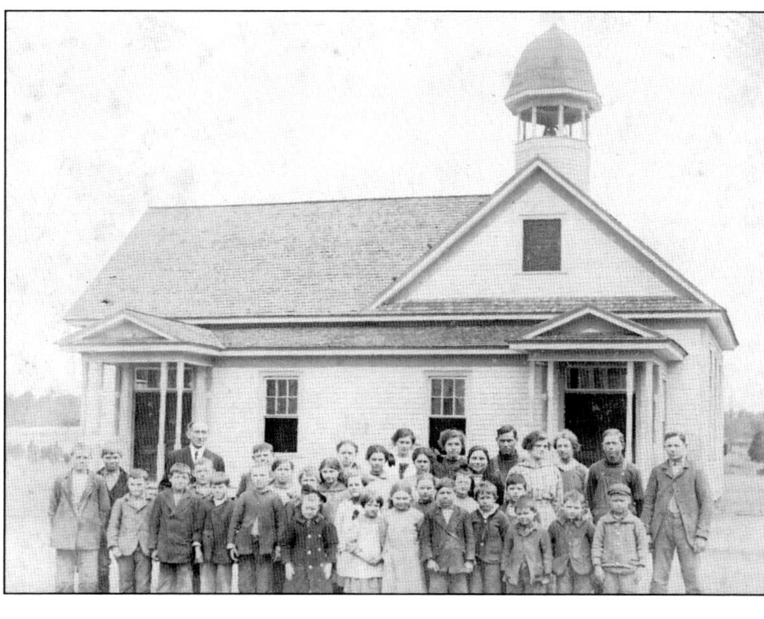

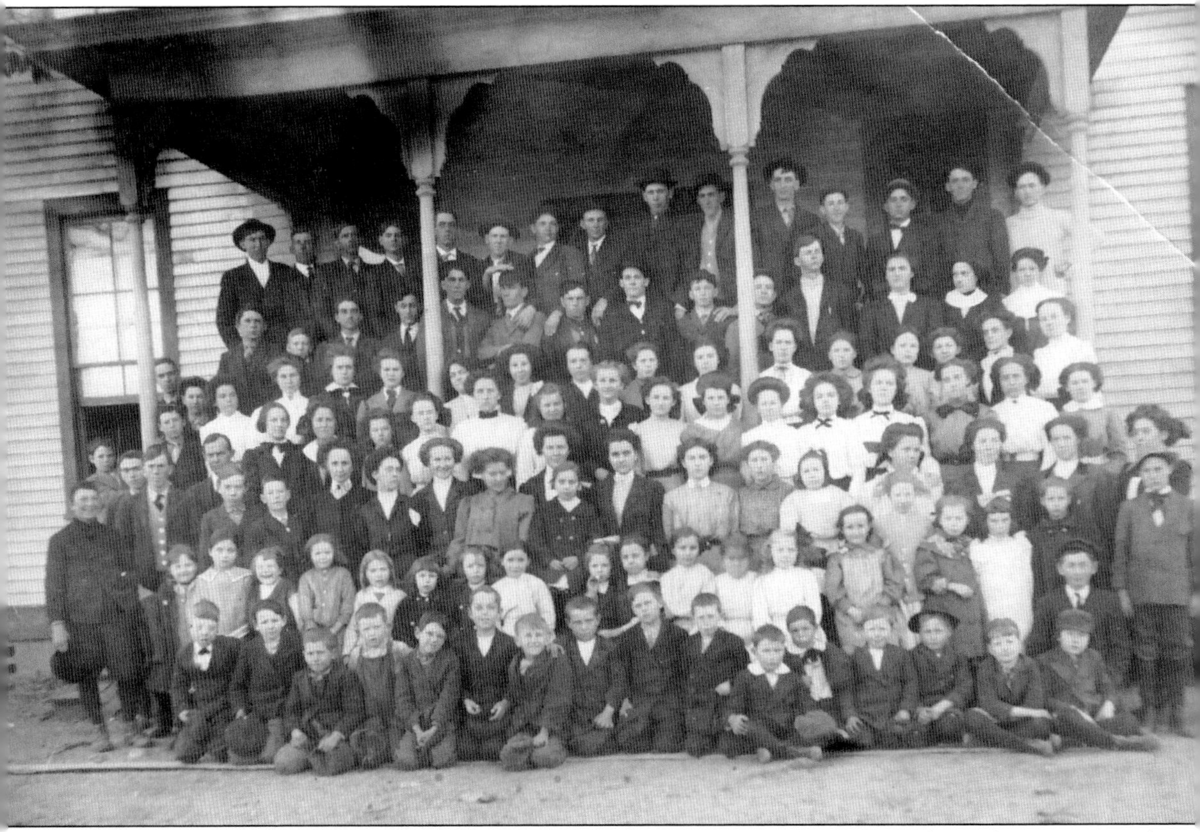

This photograph of the entire student body was made in 1909, the year Prof. Frank Foust arrived to lead Pleasant Garden High School. During his nine-year tenure as principal, agriculture and home economics became part of the curriculum when it became a Farm Life School. Two students captured the first statewide debating contest in 1913, and dormitories were built for both male and female students in 1914.

Charles Thaddeus Weatherly was chairman of the school committee for many years. He and his wife, Martha Fletcher, raised eight children in this house just north of the village. He was also a leader in farming organizations and Pleasant Garden Methodist Church. (Courtesy of NCHPO.)

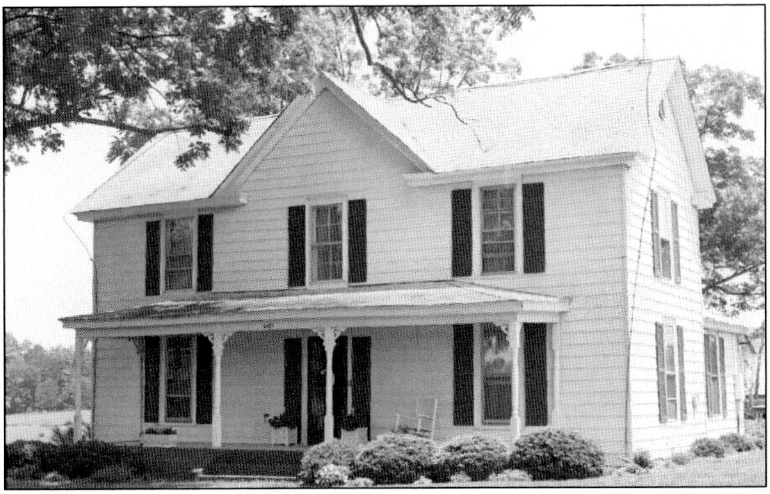

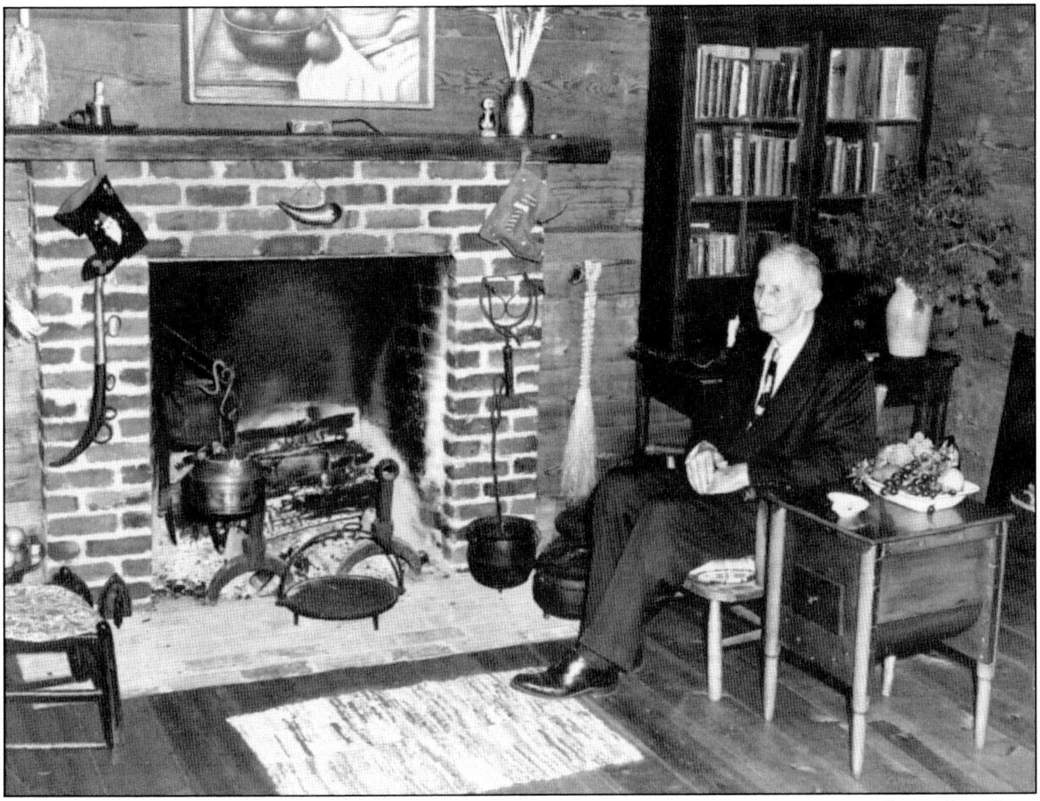

Singing master Albion Monroe Fentress chose his career as a young man. He went from church to church and community to community to teach singing classes. A grandson of Frederick Fentress, he was nearing his 93rd birthday at the time of this 1965 photograph. It was made in a cleverly designed painting studio that Angie Fentress and Lucian Riley created by combining the old Piney Grove School that her father once attended and a stable. (Courtesy of Martha Boren.)

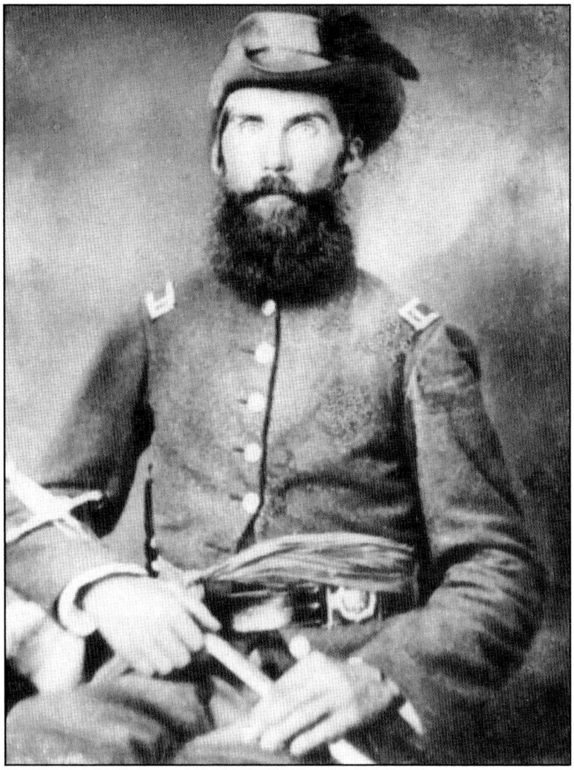

A Randolph County farmer/schoolteacher from Franklinville, 1st Lt. Clayborn Gray married in Fayetteville while serving in the Civil War. Both his wife and infant son died before the war ended. He was 35 years old when the Confederate troops were mustered out in Greensboro. Perhaps that is where he studied medicine and met Sarah Jane Thurston, daughter of a prominent cabinetmaker, Peter Thurston. They were married in 1868. (Courtesy of Martha Boren.)

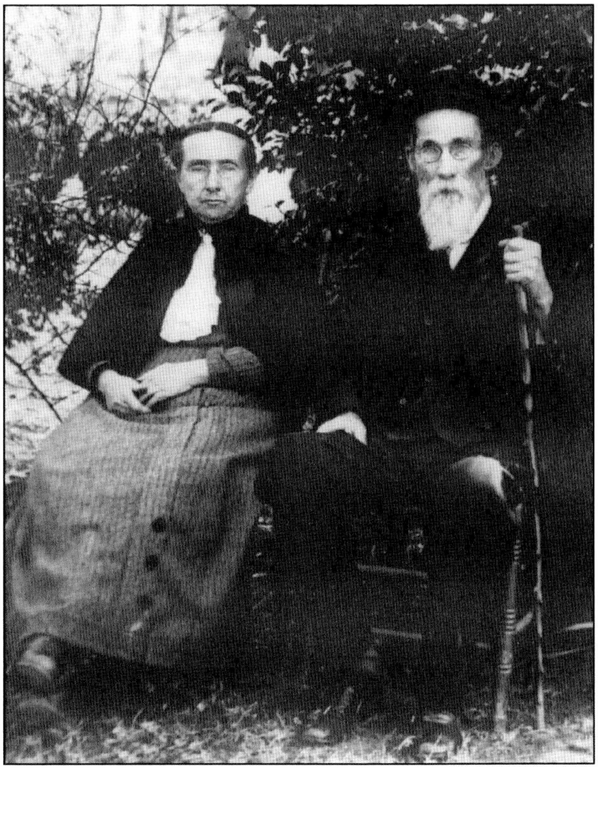

Sarah Thurston and Clayborn Gray moved to the Pleasant Garden area from Level Cross around 1890. He was known to all as Dr. C. Gray. This photograph may have been made around 1915. Four of their seven children remained in the village to raise their families—Mary Gray Riley, Hattie Gray Neelley Hendrix, Clayborn Alexander Gray, and Kate Gray Ross. (Courtesy of Tom Ross.)

Thomas Eli and Fatima "Tint" Vickery Marley began married life in a log cabin. As their family grew, the home was enlarged with a two-room frame addition attached to the back. The log cabin was removed around 1912 when a two-story addition was added to the front. A few years later, a photographer memorialized their family: Leo (left) and Joseph stand in front of, from left to right, Earl, Cecil, Arthur, Ellen, Tint, and Tom. (Courtesy of Ruth Ann Jones.)

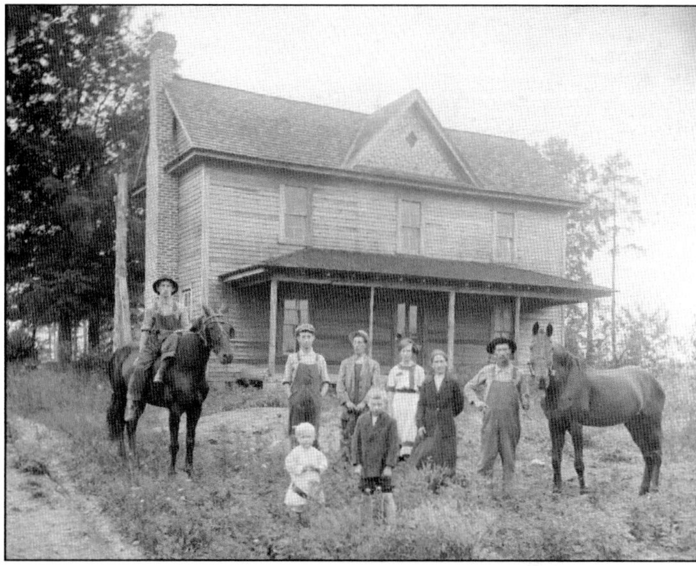

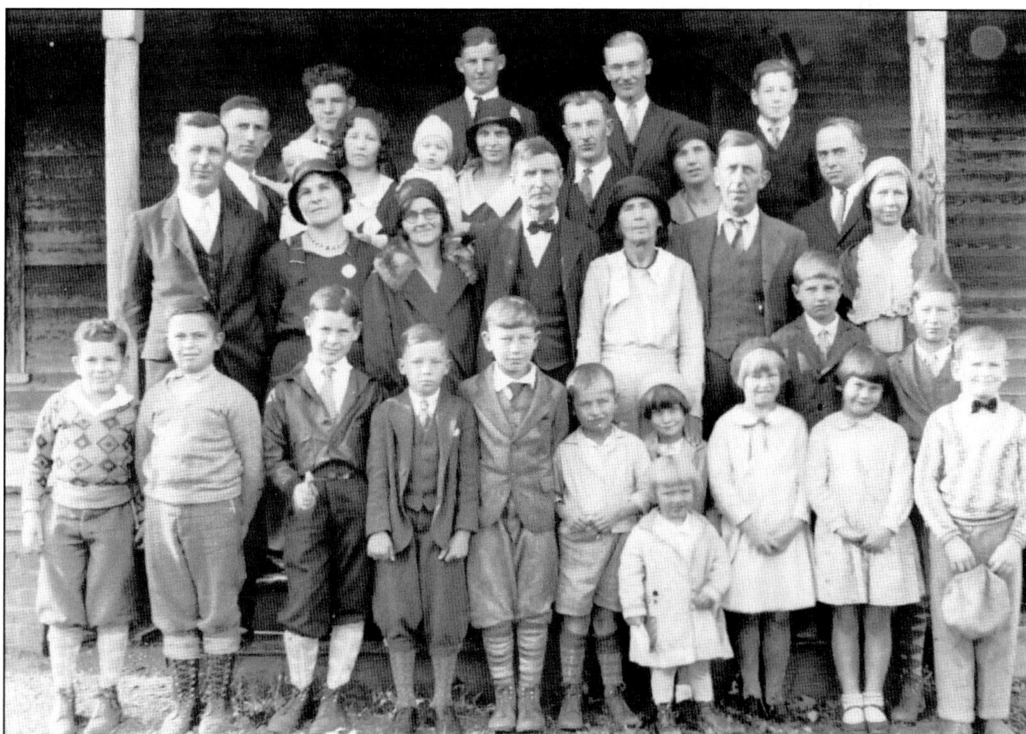

By 1931, Tom and Tint Marley's family had increased exponentially; from left to right are (first row) Bobby Marley, Bill Yow, Tom Marley, Claude Marley, Branson Marley, Phillip Marley, Linda Marley (in front), Dare Yow, Mildred Marley, Bessie Yow, and Clarence Yow; (second row) Eli and Cafer Marley; (third row) Cecil and Ann Marley, Flora Marley Daniels, Tom and Tint, Arthur and Mary Marley; (fourth row) Earl, Corky, and Jessie Marley, Buster, Myrtle, and Joe Marley, and Nell and Bill Yow; (fifth row) Buford Marley, Frank Daniels, Leo Marley, and W.C. Marley. (Courtesy of Ruth Ann Jones.)

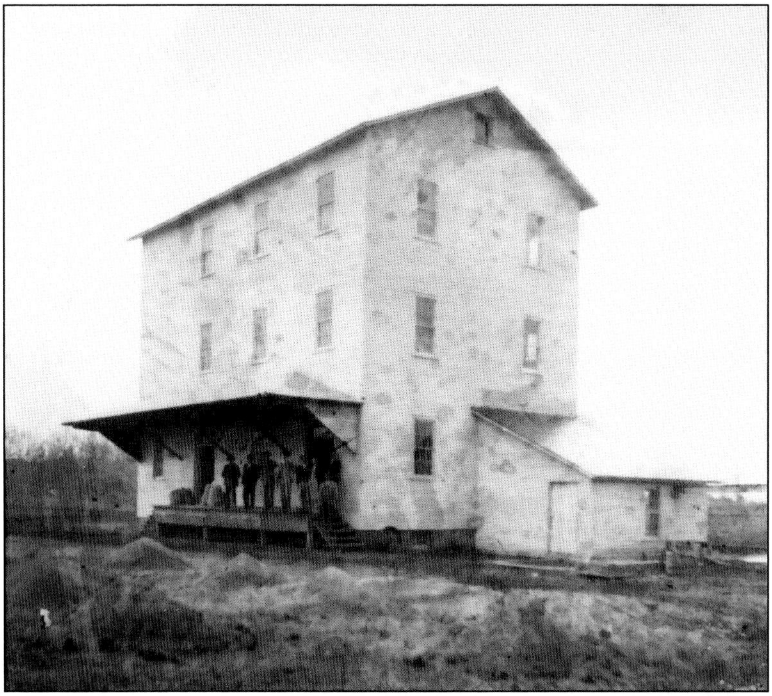

In 1907, a cotton gin was the first business opened by Pleasant Garden Company. This roller mill opened in 1909. The glass-plate negative reveals some workers standing on the porch. It was the scene of many impromptu Saturday night music sessions featuring P.F. Reddick on the fiddle, Joe Vickery and his banjo, and guitarist Gabe Latham. The building was destroyed by fire in the early 1960s. (Courtesy of Phillip Way.)

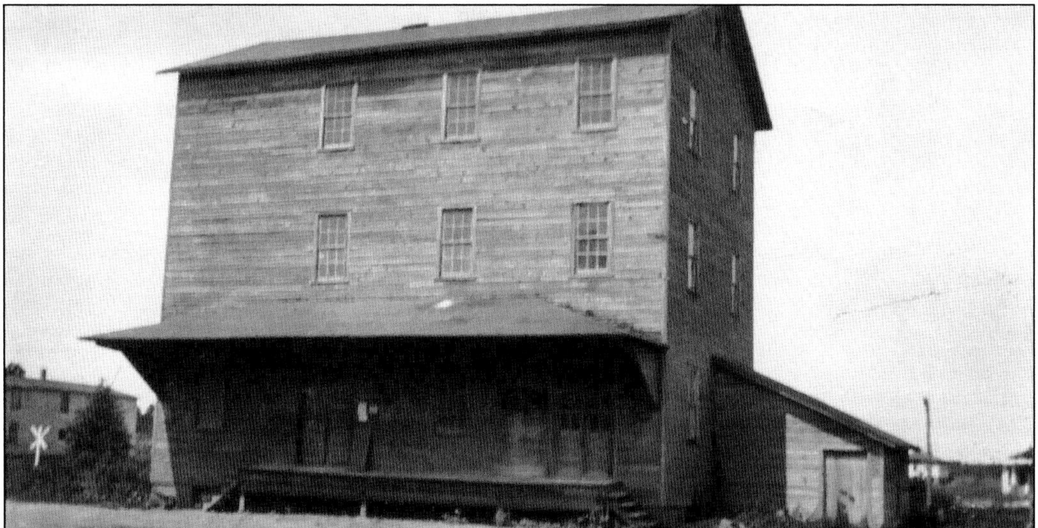

Tom Marley's blacksmith shop is on the left and across the railroad tracks from Pleasant Garden Milling Company. According to his family, he learned the craft from his wife, Tint, daughter of master blacksmith Jonathan Vickery. Tom's son Leo Marley was a third-generation blacksmith who held classes at the high school during World War II to teach farmers how to repair their tools. Donald Jones married Leo's daughter Ruth Ann, and he began blacksmithing in the 1960s. Two of their children, Mitchell and Denise, know how to shoe horses; Rene sells horse shoes. At the time of this 1936 photograph, C.H. Kirkman was manager of the Pleasant Garden Branch of Carolina Warehouse, which advertised these products: broom handles, mop handles, shade rollers, chair stock, and high-grade flour, meal, and feeds.

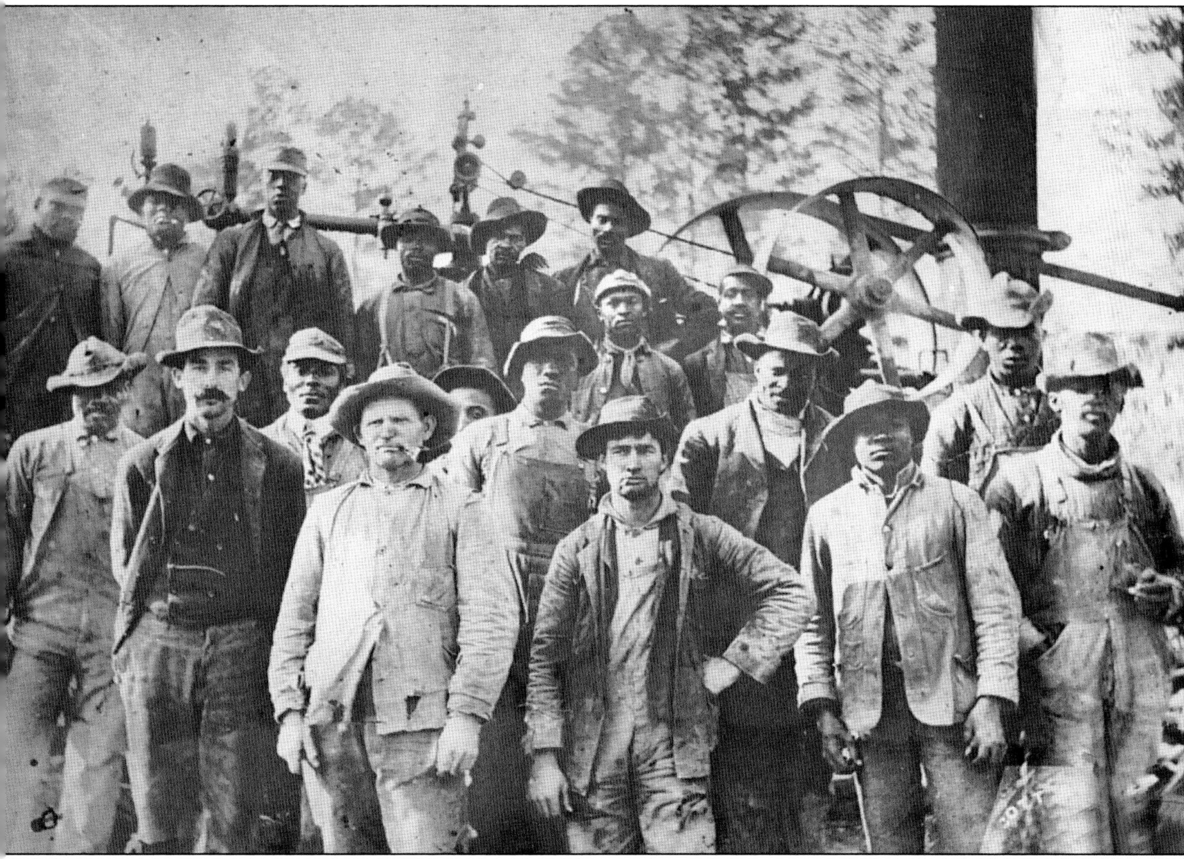

Piedmont forests produced a steady supply of hardwoods for the sawmill crew of Hockett, Hinshaw, and Johnson. Timber was loaded on cars at railroad sidings to be shipped across the state and exported to Europe. The *Patriot* noted that in May 1905, "Hockett and Johnson had the contract to furnish the framing and other rough timber for the schoolhouse that is being built in Pleasant Garden." The building was ready on October 16 of that year. (Courtesy of Ruth Ann Jones.)

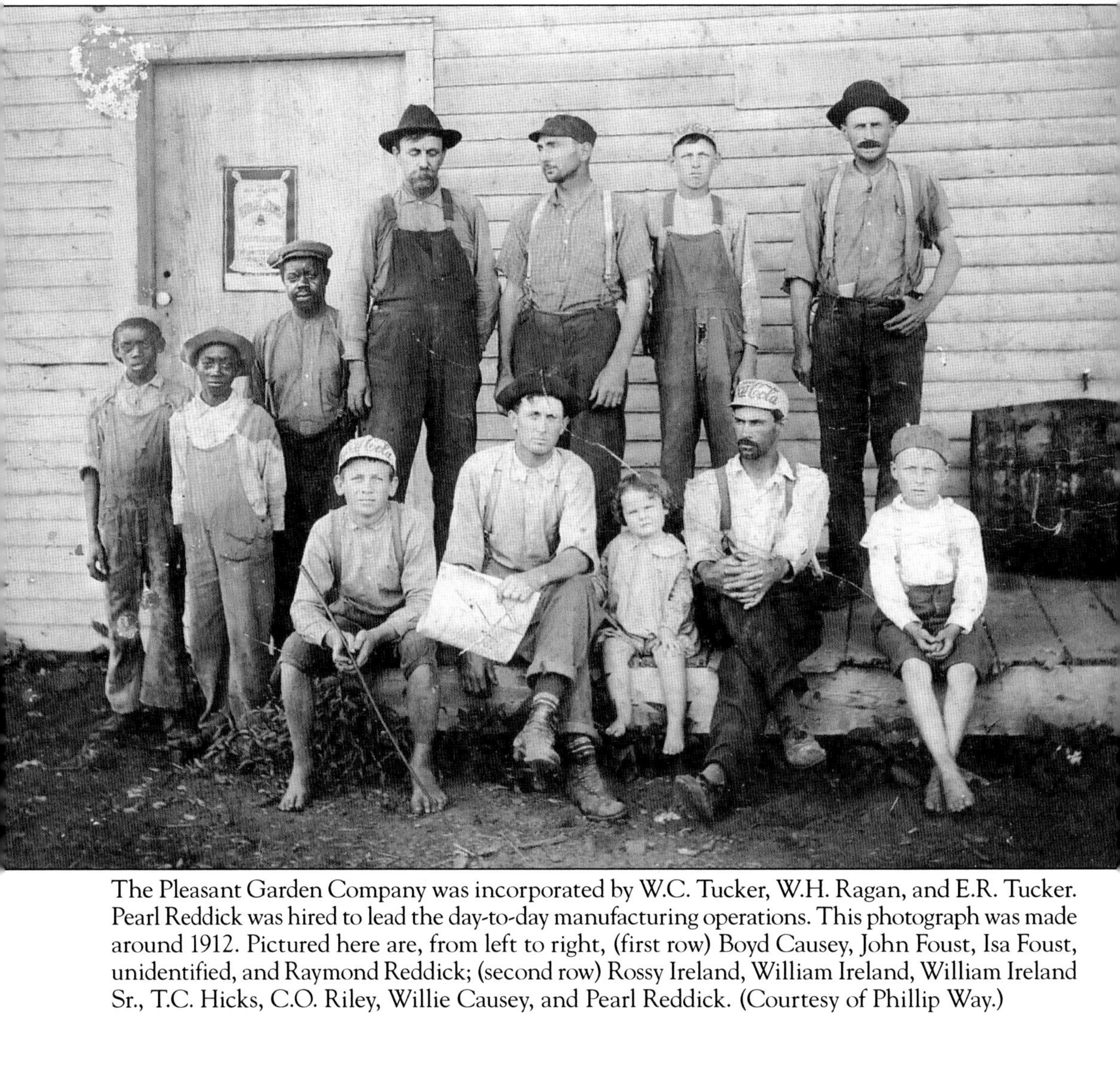

The Pleasant Garden Company was incorporated by W.C. Tucker, W.H. Ragan, and E.R. Tucker. Pearl Reddick was hired to lead the day-to-day manufacturing operations. This photograph was made around 1912. Pictured here are, from left to right, (first row) Boyd Causey, John Foust, Isa Foust, unidentified, and Raymond Reddick; (second row) Rossy Ireland, William Ireland, William Ireland Sr., T.C. Hicks, C.O. Riley, Willie Causey, and Pearl Reddick. (Courtesy of Phillip Way.)

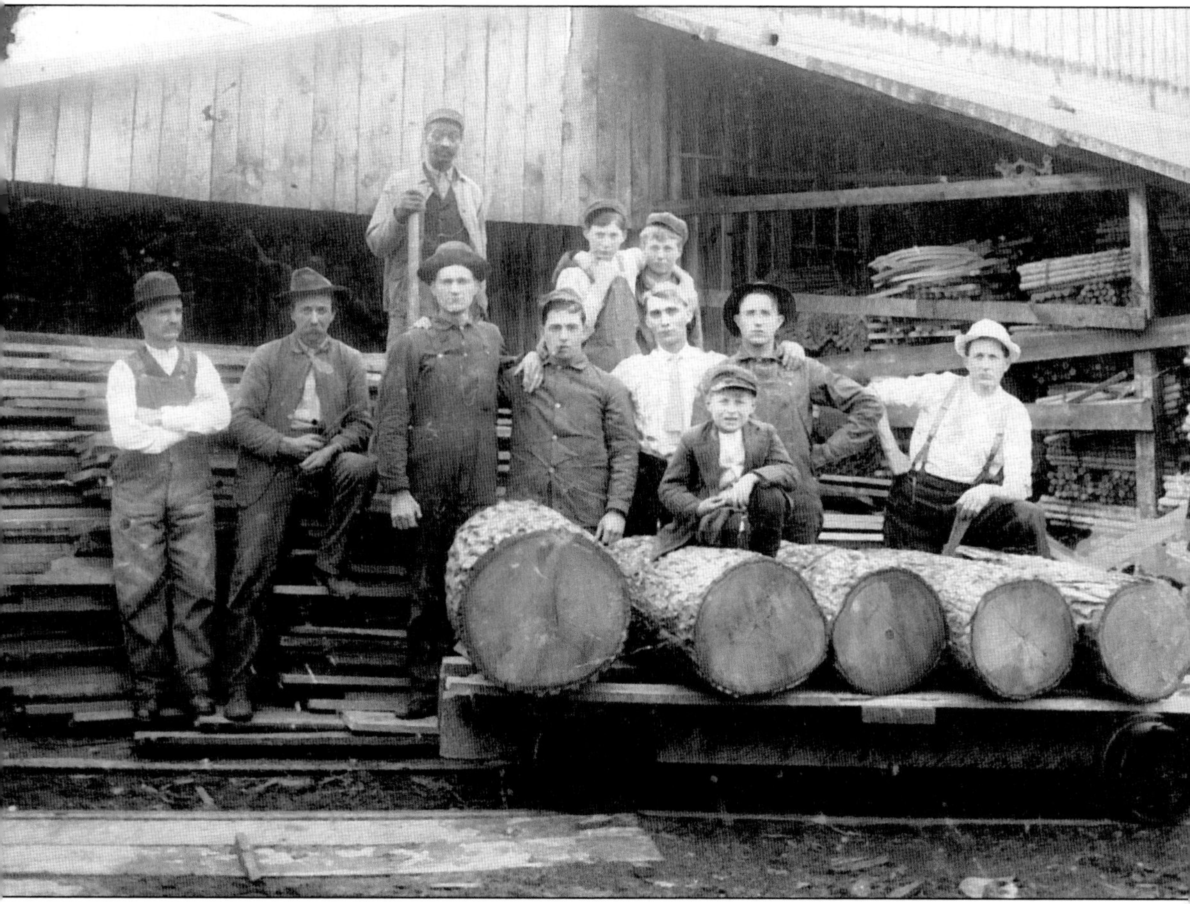

Pleasant Garden Chair Factory manufactured furniture components that were shipped by rail to a factory in High Point, where the chairs were assembled. Raymond Reddick is perched on the logs. From left to right are (first row) Pearl Reddick, T.C. Hicks, John Allred, William Yow, Clayborn A. Gray, Elmo Michael, and John Foust; (second row) William Ireland and two unidentified boys. (Courtesy of Phillip Way.)

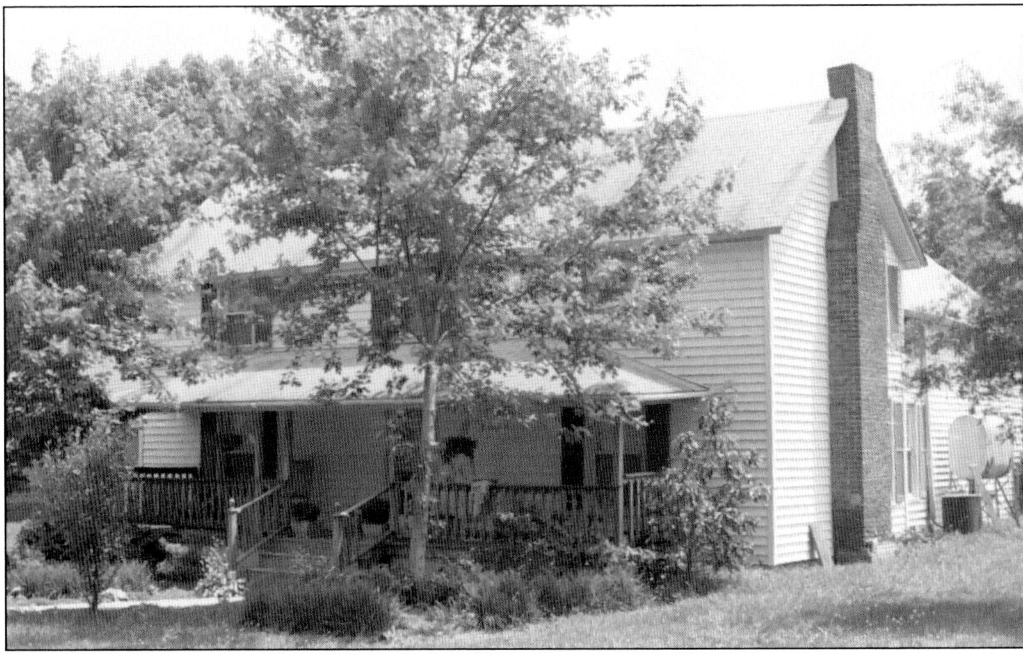

Built in 1905, the home of George Washington and Dora Bell Riley faces the railroad tracks at the intersection of Briarcrest and Laurel Knoll Roads. Riley's public work was maintaining roads. Thomas Adcock, a railroad section foreman, and his wife, Nancy, became the next owners in 1920. The A.C. Surratt family took ownership in 1947. (Courtesy of NCHPO.)

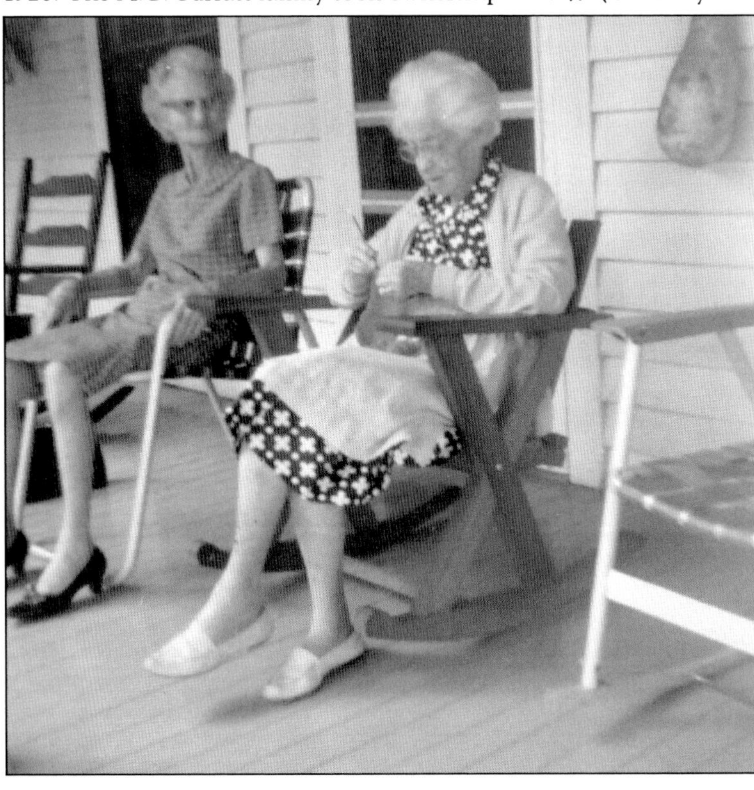

Shown in this 1970s photograph are longtime friends Nettie "Spoon" Cheek and Nannie Phillips Adcock. Adcock moved to Pleasant Garden before 1920 when her husband, Thomas M. Adcock, was named the railroad section foreman serving Pleasant Garden. They lived across the road from the depot where Cheek worked as stationmaster beginning in 1934. She managed freight, sold tickets, and operated the telegraph. (Courtesy of Phillip Way.)

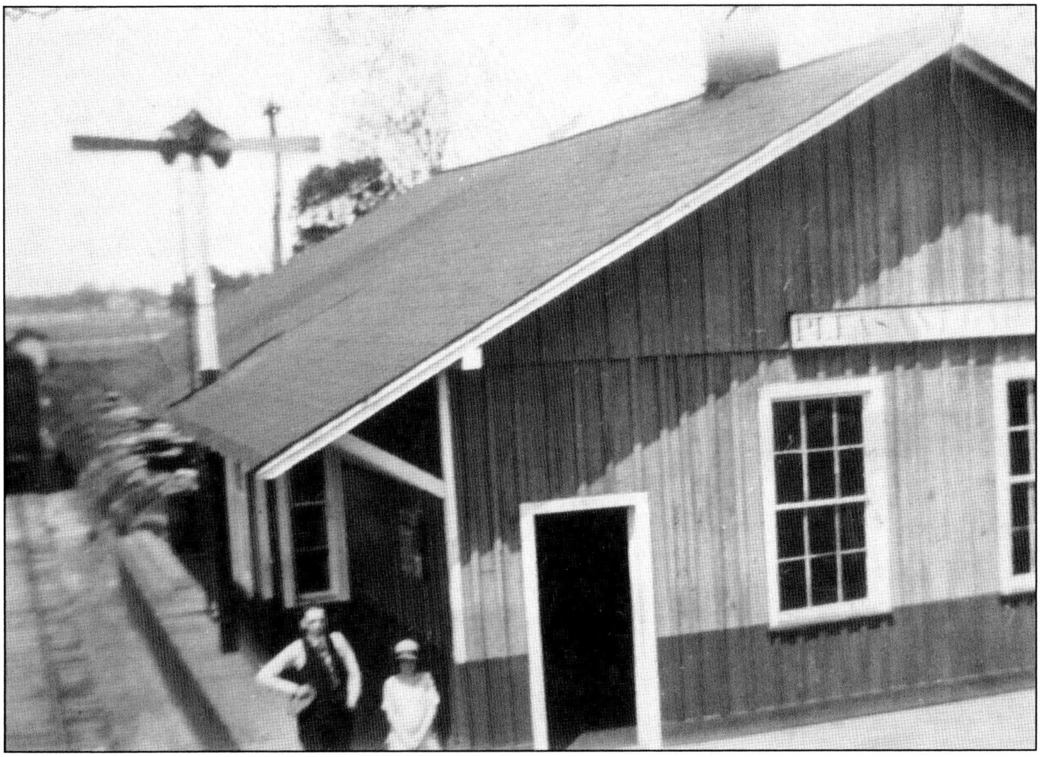

The Atlantic and Yadkin Railway extended service from Gulf in Chatham County through the Piedmont on its way to Mount Airy, reaching Pleasant Garden in 1884. At one time, there were more than eight trains serving the village each day. Riding the train was sometimes a necessity for Pleasant Garden High School students who lived in Climax and Julian because dirt roads became quagmires in rainy weather. Village residents hopped aboard for a 30-minute commute to work in Greensboro. Passenger service ended in 1939, but the tracks remained busy moving freight. These depot photographs date from the early to late 1920s. (Both, courtesy of Phillip Way.)

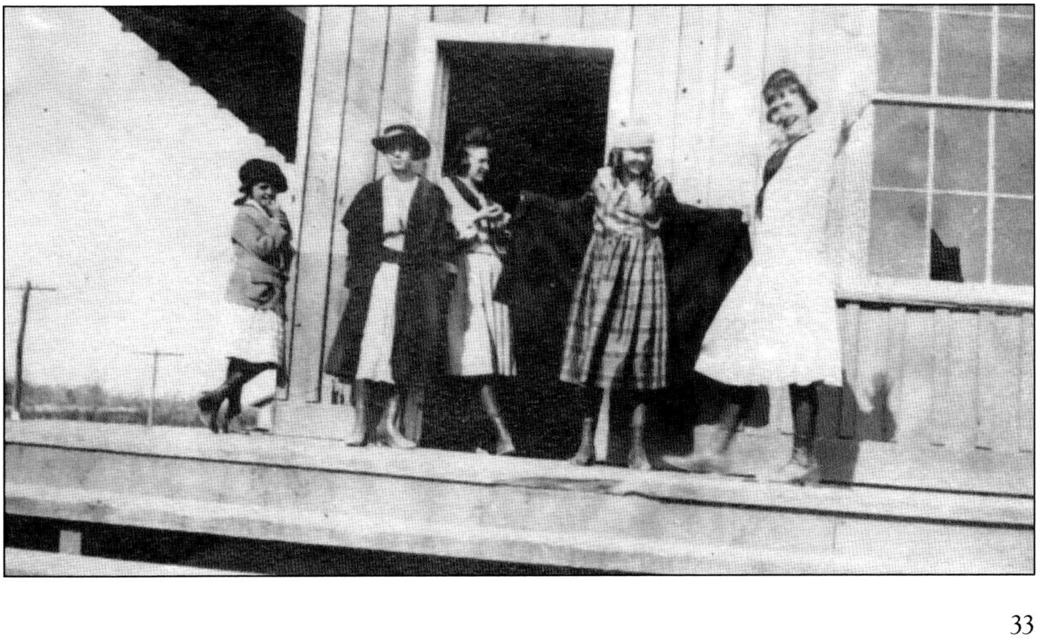

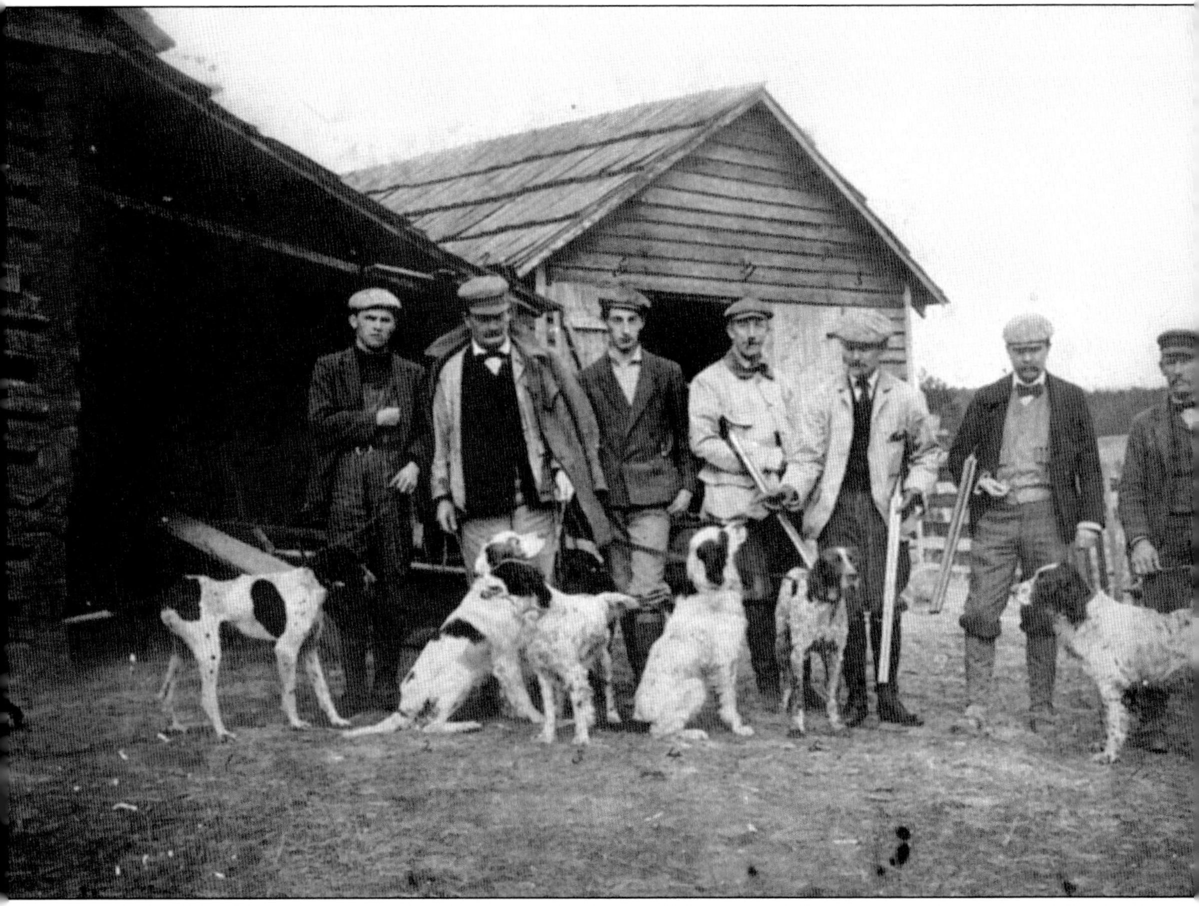

Luke W. White, a native of Ireland, was living in Baltimore, Maryland, at the turn of the 20th century. Having shown champion pointers at Westminster Kennel Club, he attracted wealthy sportsmen to hunt on property he leased from area farmers. On the back of this photograph from about 1906, he appraises each dog's skill before listing the men. The men pictured are, from left to right, Charles Ross, Luke White, Emmett White, Fred Rhinelander, George Gibbs, George Blagden, and Julius Neelley. (Courtesy of Frank Plunkett.)

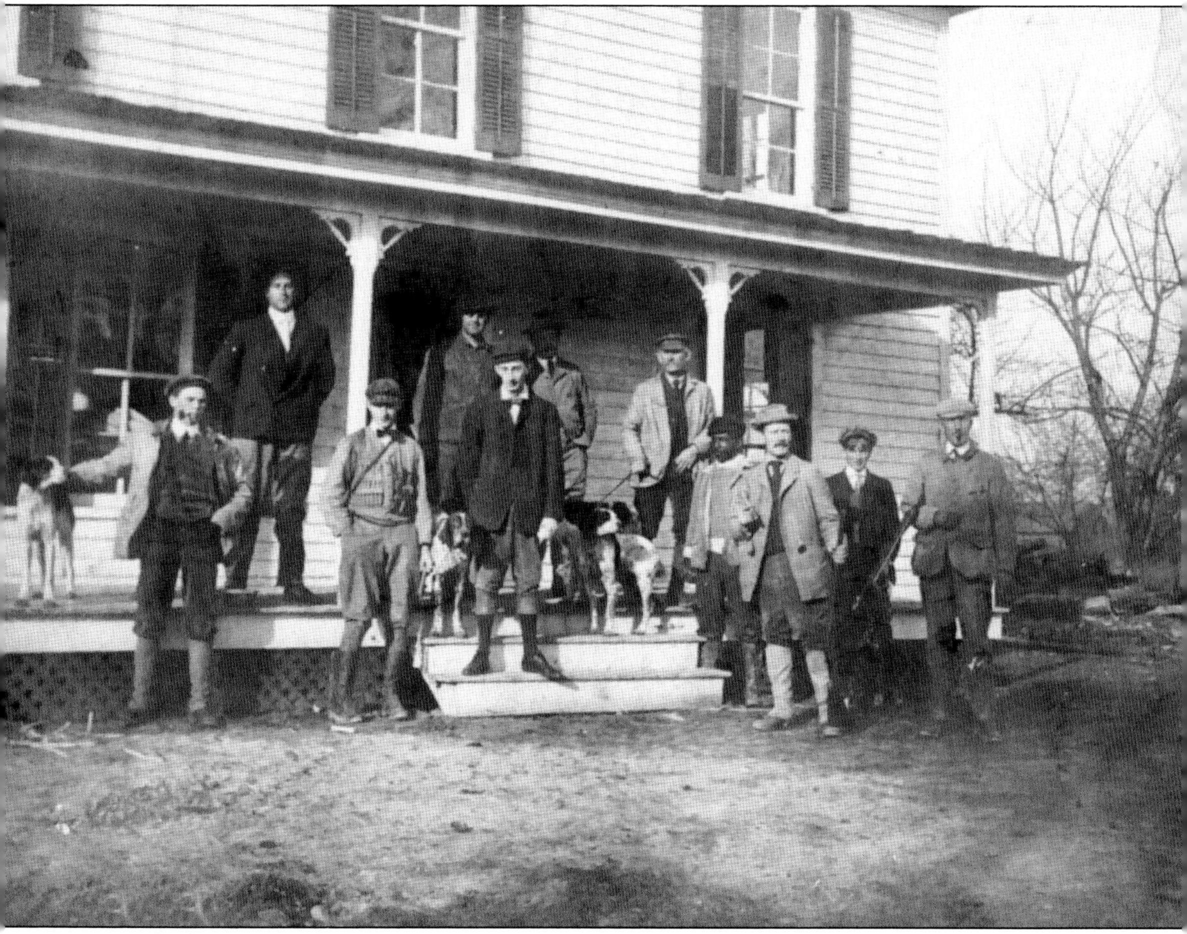

In return for his paying their property taxes, Pleasant Garden farmers leased their land to Luke White for quail hunting. They also served as guides for visiting hunters. Pictured here around 1907 are, from left to right, (first row) Charles Ross, Charles White, Emmet White, Gurney Curtis, Luke White, Shubert Smith, and Fred Rhinelander; (second row) J. Robert Ross, J. Rufus McCulloch, Albert C. Boone, and Julius Neelley. Robert Ross, McCulloch, and Boone bought the Gallberry Swamp in Bladen County and made exaggerated claims about the game they encountered.

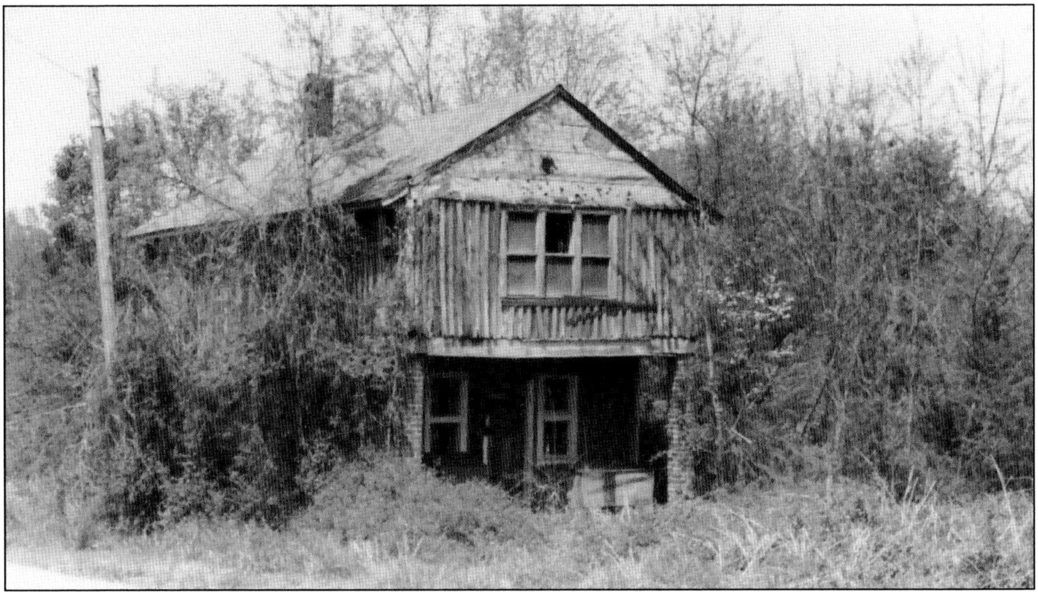

This board-and-batten structure stood by the railroad tracks for many years. Built by Luke White, it was insulated with sawdust gleaned from the nearby chair factory. It had various uses—residence, store, and/or post office. White also owned another home located between this building and the lodge. (Courtesy of Phillip Way.)

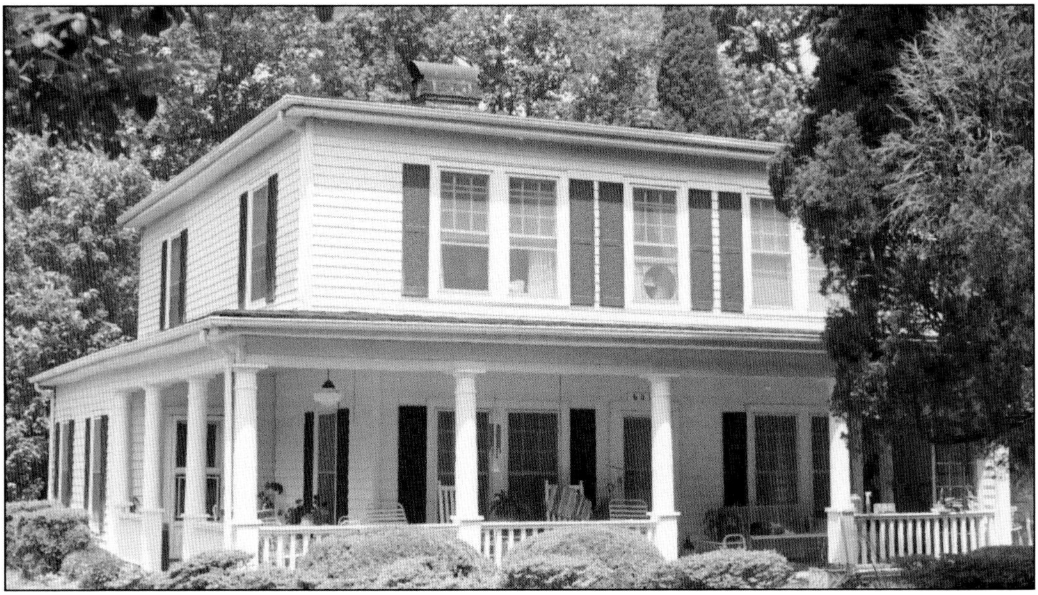

The northernmost residence on a section of town called the Hill was a hunting lodge owned by Luke W. White around 1905. Although a resident of Baltimore, he spent a good part of the year in Pleasant Garden and actively participated in the life of the village and the county. White was so affected by the plight of four local children orphaned in March 1909—Schube, Harriet, John, and Virginia Smith—that he penned a hasty letter to his wife, Lomena, suggesting that they care for the children. They raised and educated them as their own. H.C. and Frances Cannon Rudd became the owners of this house in 1923 when White focused his attention on a lodge he opened in Alabama. (Courtesy of NCHPO.)

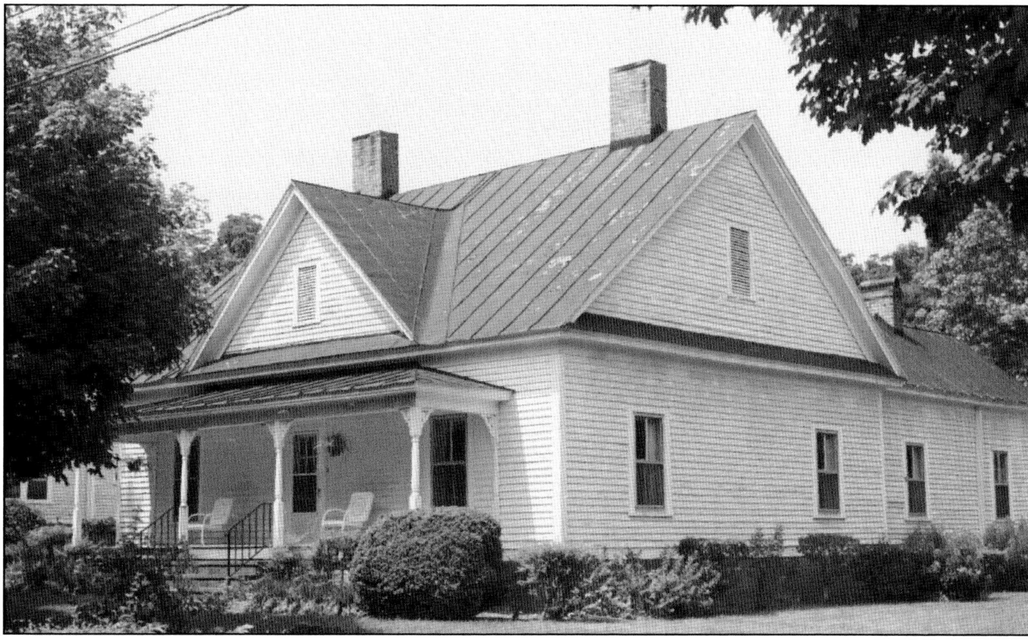

High school principal Frank L. and Mamie Rogers Foust were the first owners of this cottage. A 1903 graduate of the University of North Carolina, he followed the same career path as his brothers Thomas Foust, Guilford County school superintendent, and Julius Foust, president of the North College for Women. Frank left to become the superintendent of Hoke County Schools in 1919. (Courtesy of NCHPO.)

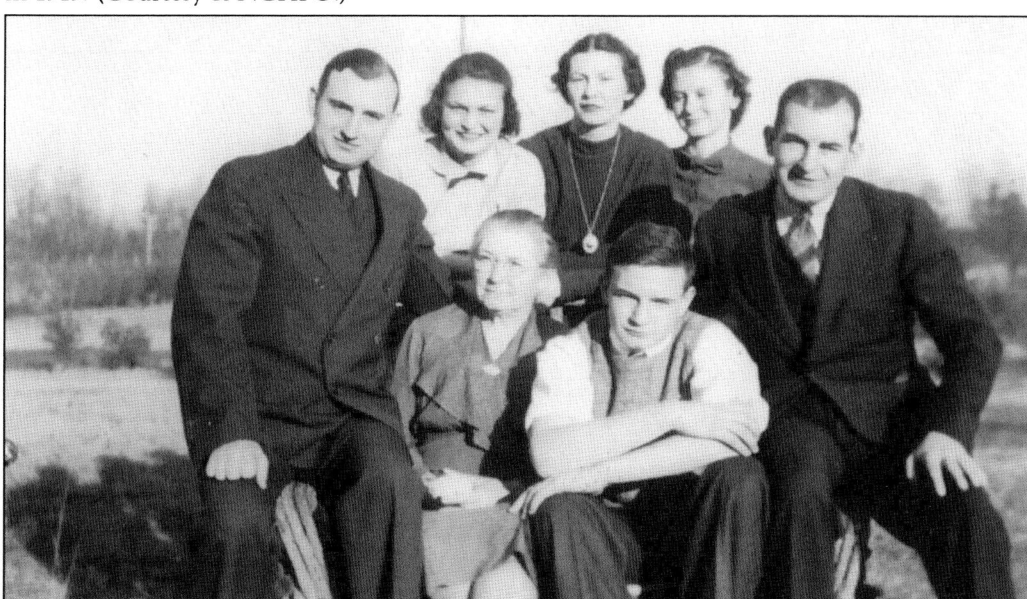

The Elton B. Shore family occupied this house for the longest period of time. Shore chose to move his family to the village from Rural Hall because of the educational opportunities it afforded. He left his job as stationmaster there and commuted by train to work at a Sanford veneer plant until his death in 1936. Pictured are, form left to right, (first row) Joseph, Nettie Poindexter Shore, C.E. "Bill," and Elton Jr.; (second row) Edith, Helen, and Virginia. (Courtesy of C.E. "Bill" Shore.)

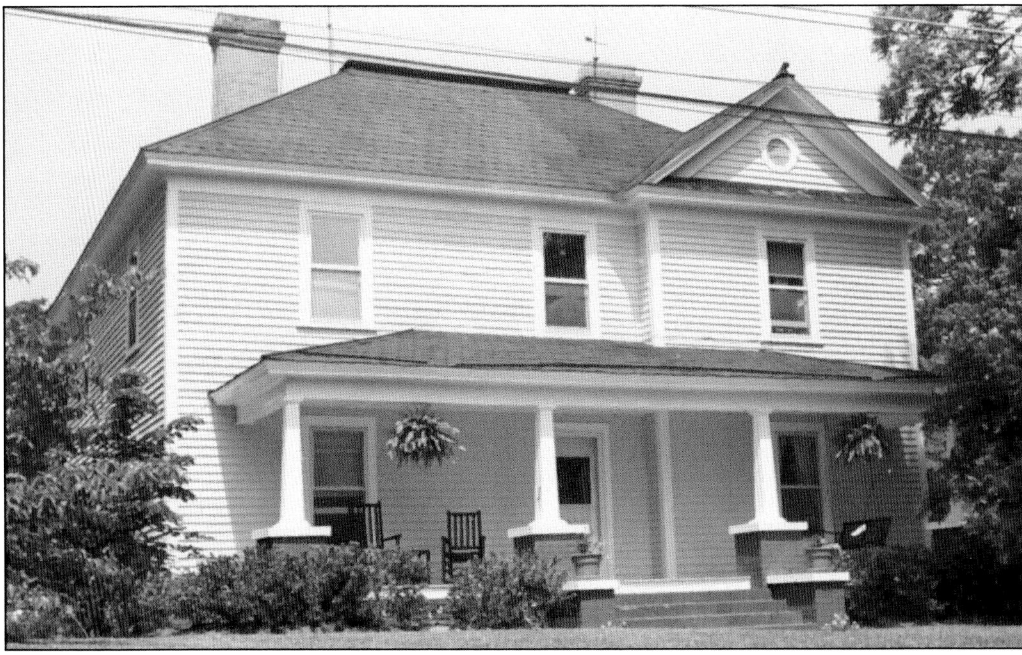

Pearl Franklin and Harriet Isom Reddick moved from Julian to the village in 1907 when he was hired to supervise the mechanical operations of the Pleasant Garden Company—a roller mill, cotton gin, and chair factory. They built this house around 1914. (Courtesy of NCHPO.)

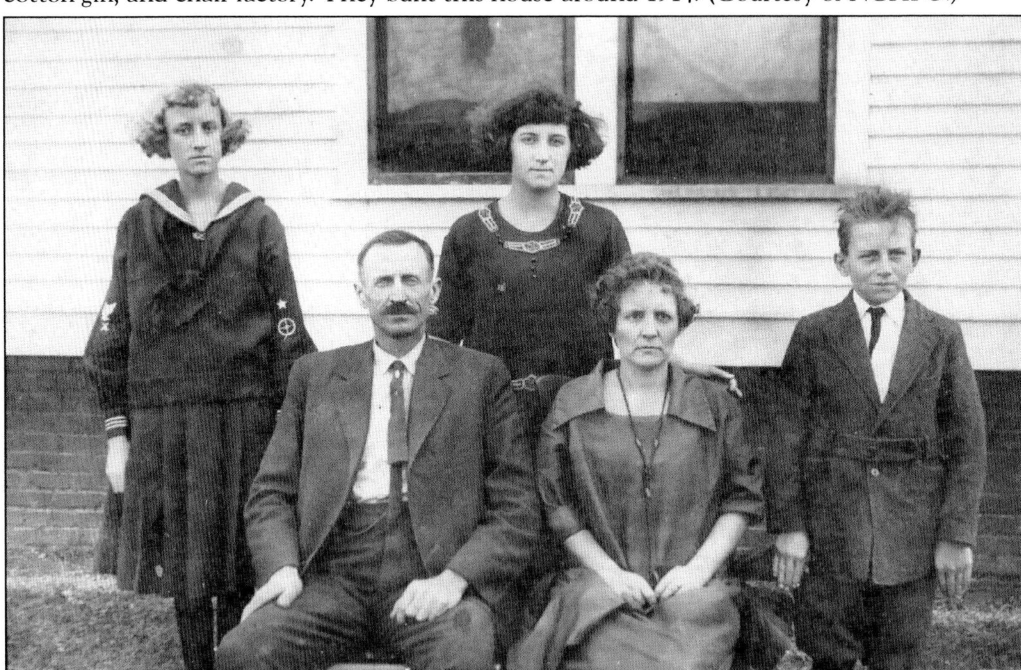

Pearl and Harriett Reddick are seated in this photograph. Marjorie (left), Ruby (center), and Roger are standing behind their parents. Raymond, the eldest son, is not in this photograph; Jack, the youngest, was born in 1924—after this image was taken around 1920. (Courtesy of Dwayne Jones.)

In 1910, Benjamin Lundy and Julia Hartsell Osborne moved into the village with two daughters, Virginia and Frances, from High Falls, Moore County, where Benjamin helped establish High Falls Mill. Family members explained the reason they returned to this area thusly: when the bridge across Deep River washed out, they could not visit their families in the Centre community. Osborne was renowned as a cabinetmaker and building contractor. The J.E. Thompson family moved into this home in the 1940s. (Courtesy of NCHPO.)

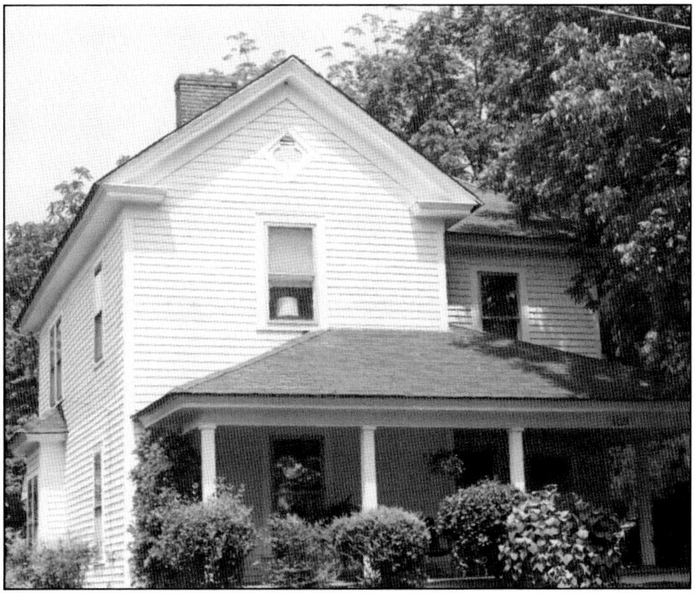

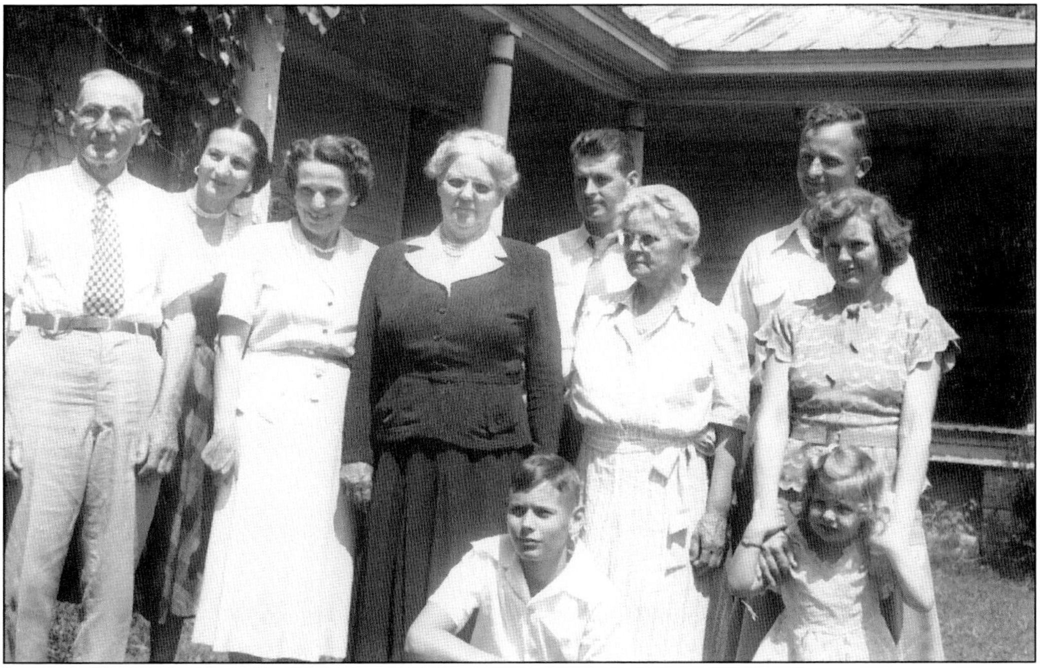

Carl O. Riley, son of Manley and Clarinda Riley, and Mozelle Murrow, daughter of John and Julia Murrow, were married when she was only 15 years old. For many years, they lived in a large house he built near the blacksmith shop. That is where the family gathered for this photograph, around 1950. Pictured are, from left to right, (first row) Sandy Tillmon and Martha Riley; (second row) Carl, Julia Ellen Tillmon, Kathleen Long, Mozelle Riley, Harvey Tillmon, Lillian McManus, Charles Riley, and Luna Riley. (Courtesy of Martha Oakes.)

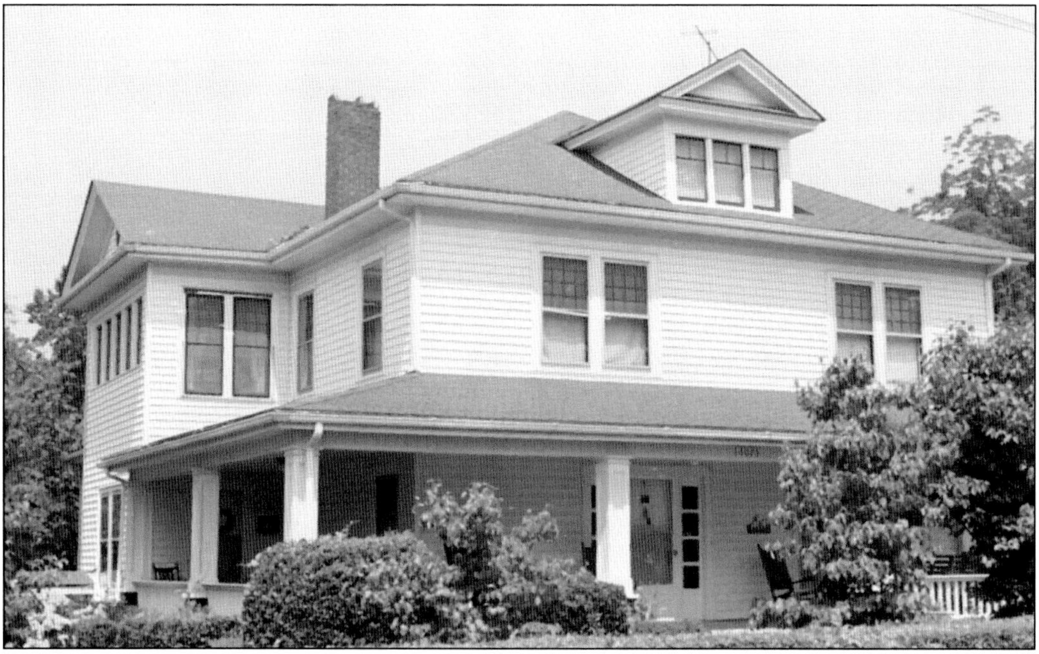

This home built in 1910 for Alta White and Dr. Thomas Tyson was their second dwelling in the village. The first one was destroyed by fire. Dr. James A. Siske's family established residency in 1920 after Tyson moved to Mebane. (Courtesy of NCHPO.)

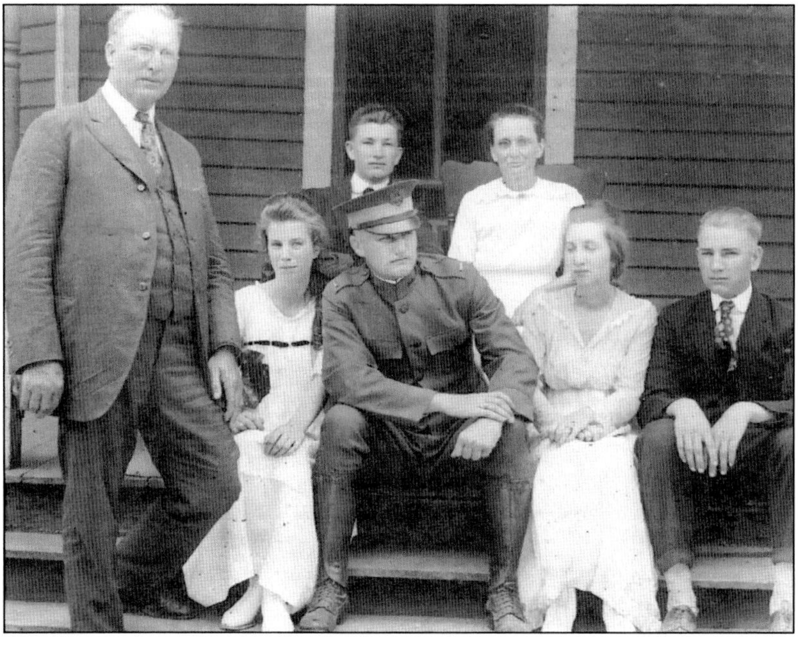

Dr. James Augustus Siske stands on the left in this 1919 photograph. Also pictured, from left to right, are (first row) Pherlie, Boyden, Ada, and Grady; (second row) Manley Arphew and Fannie. Arfew and Grady became physicians also. (Courtesy of Dr. Jimmy Siske.)

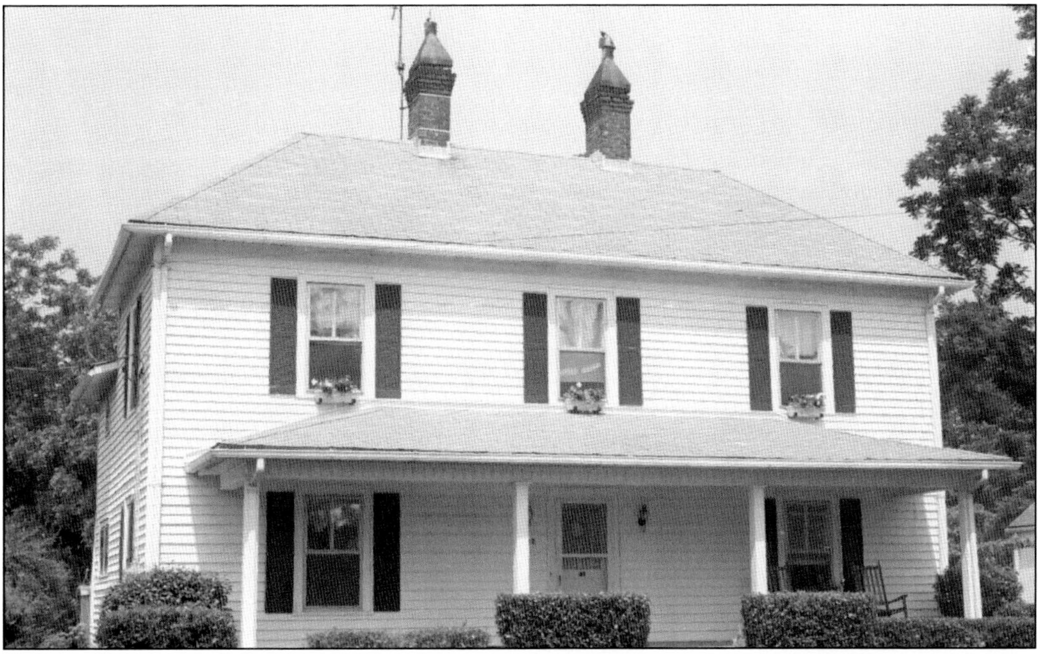

William Council Tucker built this home around 1911. In 1924, it became the residence of the N.B. Cheek family. Cheek operated Cheek's Mercantile, formerly the Pleasant Garden Company Store; Nettie Spoon Cheek worked at the depot. She had learned Morse code and how to operate a telegraph in her youth outside of Liberty, North Carolina. (Courtesy of NCHPO.)

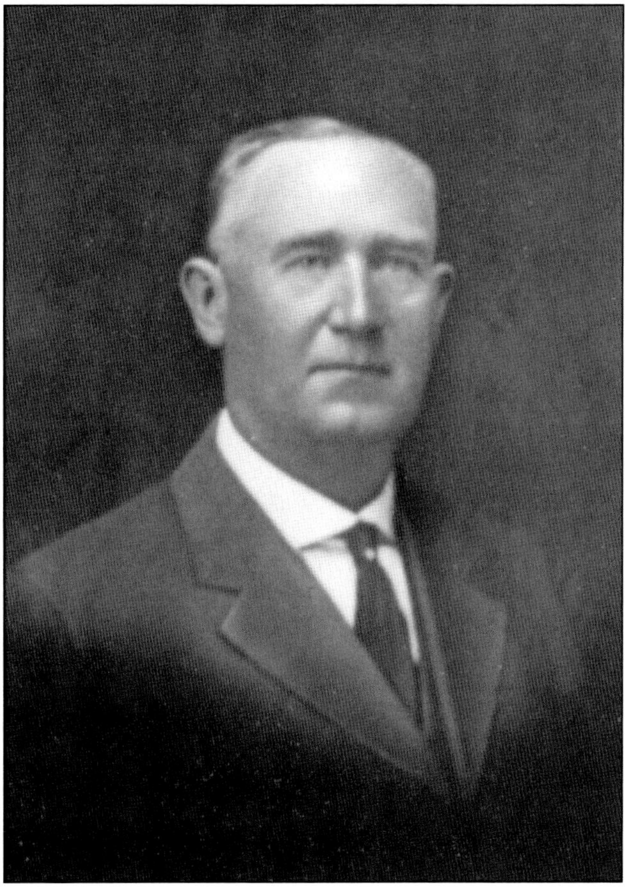

As one of the founders of the Pleasant Garden Company, William Council Tucker played a leading role in the development of the village. He served as Guilford County commissioner for 16 years, until his death in September 1921. He was chairman when the historic courthouse was built. A popular bachelor and sportsman, Tucker surprised the community when he married in 1913 at the age of 57. His bride was 28-year-old May Hinshaw, niece of May and James A. Odell, prominent Greensboro citizens. (Courtesy of Ruffin Tucker.)

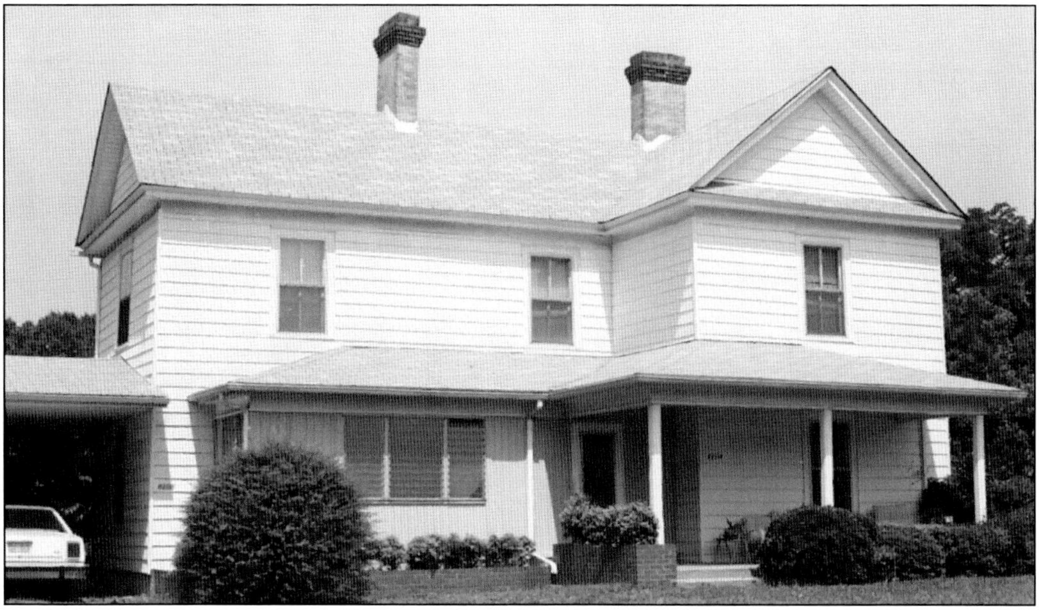

Two dormitories were constructed around 1914 at a total cost of $8,000. The Pleasant Garden High School boys' dormitory was located on the Hill. All students from the eastern half of Guilford County were eligible to attend school tuition-free; boarding cost about $8 a month. After a span of five years or so, when roads were better and there were more high schools, the need for student housing no longer existed. Clark Kirkman bought the 12-room building and converted it into apartments. Harold and Susan Gray became owners when they returned to Pleasant Garden after World War II. (Courtesy of NCHPO.)

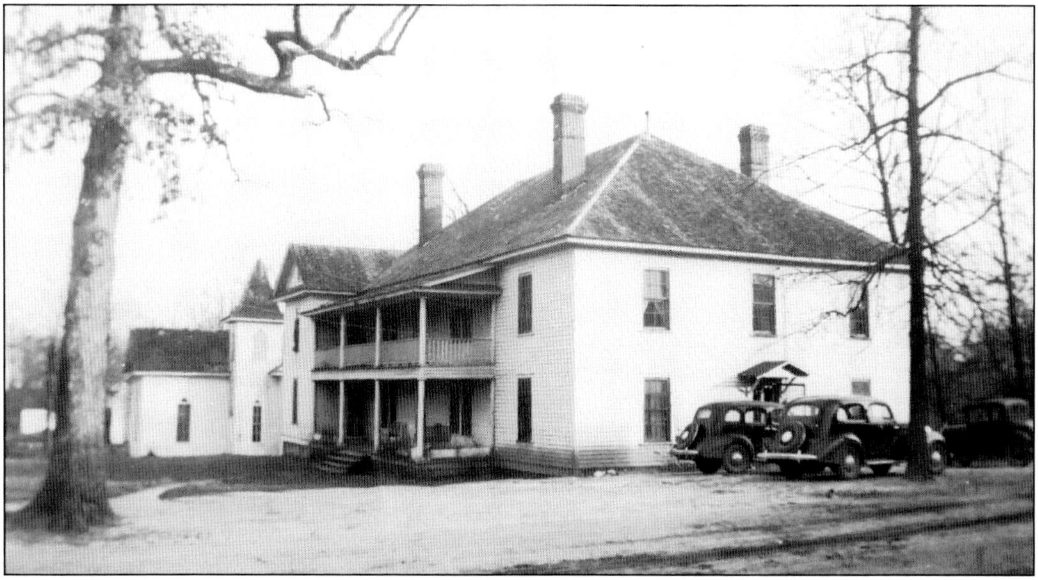

The girls' dormitory was adjacent to the school building. When it ceased to house boarding students, it was used as a teacherage for many years. In the mid-1940s, the school cafeteria and the Robert Overman family occupied the first floor. The Robert Ayers family lived upstairs. In the background is the Pleasant Garden Baptist Church. The building originally was constructed for a Presbyterian congregation.

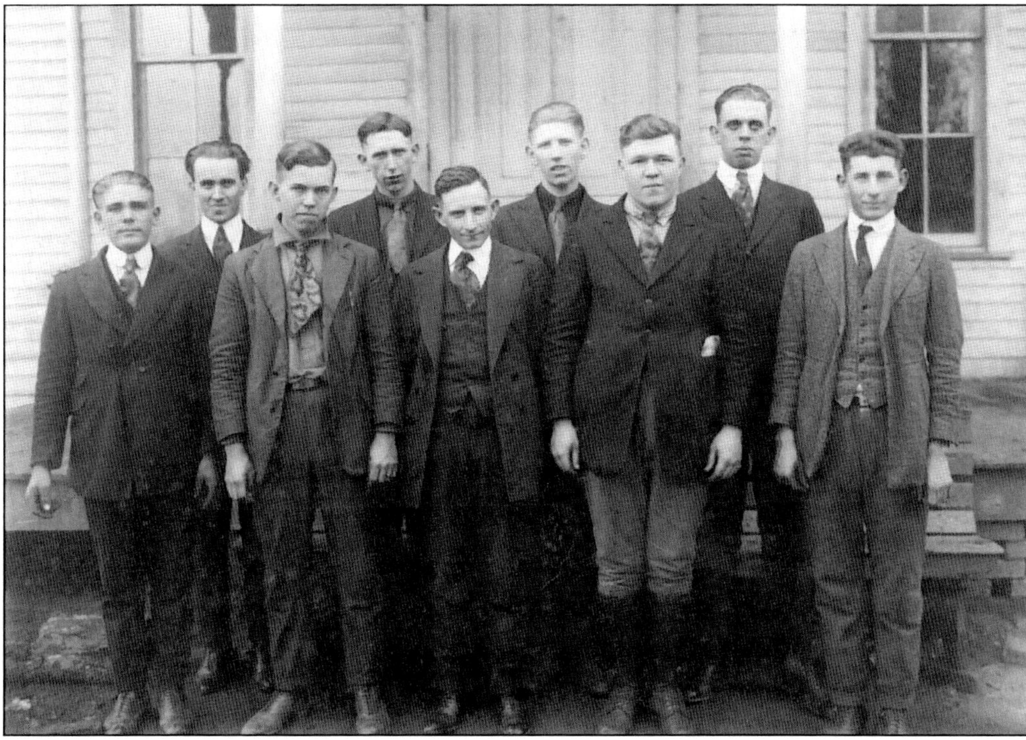

Arthur Lee Teachey, agriculture teacher, stands in the center of his students in this 1921 photograph. He attended North Carolina College of Agricultural and Mechanic Arts and Cornell University. Hugh Dixon was added to the faculty in 1922 when 72 of the 92 boys enrolled in Pleasant Garden High School were taking agriculture. It was not unusual for students to be over 19 years old before they graduated because they did not attend with consistency.

Louise Moore, a graduate of the State Normal College, was the home economics teacher when this class was photographed. According to a school catalog, the department was equipped with oil stoves, ranges, cooking utensils, and tableware. Foods and cookery were taught five days a week for 90-minute periods.

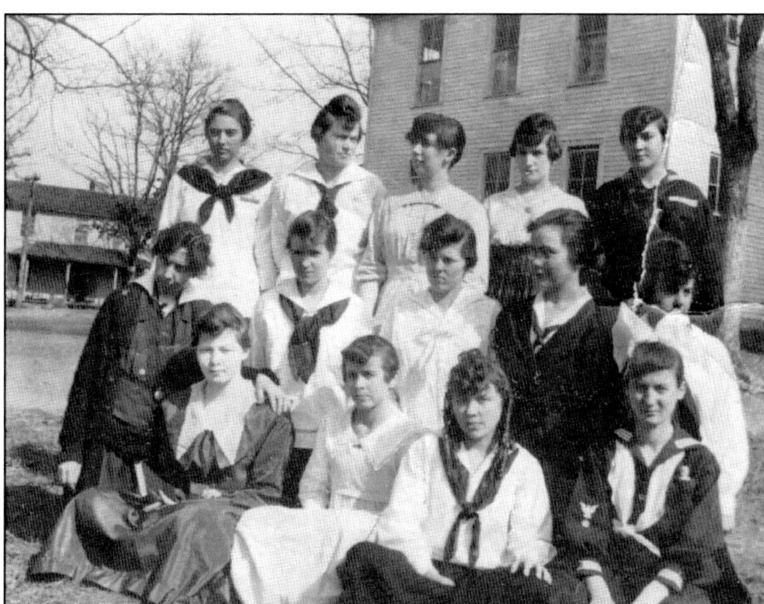

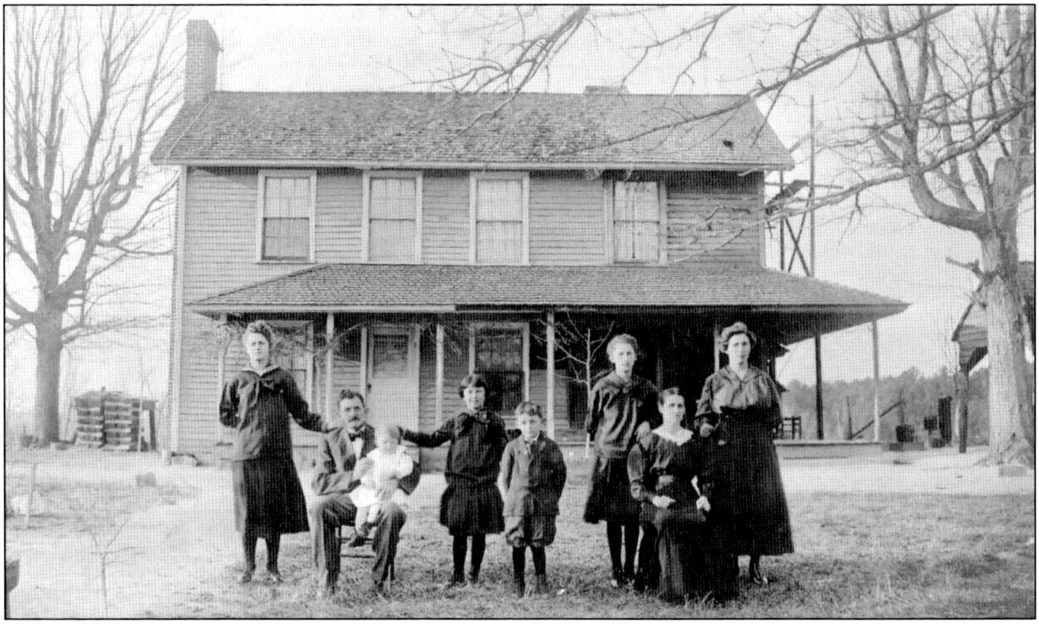

Charles E. and Minnie Fentress Kirkman had a home on the north side of Fieldview Road; the barn was across the road. When the photographer came around in 1915, Kirkman posed with his children in front of both buildings. From left to right are Lillie, Charles holding J. Norman, Callie, Floyd, Rosa, Minnie, and Carrie. (Courtesy of Ruth Ann Jones.)

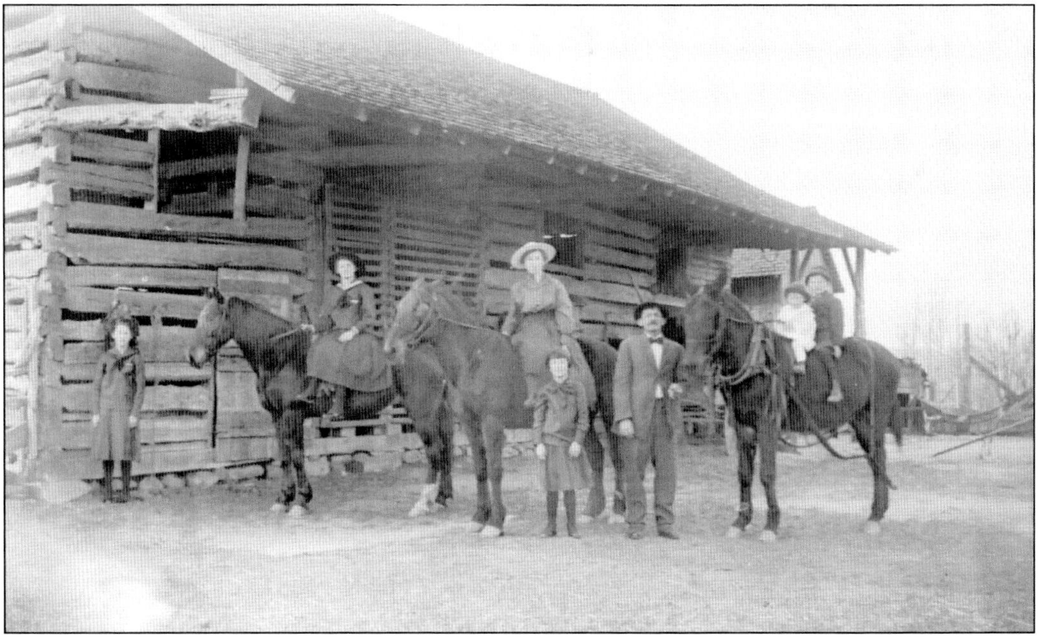

Posing in front of the log barn are, from left to right, Rosa, Lillie, Carrie, Callie, Charles, J. Norman, and Floyd Kirkman. Like most farmers in the area, Charles grew corn and grain. (Courtesy of Ruth Ann Jones.)

Two

The 1920s

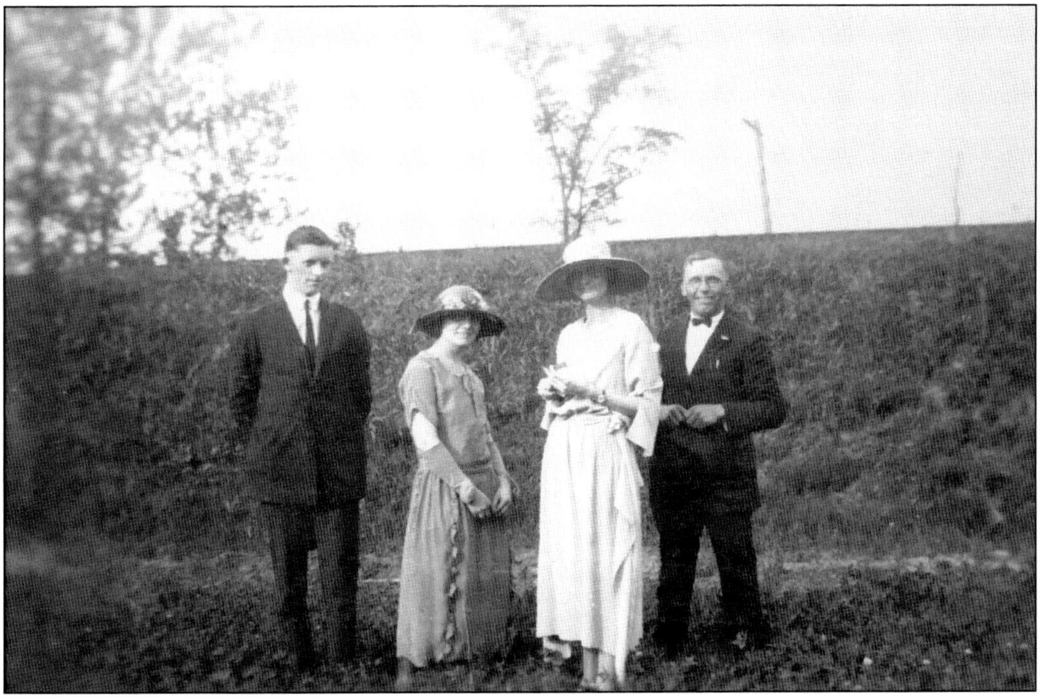

Townies Guy Ross (left) and Worth Fields (right) found a creative way to make friends with new teachers who lived in the dormitory—the young men chopped wood for them to heat their rooms. Nancy Coleman (center left) and Claudia Cates (center right) were roommates who welcomed warmth and the friendship. Coleman was one of the first young teachers to marry a Pleasant Garden man.

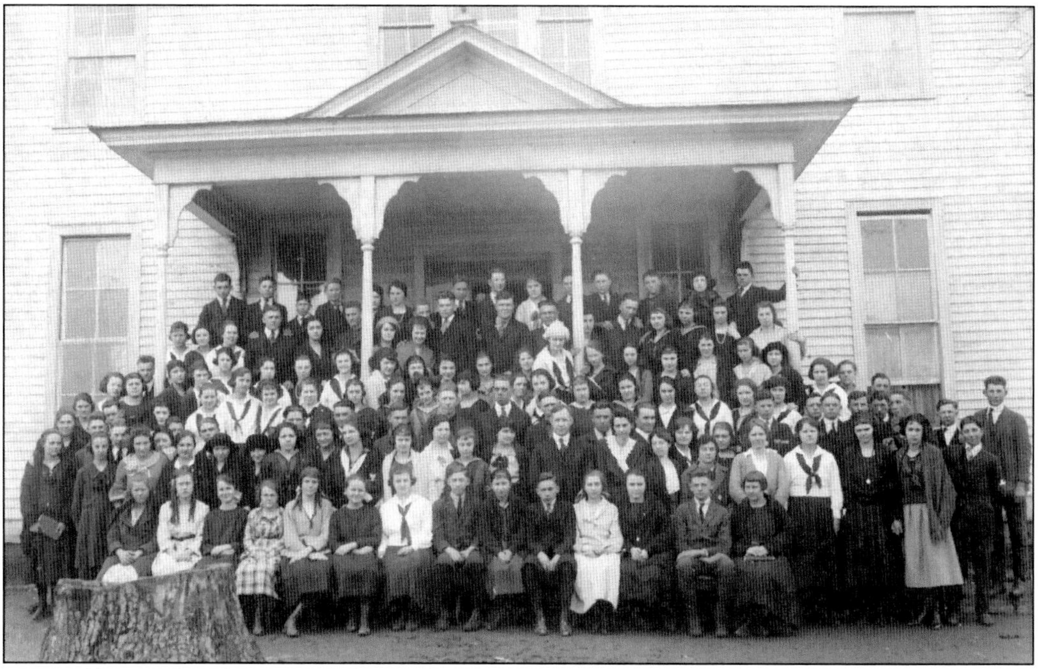

Pictured here is the Pleasant Garden High School 1920–1921 student body. Members of the faculty were Eugene D. Idol (principal), A.L. Teachey (agriculture), Louise Moore and Lillian Maynard (home economics), Laura Wiley (mathematics), Deborah Brown (English and Latin), and Ellen Raiford (science). There were students from Fentress Township and eastern Guilford. Northern Randolph students paid tuition and boarding fees.

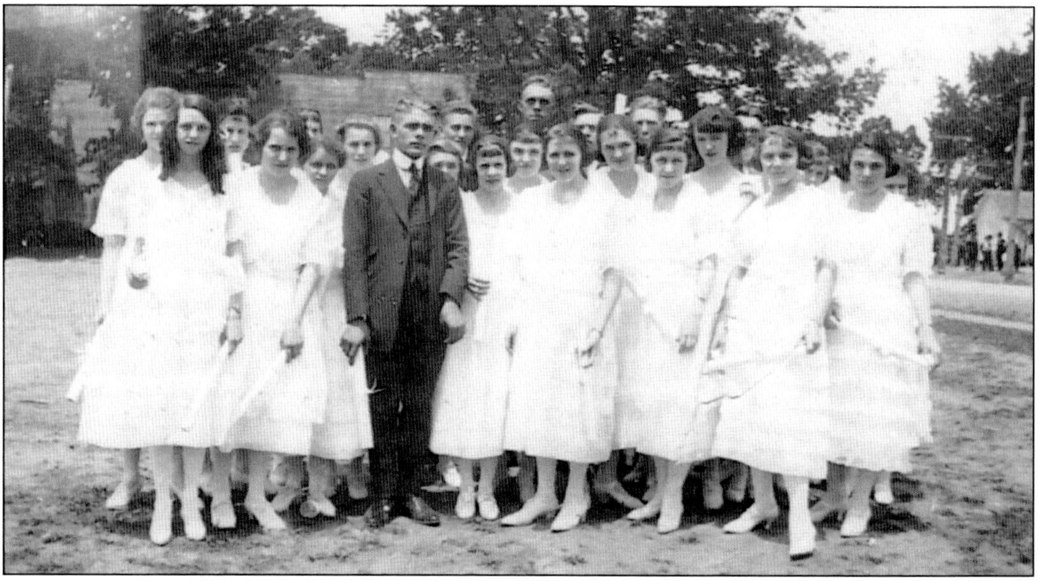

The 1921 graduates with diplomas in hand include (alphabetically) Dee Aldridge, Belton Beeson, Pansy Donnell, Mae Garrett, Esther Hicks, Stacy Hockett, Irene Holt, Ruth Holt, Verda Holt, Alma Jones, Rosa Kirkman, Mary Klinger, Esther Marley, Laura Neese, Doris Neelley, Mary Newman, Dewey McCulloch, William McCulloch, Clifton Parrish, Annie Phipps, Bessie Phipps, Elizabeth Rankin, Kathleen Riley, Pherlie Siske, Annie Rudd, Herman Sampson, and Ruth Sampson.

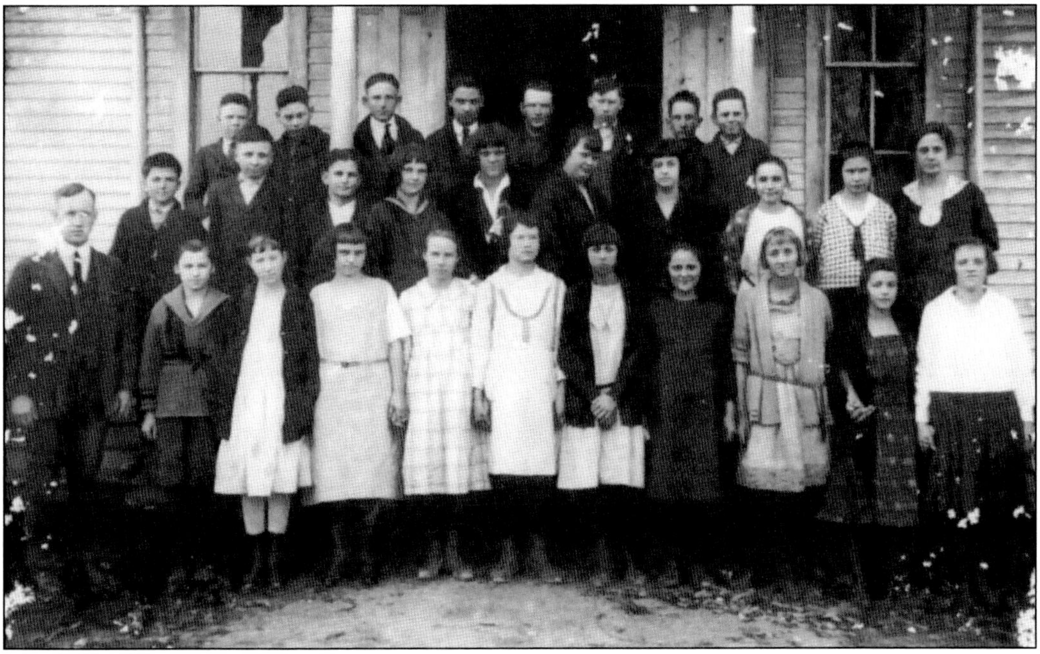

In this 1921 photograph of seventh graders, principal E.D. Idol is standing in the front row, far left; the teacher that year, Mary Cooper is standing in the second row, far right. Third from the right in the front row is Marjorie Reddick, who was born in 1908. Seventh graders received a certificate similar to a diploma because many students chose to end their education at that time.

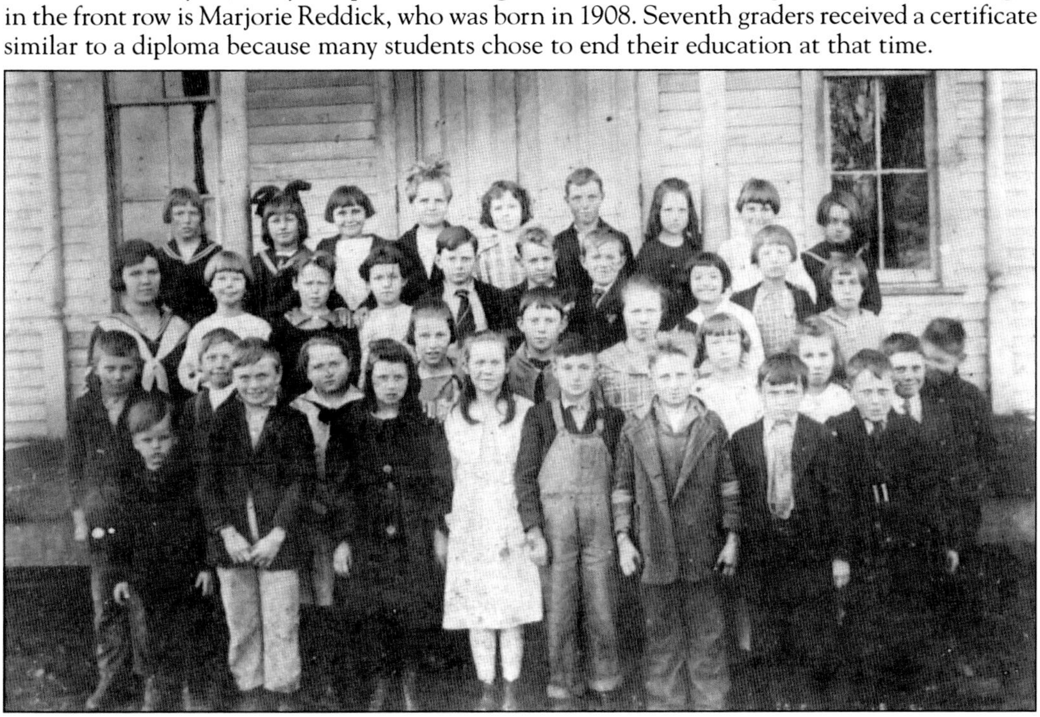

This group of students appears to be a combination grade; some were in the class of 1928. Fourth from the left in the first row is Ruby Hackett (class of 1933), and fourth from the left in the second row is Mary Riley. Sam Kirkman and Hal Ross (class of 1928) are third and second from the right, respectively. Mrs. E.B. Moore taught second and fifth grades in 1921.

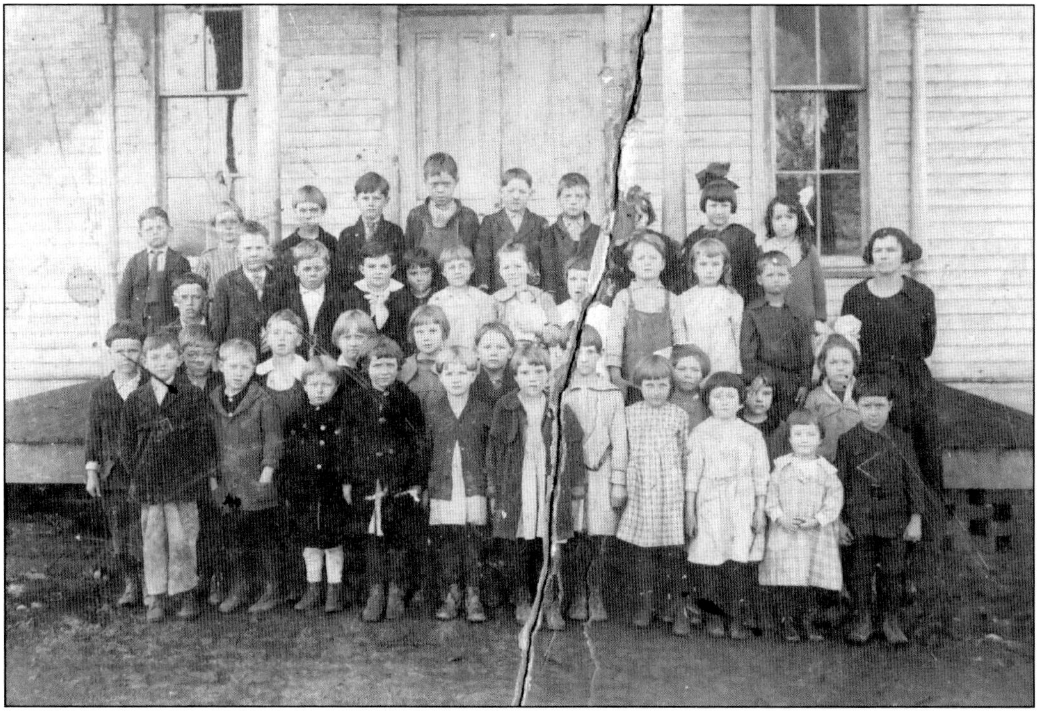

It is thought that the children seen in this 1920 photograph were in the first or second grade. Identified are (first row) Charles T. Ross, second from the left; (second row) Dena Ross, fourth from the left; (third row) Helen Gray, sixth from the left. Cora McNeil taught first grade at that time. (Courtesy of Tom Ross.)

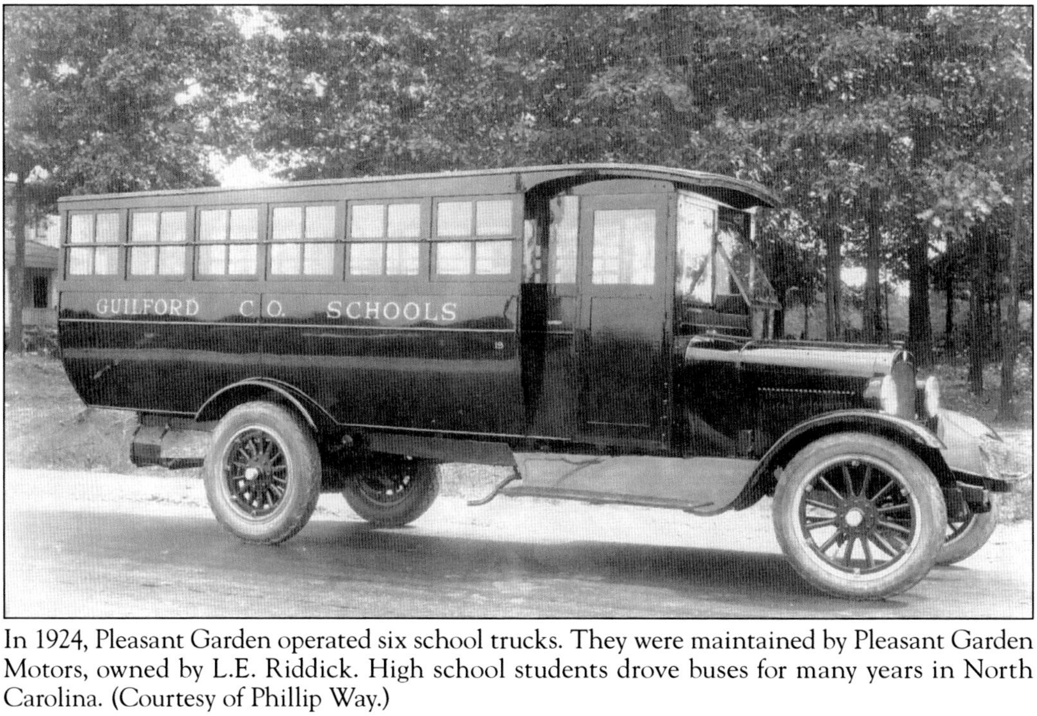

In 1924, Pleasant Garden operated six school trucks. They were maintained by Pleasant Garden Motors, owned by L.E. Riddick. High school students drove buses for many years in North Carolina. (Courtesy of Phillip Way.)

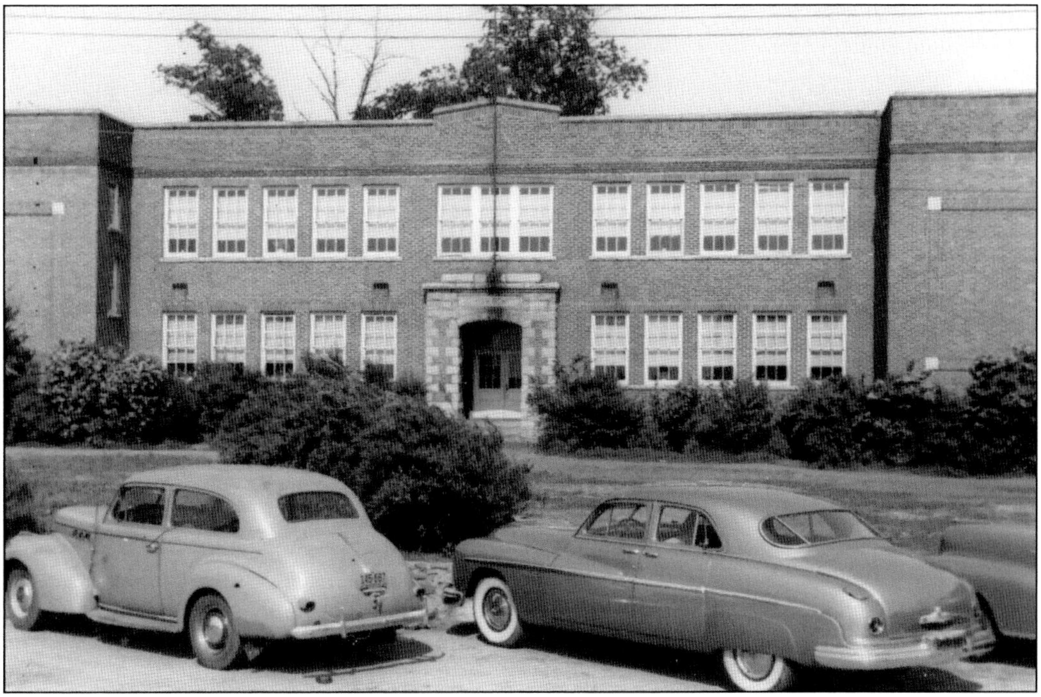

Contractor W.B. Hunt won the bid to construct the $35,000 "Economy Eight-Room Consolidated School House" that opened in 1923. The plan was modified, omitting the auditorium to provide 12 classrooms and four offices. The basement housed a shop, forge, lumber storage, and an incubator room. At the time, there were two other standard high schools in the county, Jamestown and Pomona. The schoolhouse is pictured here around 1949.

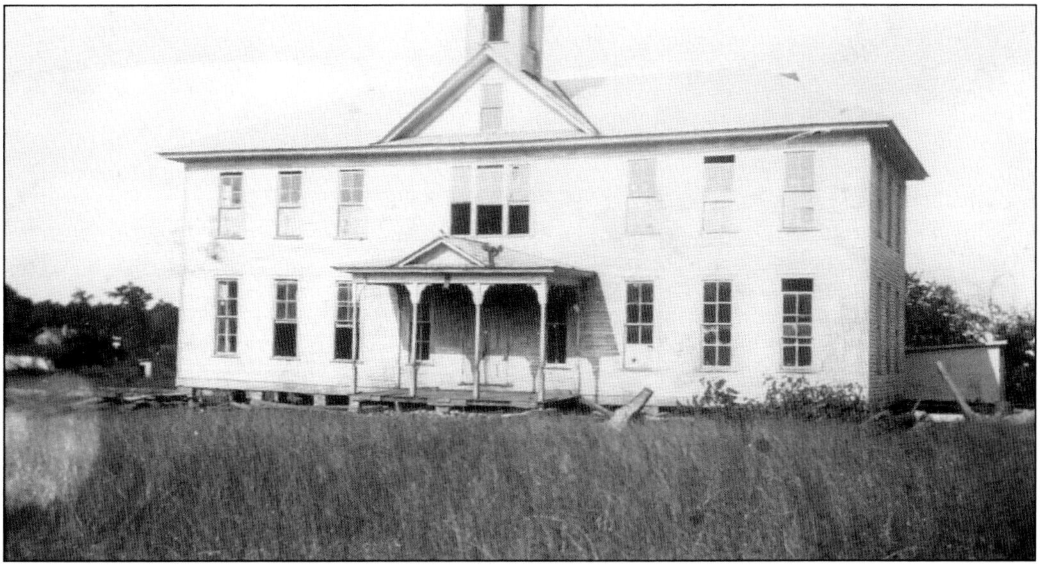

In 1925, the old high school building was unceremoniously rolled toward the railroad tracks to make room for a brick building to house elementary students. The former high school became the location of Buffalo Broom Works for a brief time before it was destroyed by fire.

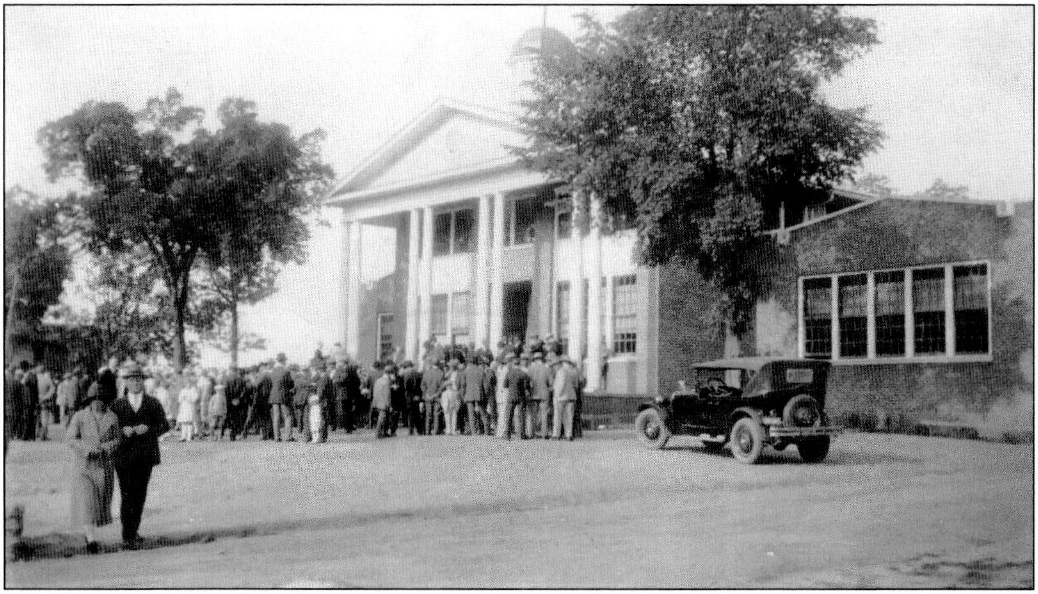

This building opened in 1926. It housed six classrooms and an auditorium, making it the scene of many school and community performances. It also had an office and library room. Wade H. Crawford was the principal.

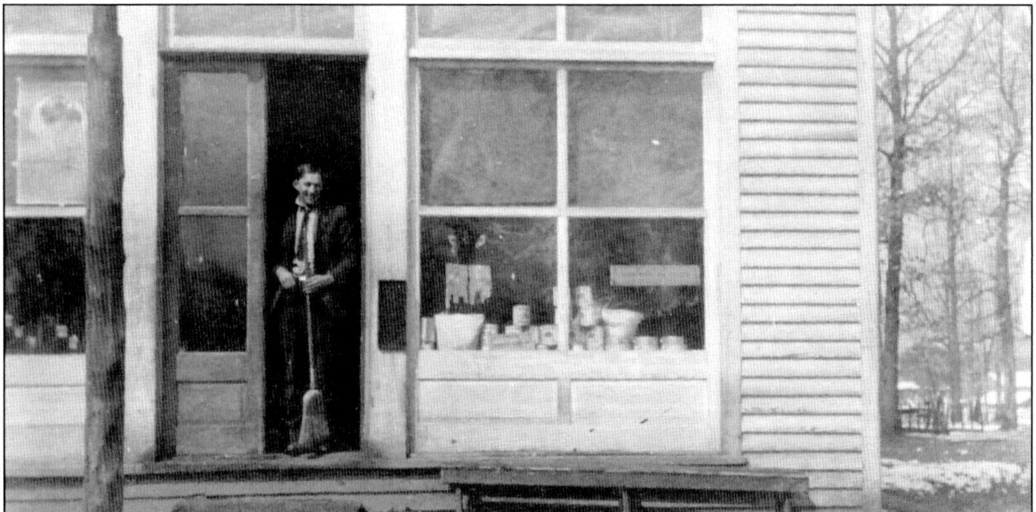

J. Frank Ross is all smiles as he stands in the doorway of his store, located across the street from the school. J.F. Ross Cash Store carried groceries, gas and oils, rough lumber, and framing cut to order.

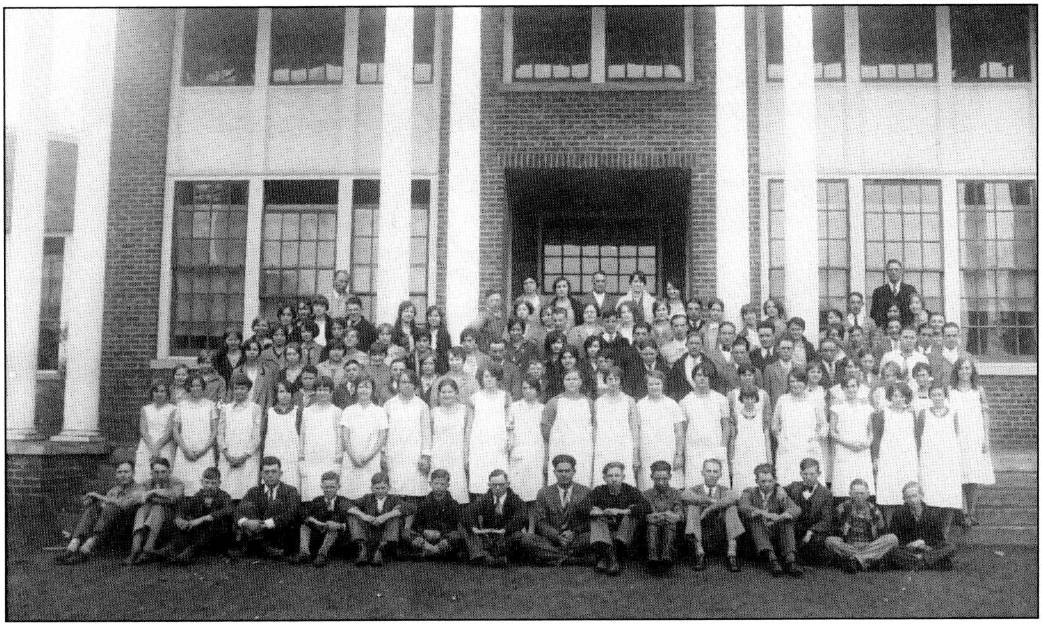

The new building became the backdrop for many school photographs. First-year home economics students are attired in aprons they made in class. Wade H. Crawford was the principal at the time of this 1928 photograph.

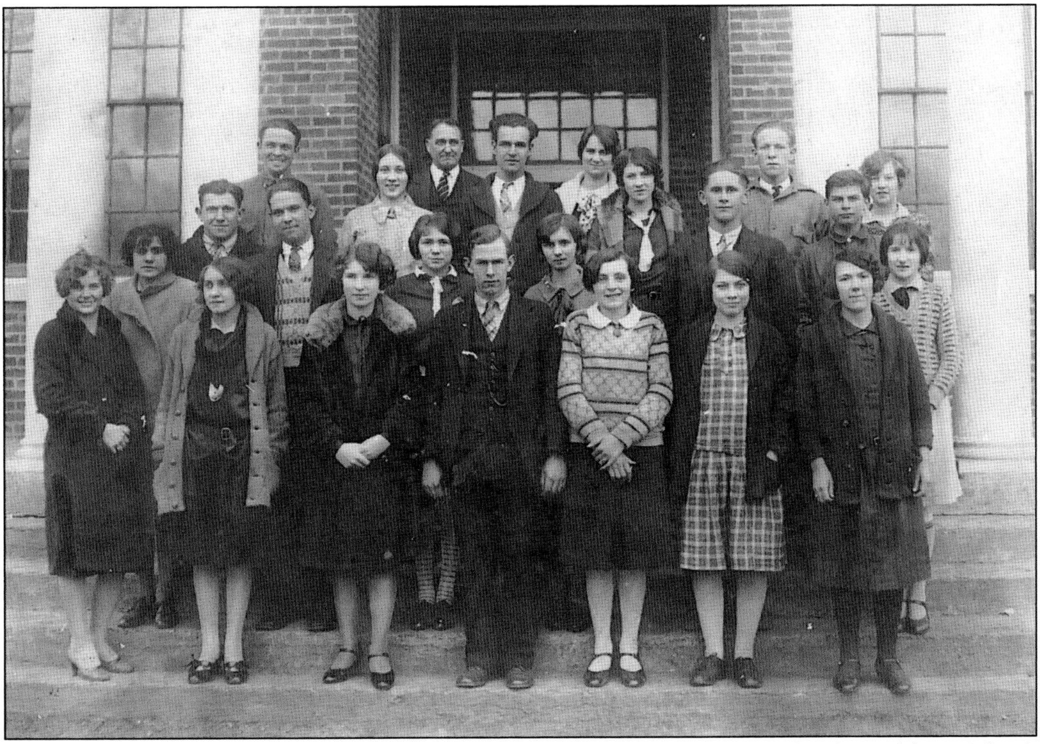

The class of 1928 was small. Some of the members were Mary Katherine Adcock, Kathleen Allred, Chris Bayer, Clada Berry, Martha Fulgram, Kate Garrett, Lucille Latham, Helen Lasley, Sam Kirkman, George Reynolds, Jeanette Reynolds, Hal Ross, Paul Smith, and Villa Underwood.

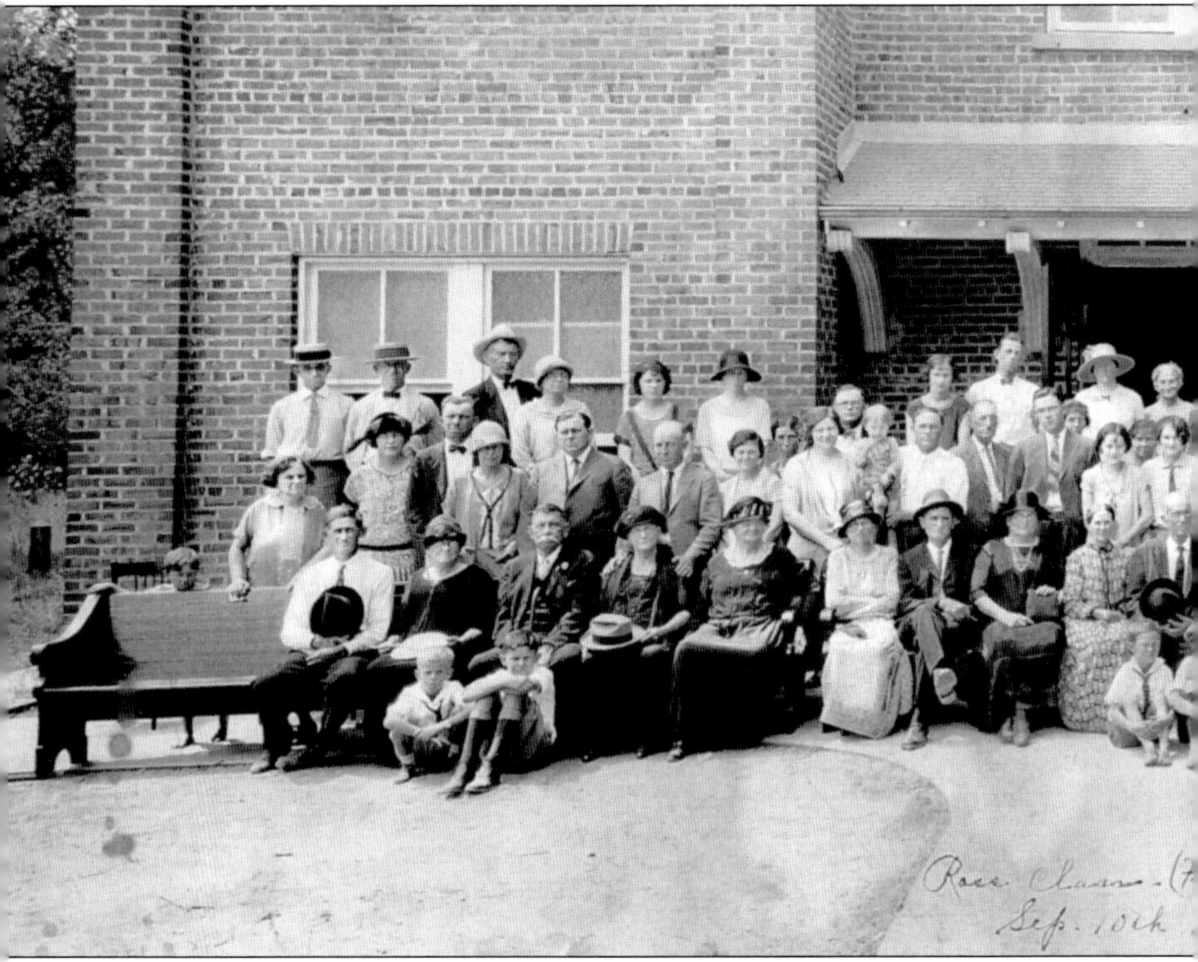

Discovering one's lineage was fashionable in September 1925 when the first Ross Reunion was held. Most of the attendees were descended from Leven Ross and his two wives, Elizabeth Neelley and Margaret Denny. In deference to age, the older cousins were seated on the first row. The following list of names is arranged by residency and is not a seating chart: Rom and Ellen Ross, George and Margaret Ross, George Ross Jr., William Goley Ross, and Esther Ross came from Asheboro. Amelia Cranford, Jack Cranford, Mary and Henry Phipps, Alta Phipps, Ethel and Gurley Coble, Ruth and W.F. Ross, Tela and Joe Manson, Bette and Jim Landreth, Mabel Landreth, Frances Landreth, Alia Josephine Ross, Laura Ross Smith, Lelah Perkins and Aubrey Perkins came from Greensboro. Julia and Joe Hodgin, Blanche Hodgin, Blanche Hodgin and Ona Hodgin lived in the Centre community. Mary and W.B. Hunt, Lynn Hunt, Paul Hunt, James Hunt and Mary

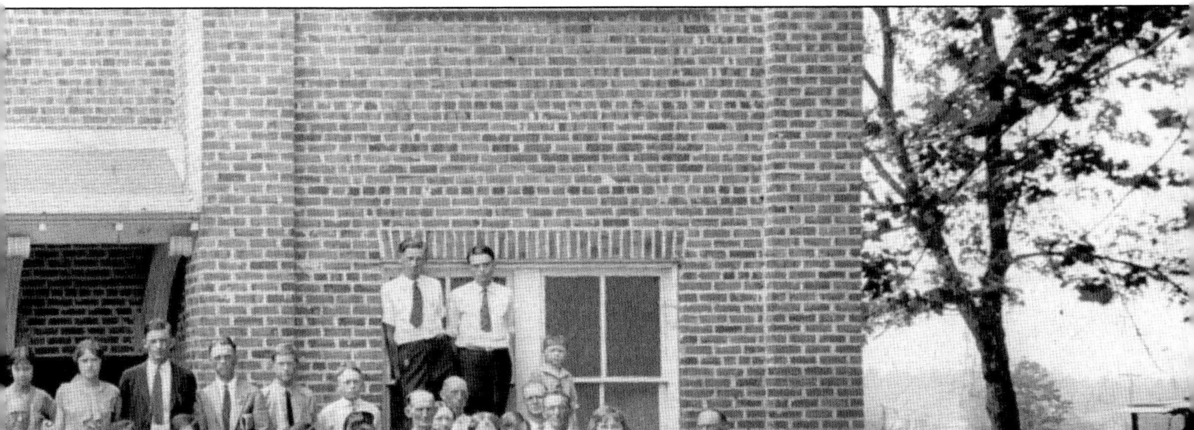

Elizabeth Hunt, Kate and B.W. Kirkman, David Kirkman, Mary Moling Kirkman, John Hardin, Annie Hardin, and Estella Fentriss lived south of the church. Oliver Ross, Claude Ross, Ila Ross, Clay Ross, Menzell Ross, Hal Ross, Dena Ross, and Wynne Ross lived near the old homeplace. Charles and Kate Ross, Minnie Ross, Charles Ross, Laura Ross, and Delbert Ross lived in the Col. Neelley house. Percy King, Mary Burgess, Jimmy Burgess, Octavia Fentress, Annie Ross, Nannie Tucker Ross, J. Frank Ross Jr., Robert Ross, and Nancy and Guy Ross lived near the center of the village. Clark Kirkman, C.H. Kirkman, Stacy Kirkman, Mary Kirkman, Marian Kirkman, and Lelia Kirkman lived on the farm that became the Pleasant Garden Municipal complex. Special guests were L.D. Mendenhall and Rev. Filmore McCulloch, a Methodist minister.

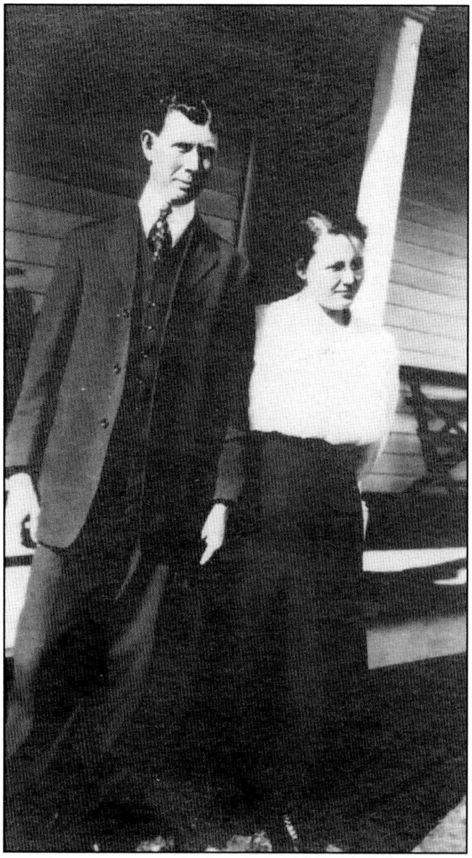

Cora John, a Pleasant Garden teacher, and Clark Kirkman married in 1918. She was from Robeson County. He farmed and managed the company store across the road from the school. They were the parents of four children—C.H., Stacy, Marian, and Mary. (Courtesy of Mary Routh.)

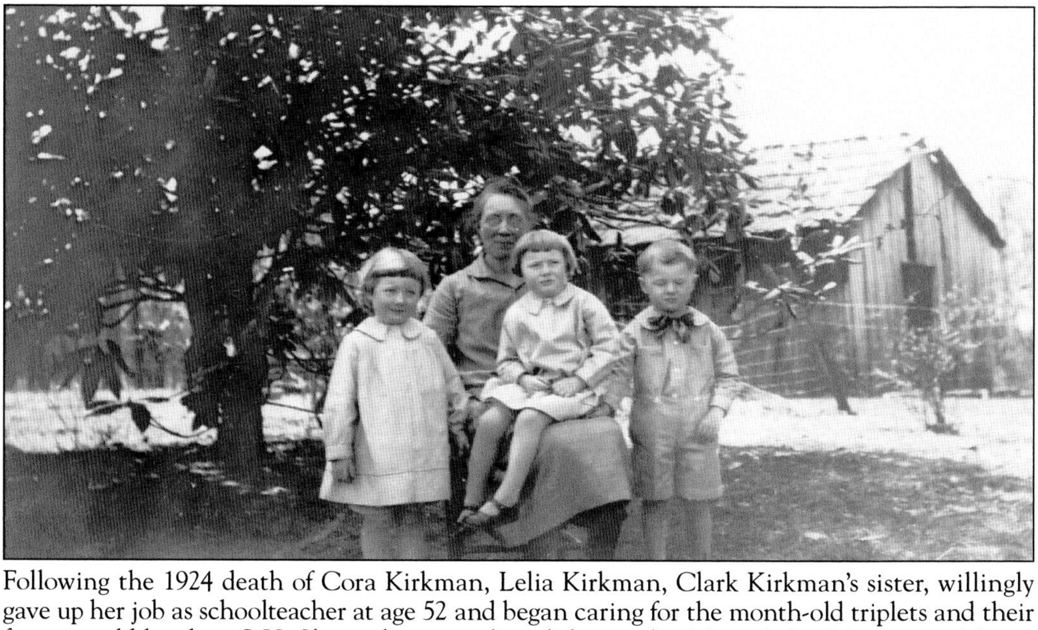

Following the 1924 death of Cora Kirkman, Lelia Kirkman, Clark Kirkman's sister, willingly gave up her job as schoolteacher at age 52 and began caring for the month-old triplets and their four-year-old brother, C.H. Shown here are, from left to right, Mary, Lelia, Marian, and Stacy Kirkman. (Courtesy of Mary Routh.)

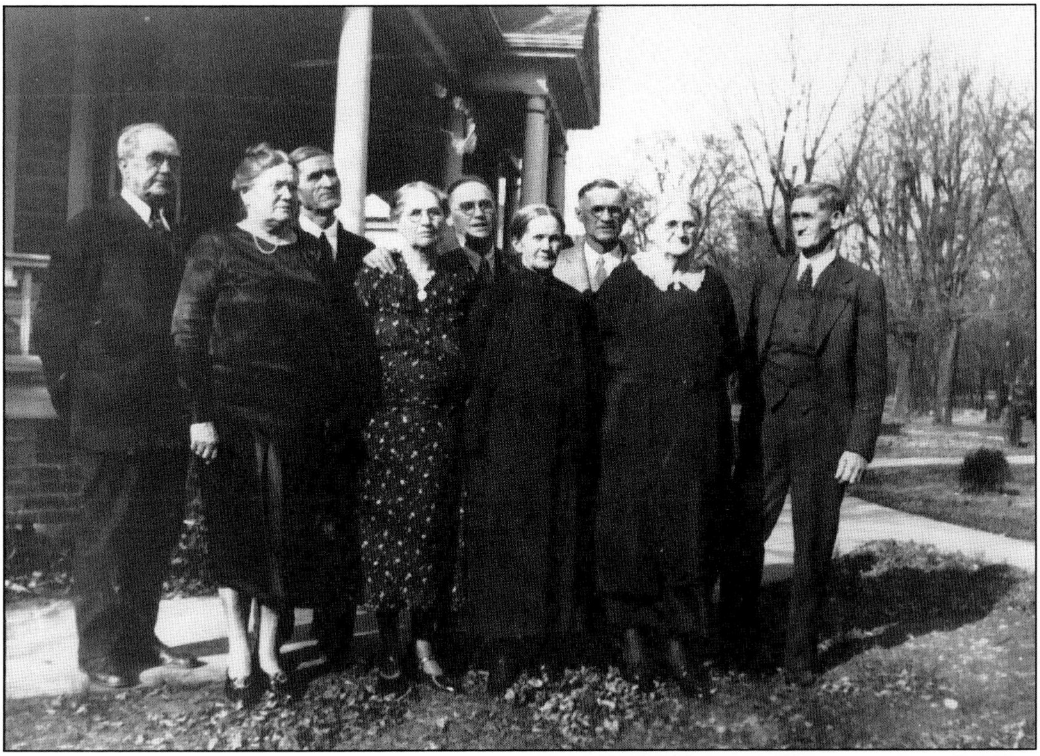

The children of Addison and Letitia Ross are pictured here at the A.N. Perkins residence on Asheboro Street. From left to right are Robert Ross, Lelah Perkins, Oliver Ross, Mary Hunt, Charles Ross, Bette Landreth, Will Ross, Julia Hodgin, and Claude Ross.

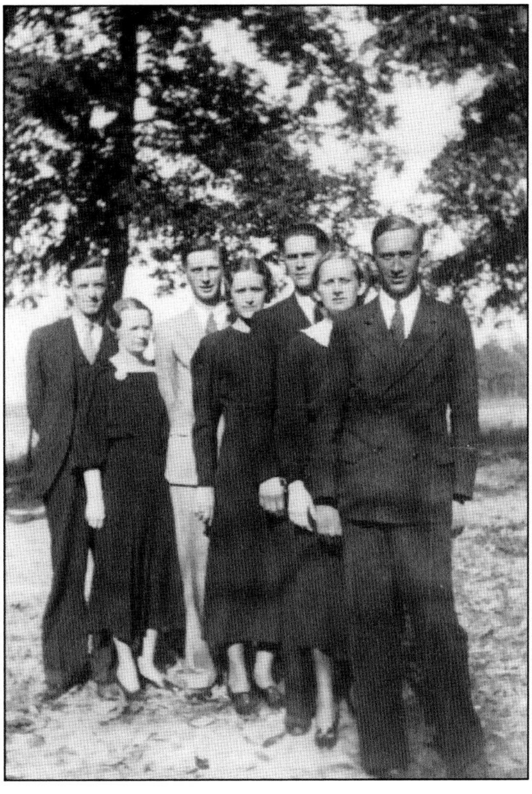

Claude and Maude Matthews Ross's children line up around 1940 from oldest to youngest. From left to right are Guy Ross, Ila Holt, Clay Ross, Menzel Fields, Hal Ross, Dena Kirkman, and Wynne Ross. When their mother died, Guy was 13 and Wynne was just seven months old. Maude's aunt Mary Matthews, a former schoolteacher and nearly 65 years old, stepped in to keep the family together.

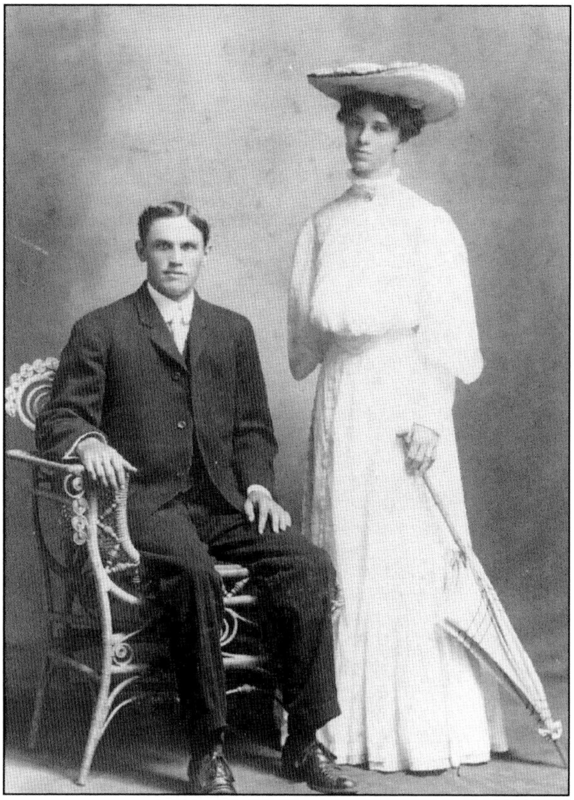

Charles T. Ross and Kate Gray were married at Pleasant Garden Methodist Episcopal Church on June 21, 1905. The *Patriot* reported, "After the ceremony there was a reception at the home of the bride's father, Dr. C. Gray. The following day a reception was given the happy couple at the home of the groom's mother, Mrs. A.S. Ross. The wedding presents were numerous and beautiful." (Courtesy of Tom Ross.)

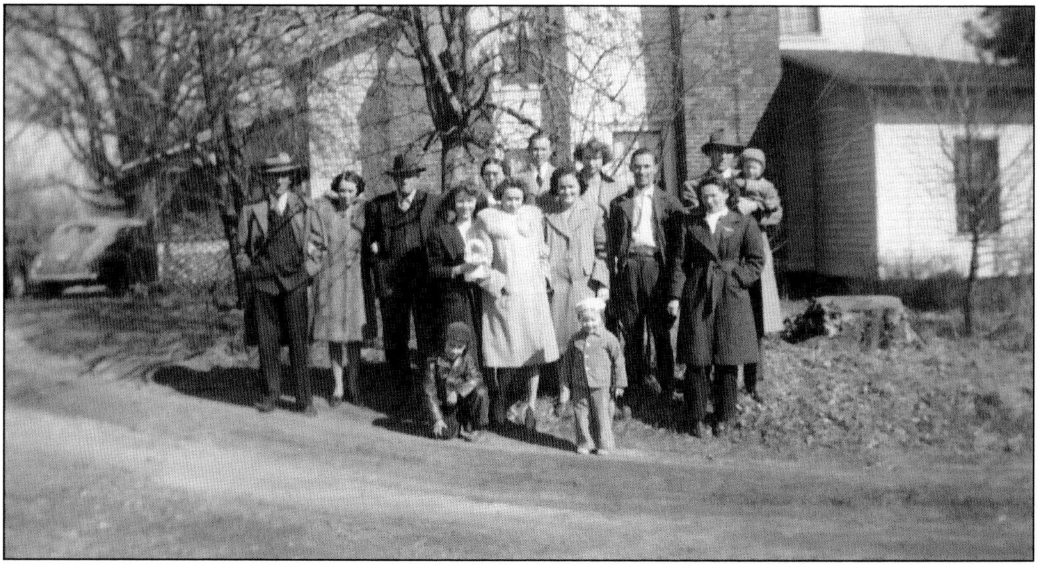

Charles and Kate Ross reared their family in the Colonel Neelley house that is in the background of this photograph from about 1942. From left to right are (first row) Frank Plunkett and Libby Jo Ross; (second row) Betsy and Minnie Brown, Lorene and Delbert Ross, and Eva Ross; (third row) Frank and Inez Plunkett, Charles and Kate Ross, George and Sarah Kate Redmond, and Charles Ross holding his son Tom. Two other children, Laura Ross and Jack Ross, were not present. (Courtesy of Tom Ross.)

W.B. and Mary Ross Hunt moved to Pleasant Garden in 1919. He was a farmer and builder. Three of their five sons later married and lived near the village. W.B. Hunt Jr. and his wife, Ruth Huffman, lived in the homeplace, formerly the residence of Frederick Fentress. In this mid-1920s portrait are Lynn Ross Hunt and Emma Ruth Hadley, who were married in 1926 and settled near Pa and Ma Hunt. They met while Lynn lived near Greensboro College, where Ruth was enrolled. The parents of three children, they were active in the Methodist church, the Lions Club, and the American Red Cross. (Courtesy of Polly Dickson.)

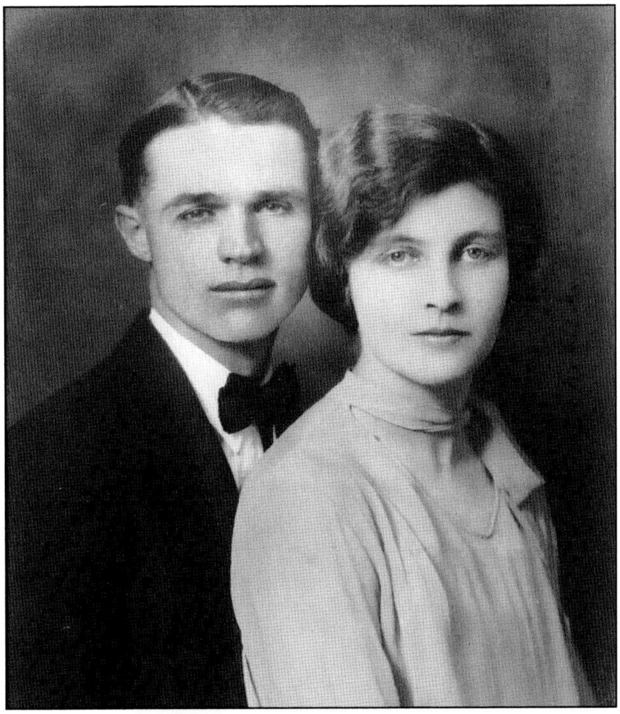

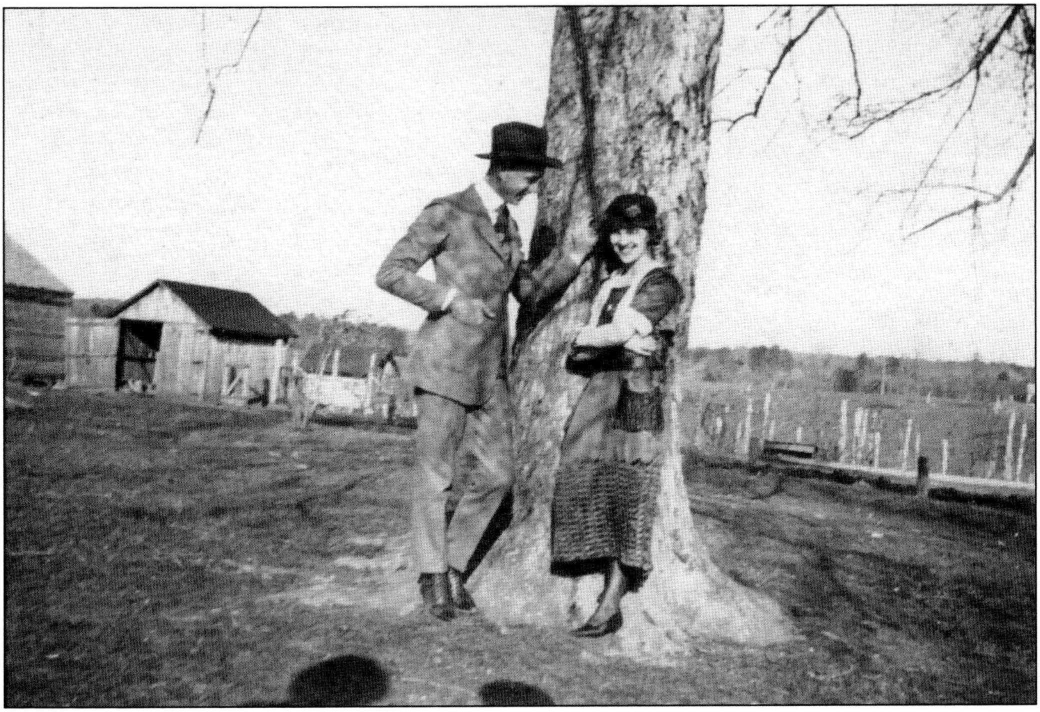

This image captures a young courting couple, Charles Jackson Hunt and Frances McLeod, who married in 1923. They settled next to his parents, where he operated Piney Grove Dairy, worked as a builder, and later served as Guilford County commissioner for 20 years. A mother of four, Fannie was active in Pleasant Garden United Methodist Church. (Courtesy of Ann Harden.)

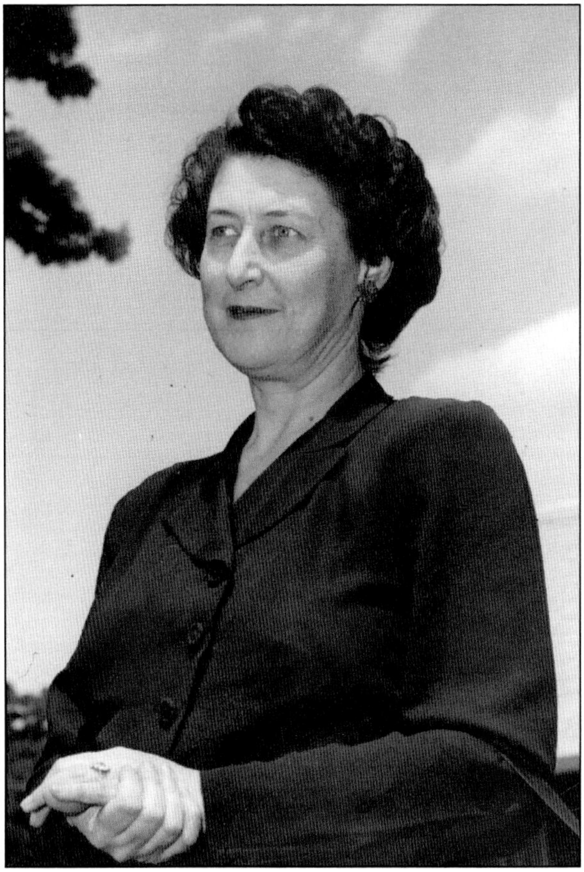

After graduating from North Carolina College for Women, Nell Kennett returned to Pleasant Garden High School to teach home economics in 1930. After five years, she became a home extension agent. She retired as a state home economics agent at North Carolina State University.

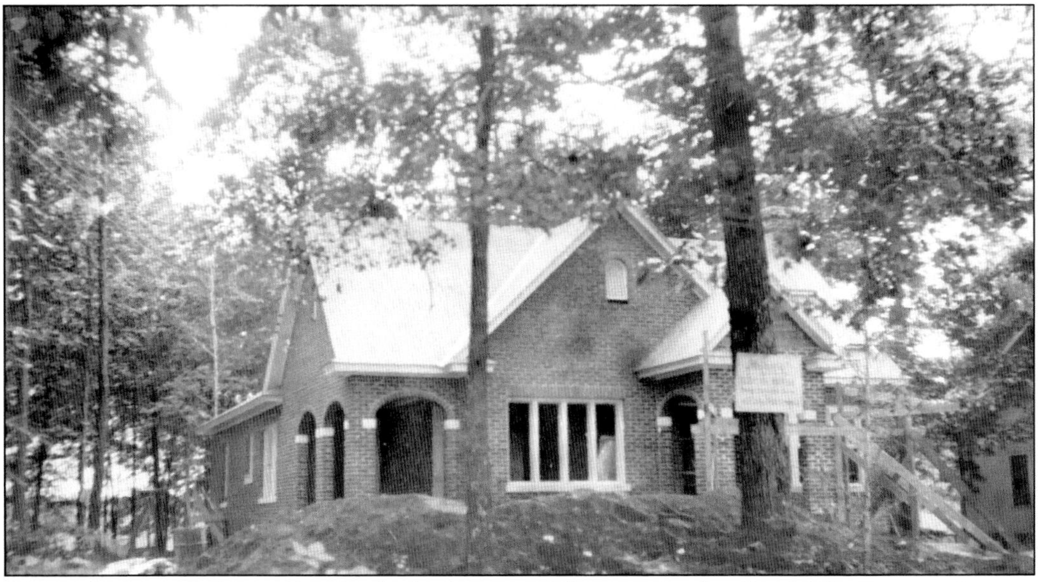

Guy and Nancy Coleman Ross built this home on Pleasant Garden Road. The sign on the tree boasts that it is to have a Hotpoint stove. Due to economic conditions of the era, construction ceased for a year until finances could be attained. It was completed in 1929.

Three

The 1930s

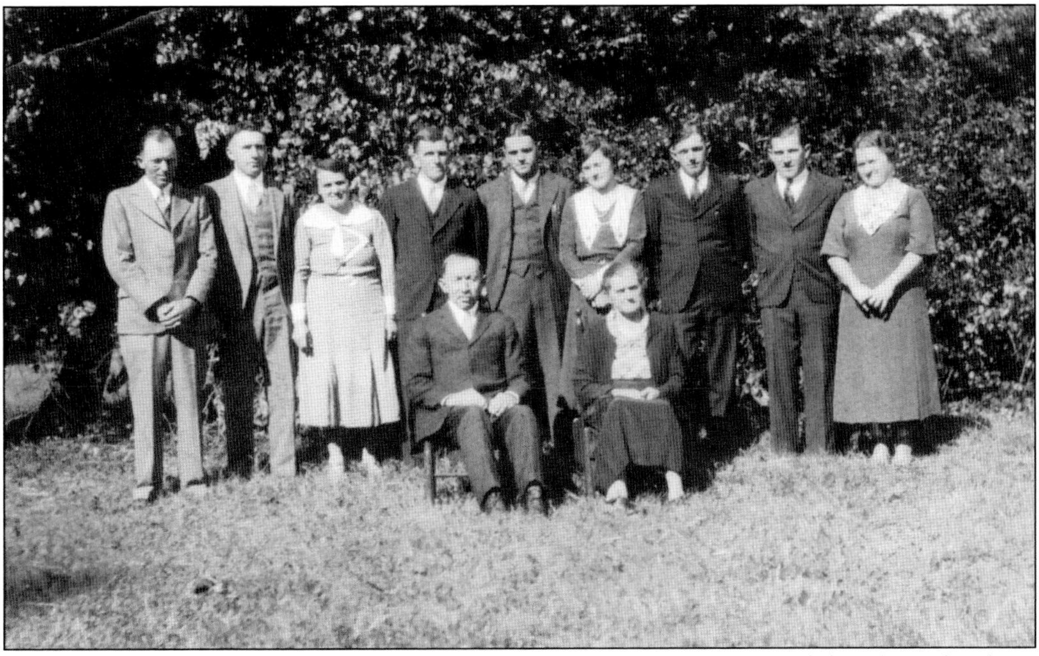

William Charles and Georgia Greeson Kirkman proudly pose in front of their large family in the early 1930s. From left to right are Thomas, John, Nancy, Robert, Charles, Margaret, James, Samuel, and Rosa Mae. The elder Kirkman was a farmer, as were most of his children. (Courtesy of Jane Kimel.)

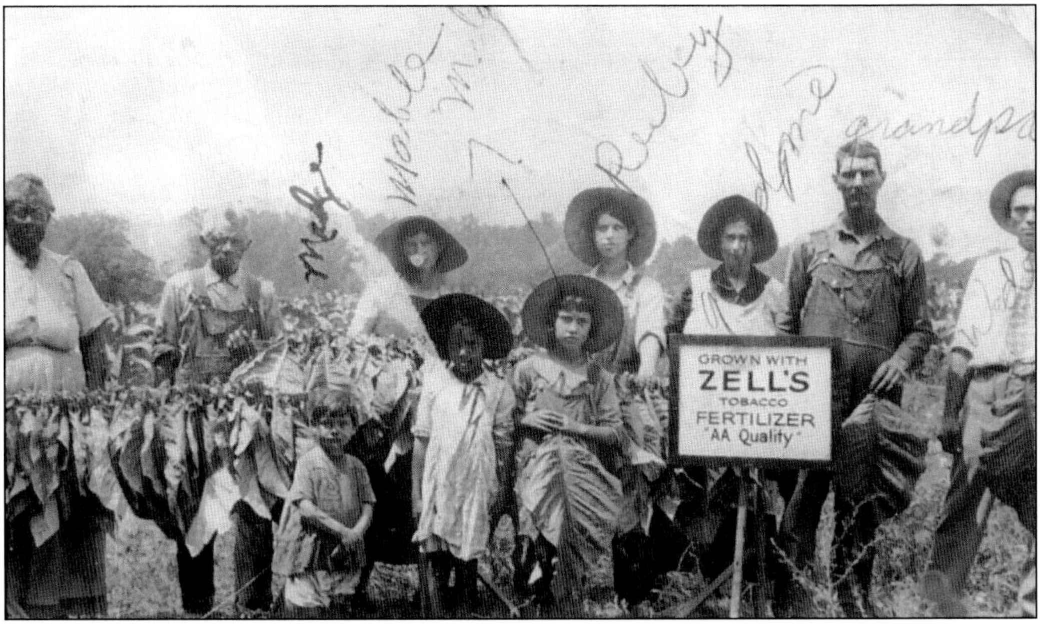

John and Clara "Kate" Fields Hackett lived on a farm she inherited from her family. They began growing tobacco in 1910. Fertilizer companies offered photographs as an incentive to tobacco growers who used their product, and this one was taken around 1929. Pictured are, from left to right, (first row) Madge Hackett, Clara May Avant, and Mildred Hackett; (second row) "Aunt" Susie and "Uncle" Henry McAdoo, Mable, Ruby, Clara, and John Hackett, and Wade Kearns. The McAdoos were tenant farmers and lived on the property; Avant was their grandchild. (Courtesy of Ruth Ann Jones.)

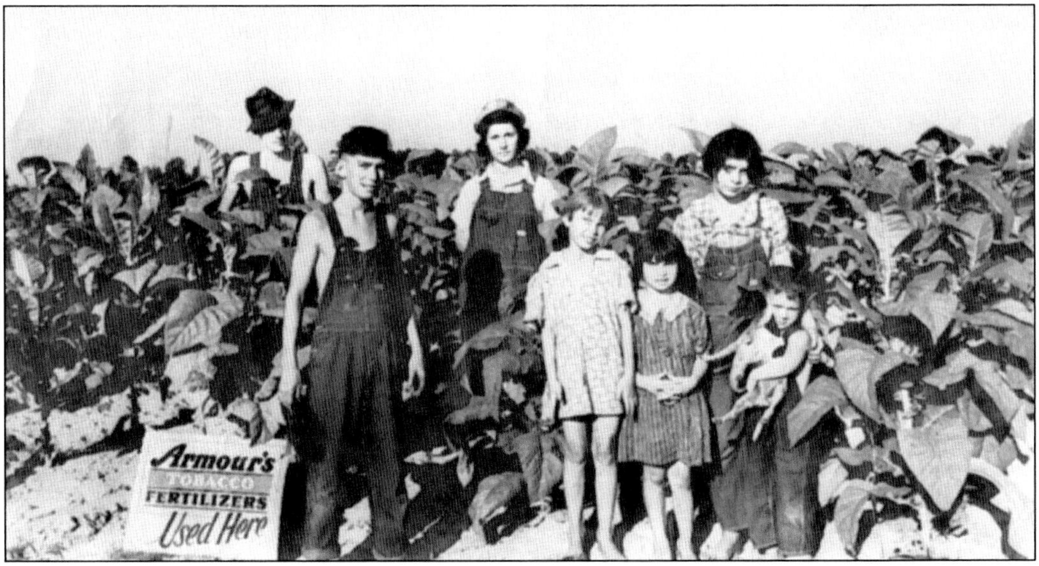

These are the workers in John Hackett's tobacco field a few years later. Pictured are, from left to right, Darius Hinshaw, Jack, Mildred, Mary, Barbara, Madge, and Joe Hackett, the youngest cradling Fritz, a favorite dog. Hackett also raised wheat and corn. Hinshaw was the youngest son of Marshal Hinshaw, whose family tenant-farmed with John and Kate Hackett for 17 years. (Courtesy of Ruth Ann Jones.)

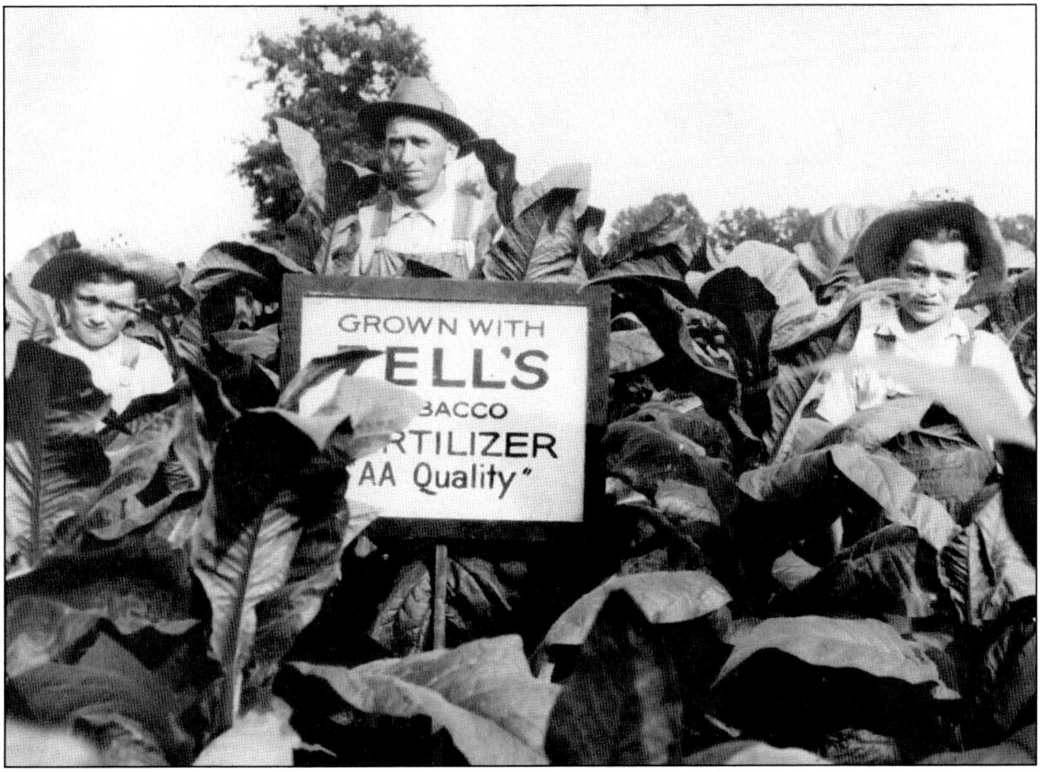

Marcus Kearns's farm adjoined Hackett's. He and his sons J.C. (left) and Thomas pose in a field of tall tobacco in the early 1930s. Thomas Kearns later attended North Carolina State, where he lettered in baseball. He organized a Little League baseball team in the village in the 1950s. (Courtesy of Anne Hice.)

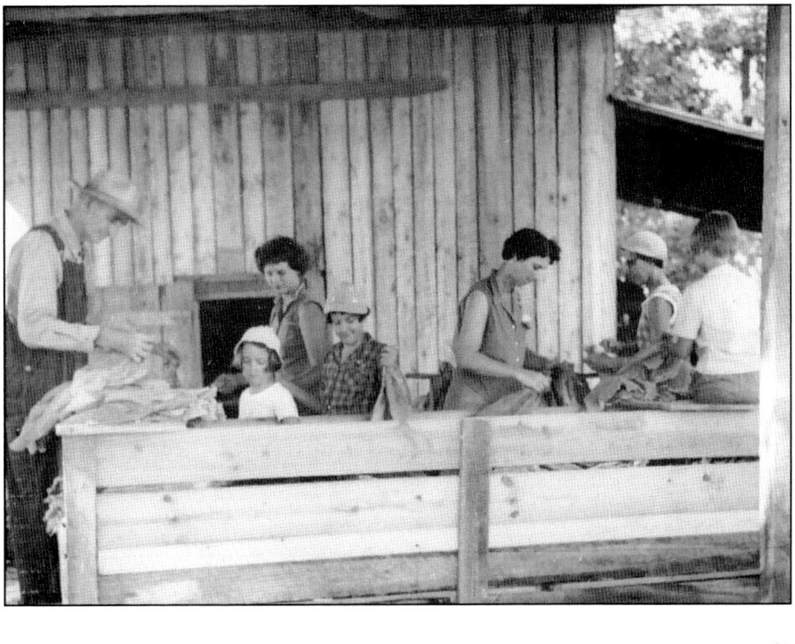

In this 1950s scene, from left to right, Wilbur Hockett, Diane Priddy, Ernestine Williams, Patricia Priddy, Ruby Marley, Phoebe Priddy and Donna Marley load a barn of tobacco by tying leaves to sticks that will be hung in the barn to dry and turn to gold. (Courtesy of Ruth Ann Jones.)

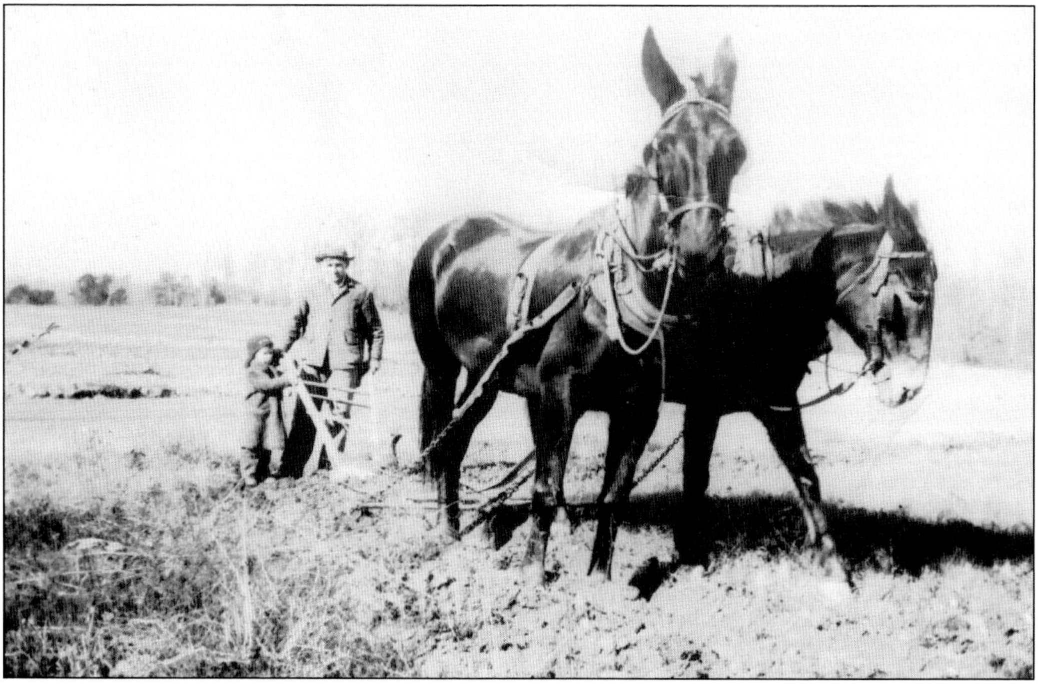

Robert Kirkman is pictured here teaching his son Charles how to grasp the handles of a plow around 1940. The elder Kirkman tilled the soil on a farm his father, William Charles Kirkman, acquired earlier in the 20th century. (Courtesy of Charles Kirkman.)

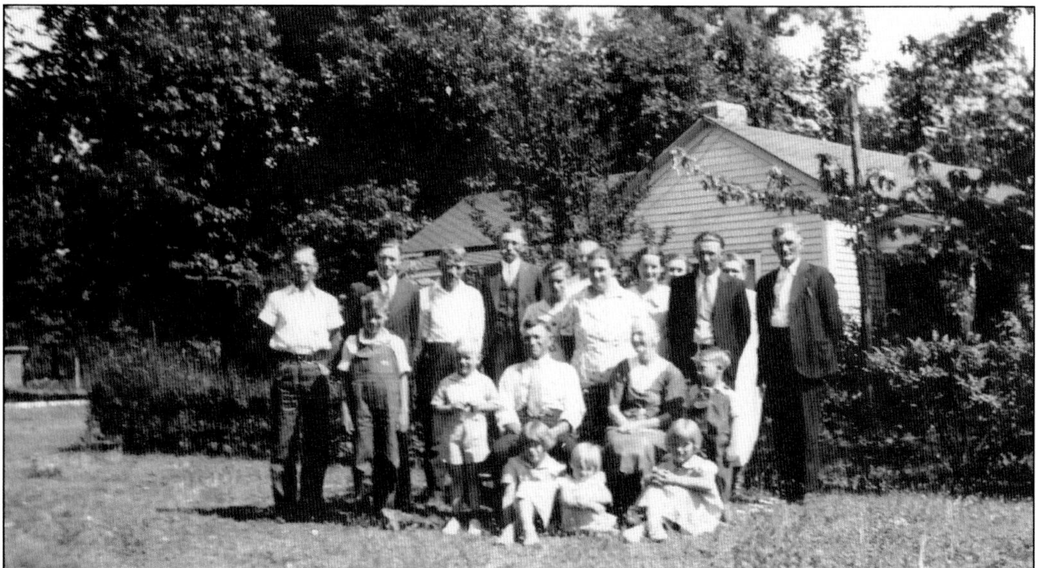

Two men named John Berry lived side by side in the curve on Steeple Chase Road. One was called "Road John" because he worked on the roads. In this mid-1930s photograph is the extended family of "Mule John," so named because of the teams of mules he used to plow and tend crops around the village. (Courtesy of Wilbur Berry.)

The Great Depression impelled families to move from an impoverished Bladen County. That is when William and Jane Melvin Dunham and 11 of their 12 children moved to Pleasant Garden to tenant-farm. Their nine sons formed the nucleus of many championship baseball teams. (Courtesy of Ruth Ann Jones.)

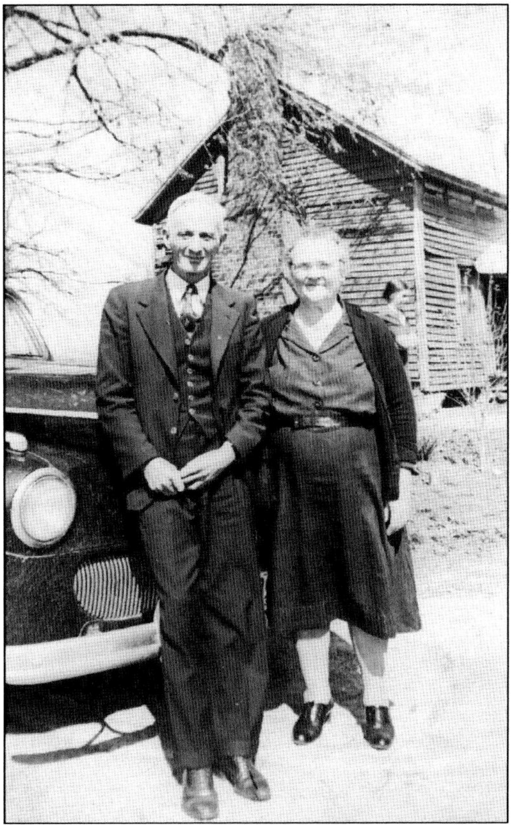

James Marley may have courted Mary Dunham in this roadster. She had recently moved to Guilford County with her parents, William and Jane Dunham. James and Mary were married in 1933. He farmed, and worked as a carpenter with his brother Ervin during the winter. (Courtesy of Audrey Rumley.)

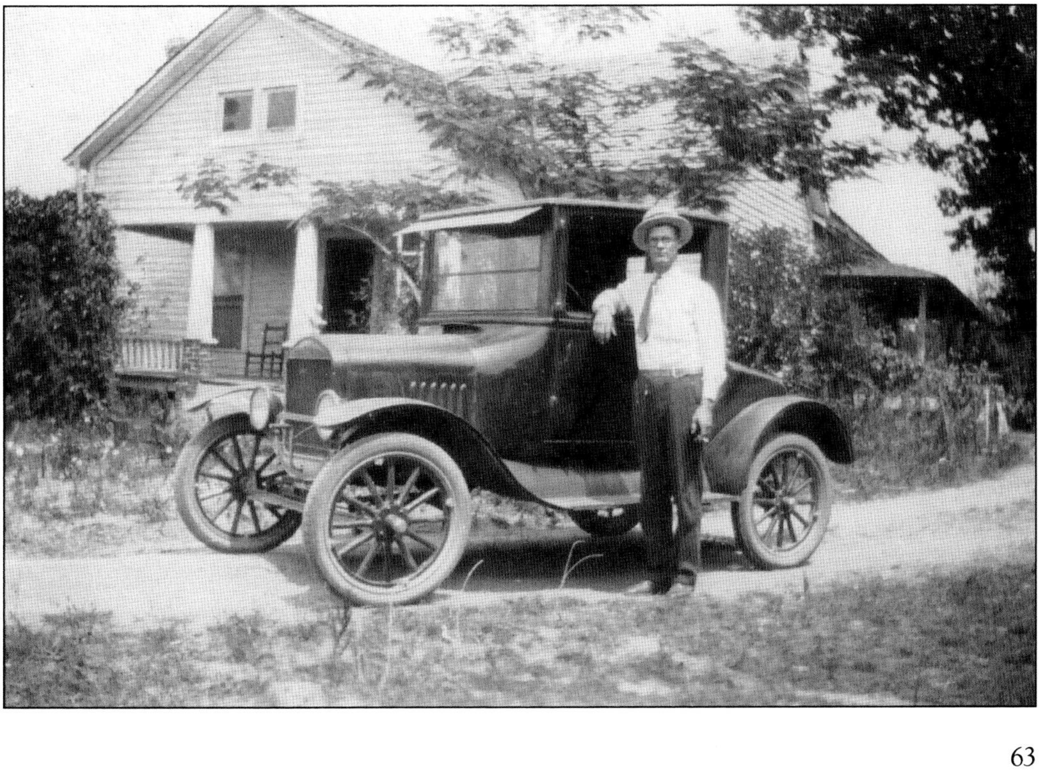

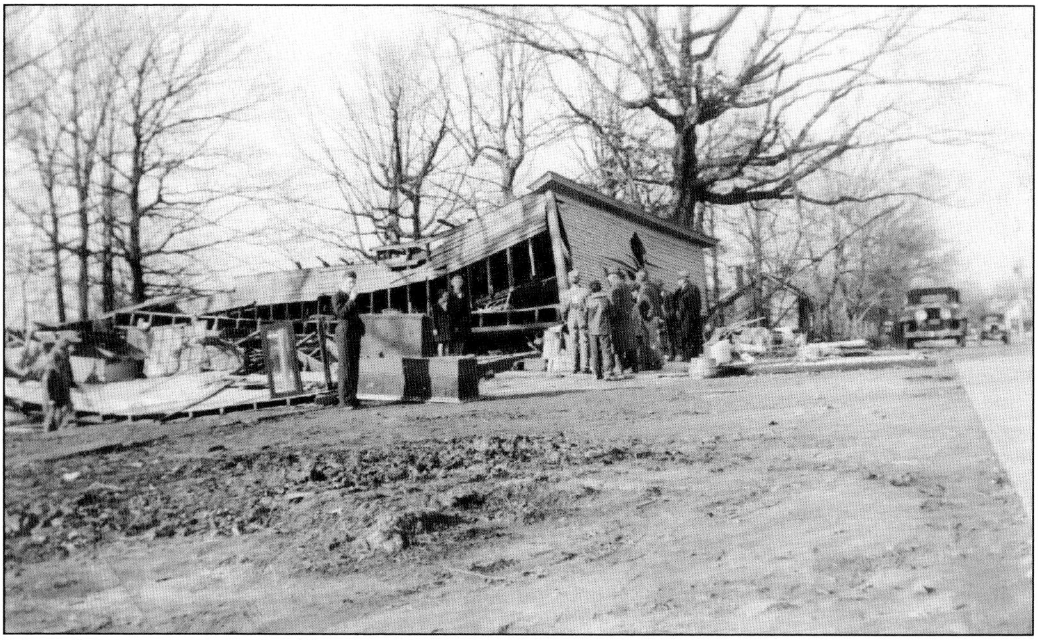

J. Frank Ross's two-story building was decimated by "winds of cyclonic proportions" that flattened and pushed it east into the road on a Sunday morning in April 1936. E.R. Tucker was operating a store and John Foust a barbershop on the first floor. Emory and Eva Bowman were able to escape with cuts and bruises from their second-floor living quarters as the structure collapsed. (Courtesy of Phillip Way.)

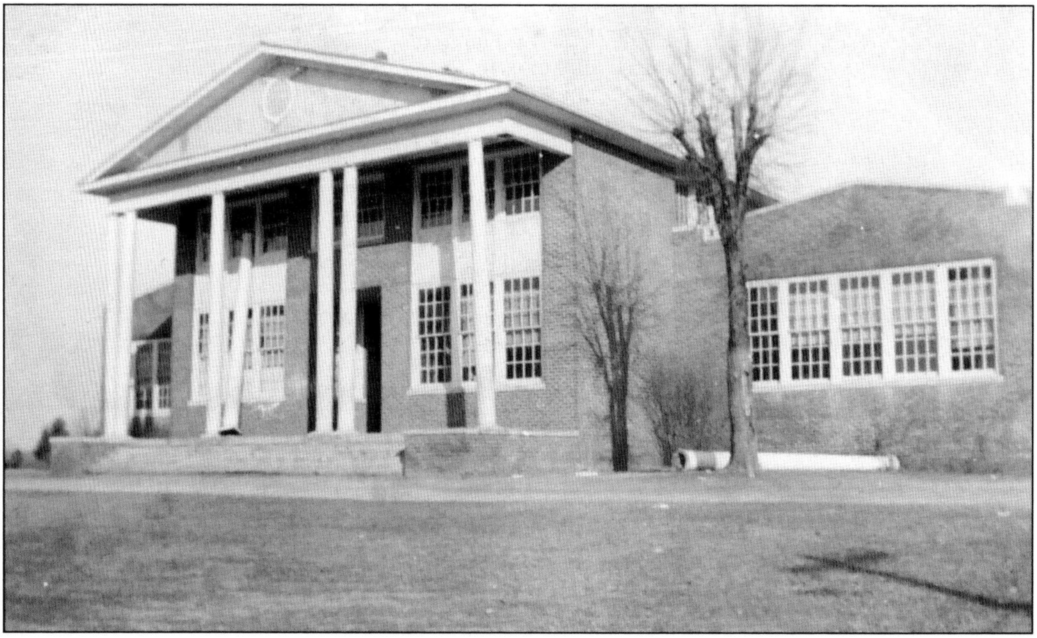

Way Lumber Company was west of the store and suffered very little damage. However, to the east, strong winds dislodged columns of the school auditorium and blew one out of place. The belfry was carried away, leaving holes in the roof that caused significant water damage from the heavy downpour. (Courtesy of Phillip Way.)

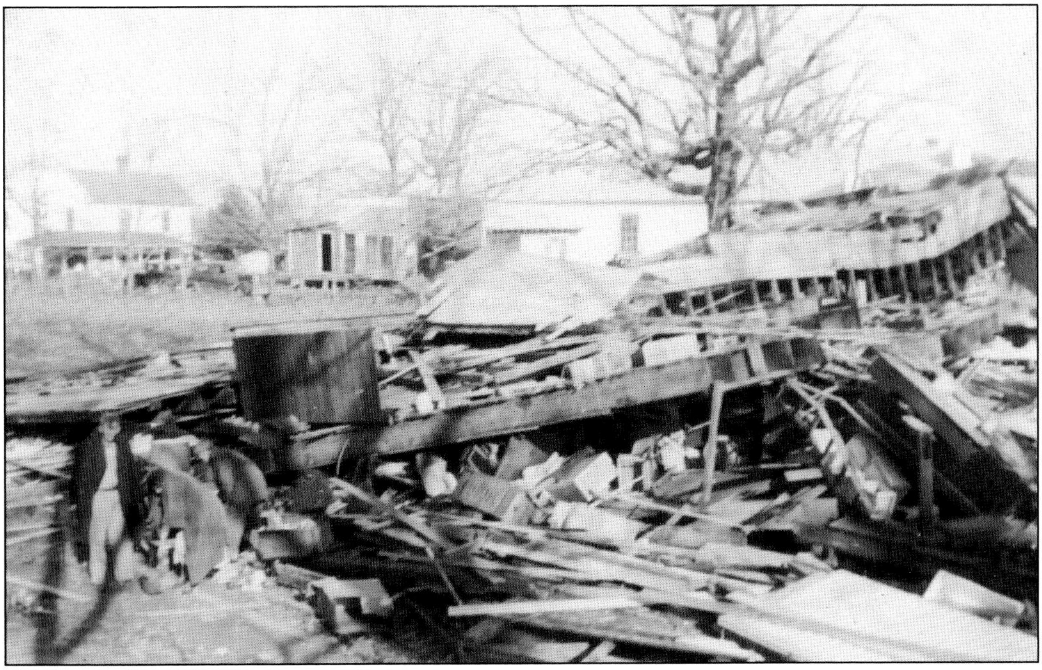

Gleaners harvested what was salvageable in the debris. John Foust and his son J.W. found enough wood to build a small barbershop. The Gray/Hendrix house is in the background. (Courtesy of Phillip Way.)

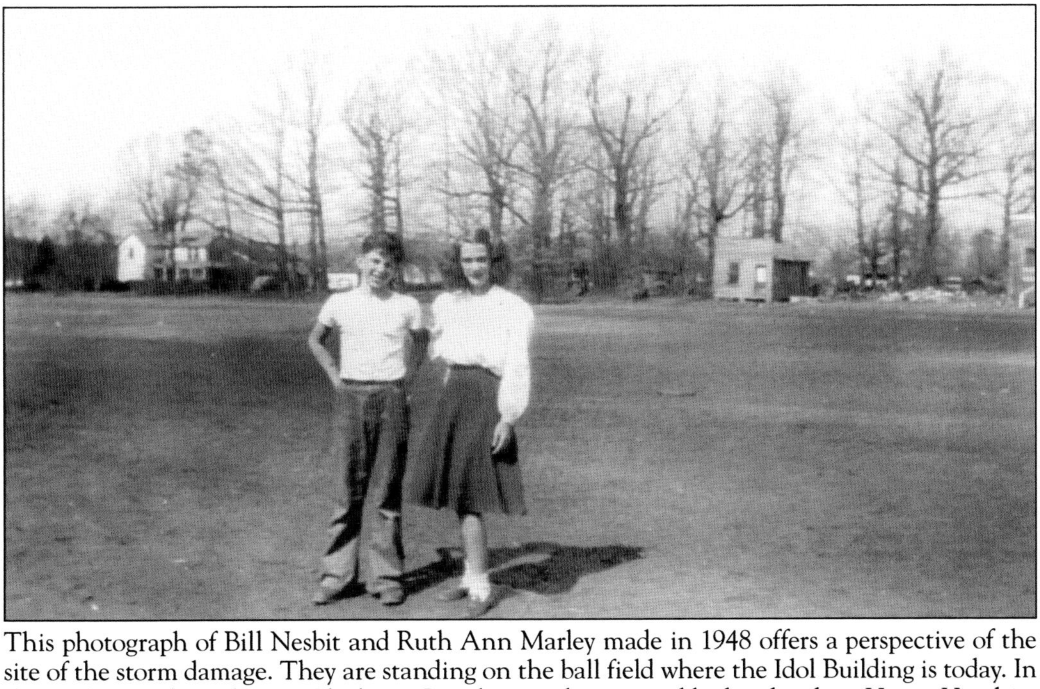

This photograph of Bill Nesbit and Ruth Ann Marley made in 1948 offers a perspective of the site of the storm damage. They are standing on the ball field where the Idol Building is today. In the background are the Dr. Clayborn Gray house, then owned by his daughter Hattie Hendrix, and the barbershop John and J.W. Foust built. (Courtesy of Ruth Ann Jones.)

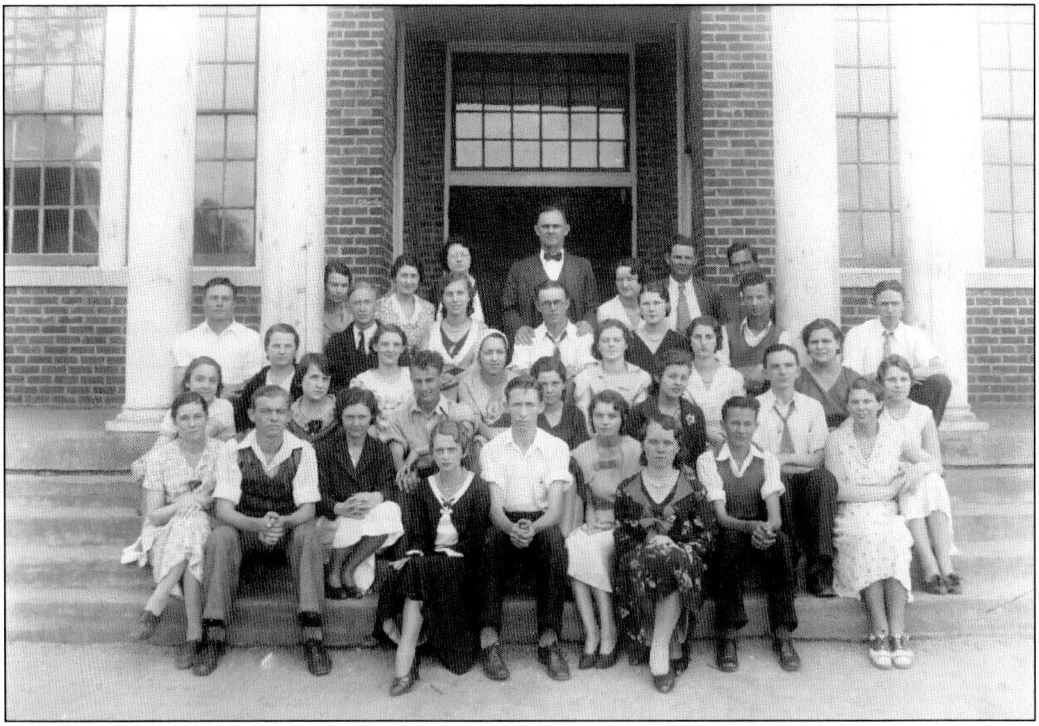

Members of the class of 1932 are (alphabetically) Margaret Baynes, Marnee Burgess, Frances Fentress, Florence Fields, Louise Foust, Harold Gray, Mary Emily Jones, Clarence Hinshaw, Lee Kirkman, Sarah Kirkman, Helen Lasley, Starr Layton, Julia Ledbetter, Frances Michael, Dozier Moser, William Newman, Ruth Overman, Allene Pugh, Charles Riley, Wynne Ross, Edwin Sharpe, Clara Sillmon, Henry Clay Smith, Edith Staley, Sarah Thompson, Frank Tucker, Hallie Ree Underwood, Pauline Watts, and Irene Weatherly. (Courtesy of Martha Oakes.)

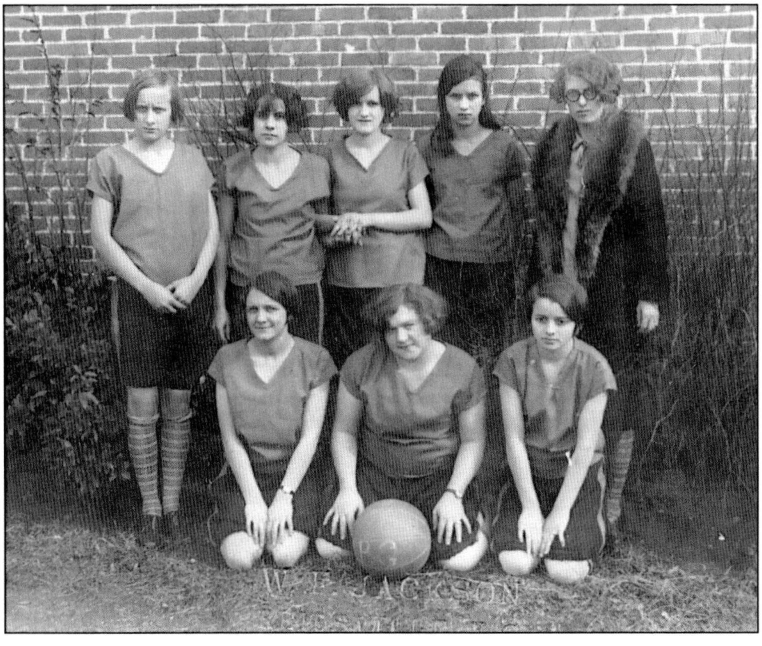

Pleasant Garden girls began playing competitive basketball as early as 1914. They played outdoors until the gymnasium was built in 1941. Rosa Mae Kirkman is in the center of the first row; the other two girls are unidentified. In the second row are, from left to right, Dena Ross, Gladys Maness, Mary Riley, Myra Reynolds, and coach Ruth Hockett. (Courtesy of Anne Hice.)

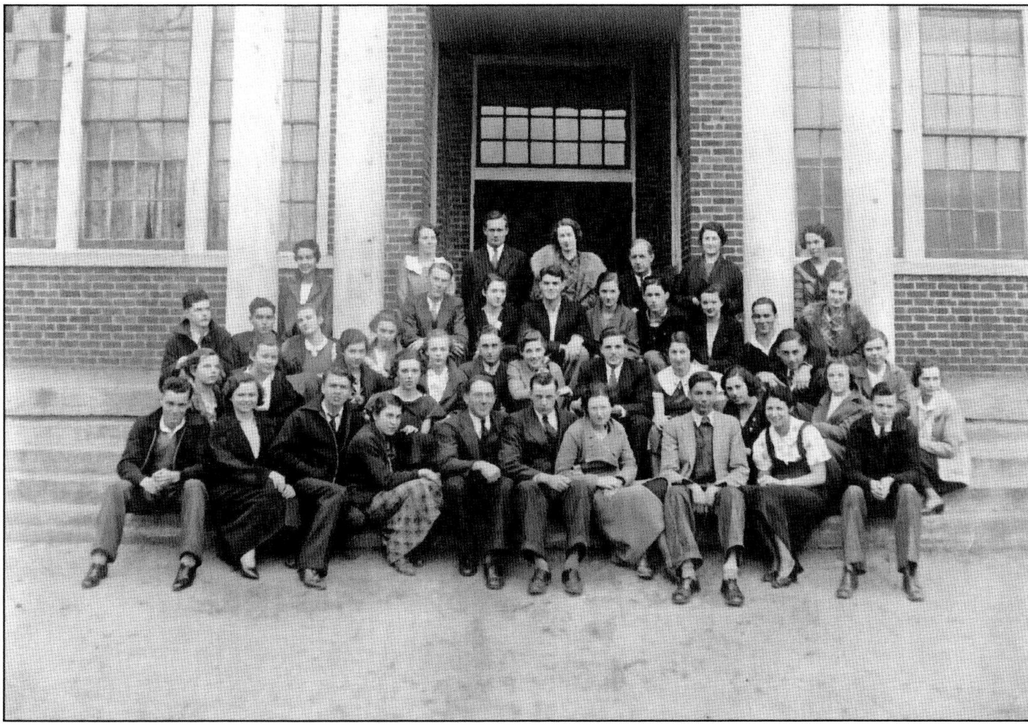

The class of 1934 and faculty pose for the traditional end-of-year photograph. From left to right are (first row) Jack Collins, Margaret Kanoy, Ronald Otwell, Hallie Kirkman, Dewey Sizemore, John Fields, Fannie Belle Marley, Harvey Garrett, Myra Reynolds, and Paul Moore; (second row) Cletus Underwood, Maurine Fields, Lara Mae Whiteley, Mildred Hockett, Martha Smith, Woodrow Smith, Lois Tucker, Victor Neese, Donavee Fentress, Moselle Shaw, C.E. Moser, Eunice Belle Vickery, Kate Freeman, and Thelma Redmond; (third row) Guy Causey, Herick Ledbetter, Lelia Belle Tucker, Dorothy Hudson, Bill Whitty, Pauline Underwood, Russom Ledbetter, Frances Reynolds, R.L. Jones, Nellie Coble, A.G. Toomes, and Ruth Smith; (fourth row) Estelle Shaw, Nell Robbins, C.J. DeLoach (agriculture), Frances Tucker (music), E.D. Idol (principal), Nell Kennett (home economics), and Elsie Brame (English). (Courtesy of Brenda Boyce.)

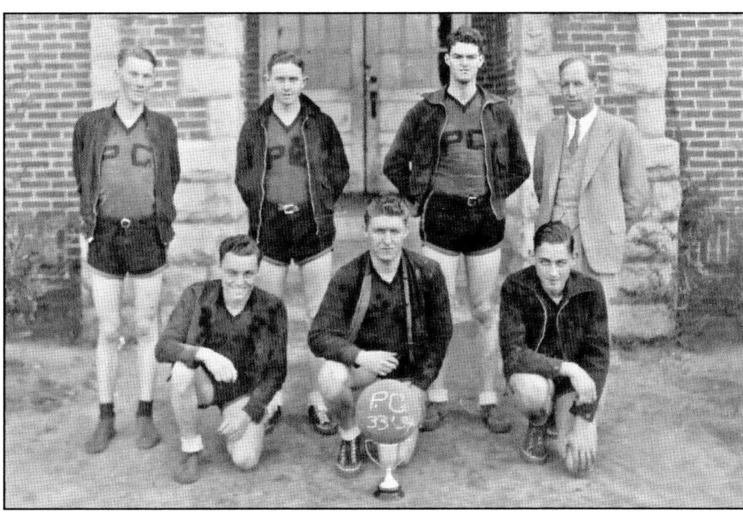

Pictured in this 1934 basketball team photograph are, from left to right, (first row) Jack Collins, Ward Allred, and C.D. Moser; (second row) William Whitty, Woodrow Smith, Russom Ledbetter, and principal and coach E.D. Idol. (Courtesy of Brenda Boyce.)

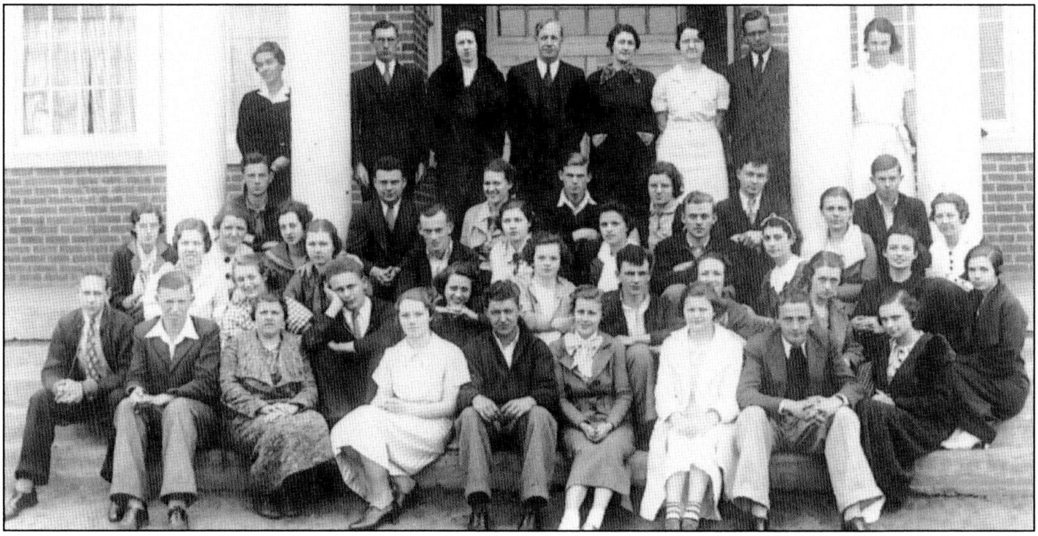

Members of the class of 1935 pictured are (alphabetically) Ward Allred, Mildred Coble, Virginia Curry, Rudolph Dunham, Elizabeth Fogleman, Edna Hackett, Mabel Hanner, Emma Hemphill, J.C. Hendrix, Reba Hendrix, Harry L. Holton Jr., Irma Grey Hornaday, Wayne Hornaday, Margaret Idol, Fay Jones, Ruby Kanoy, Frances Kirkman, Lynda Vaughn Kirkman, Violet Kirkman, James Latham, Elizabeth Michael, Ruby Monnett, Doris Montgomery, Evelyn Preston, Martha Reynolds, Guilford Ross, Mary Samuels, William Saunders, Daniel Sharpe, Grace Sharpe, Juanita Shoffner, Walter Smith Jr., Pauline Vaden, Linda Witty, and John Worth Wright. Unidentified faculty members are also pictured. (Courtesy of Grace Draper.)

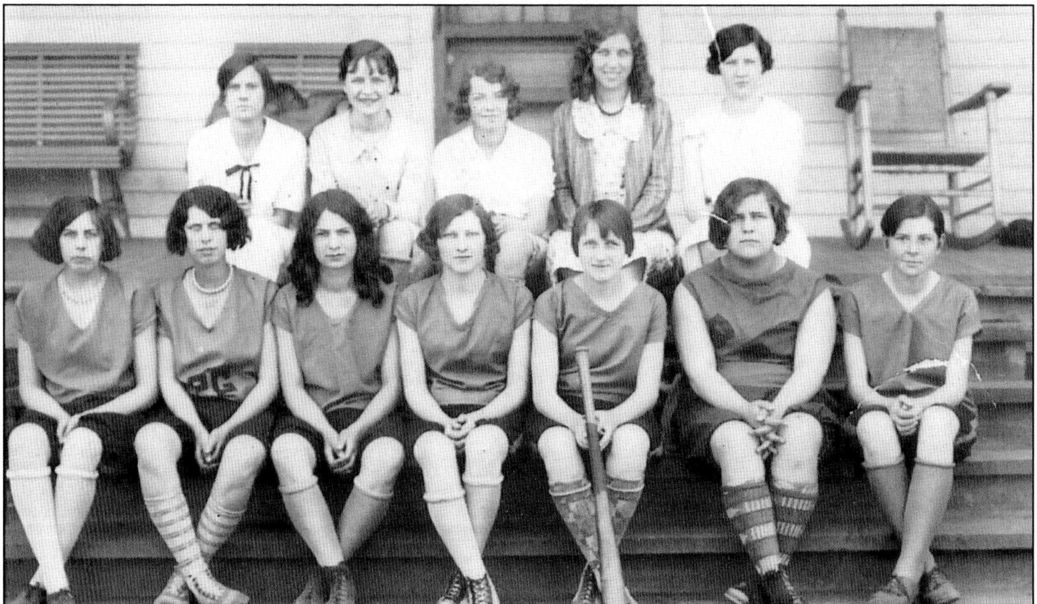

This girls' ball team poses on the steps of the Burgess home. From left to right are (first row) Mozelle Hackett, Ruby Hackett, Myra Reynolds, Tressie Gamble, Mary Riley, Clara Sillmon, and Louise Foust; (second row) Gladys Maness, Ruby Fogleman, Lillian Alexander, Margaret Bain, and Margaret Fogleman. (Courtesy of Mary Clapp.)

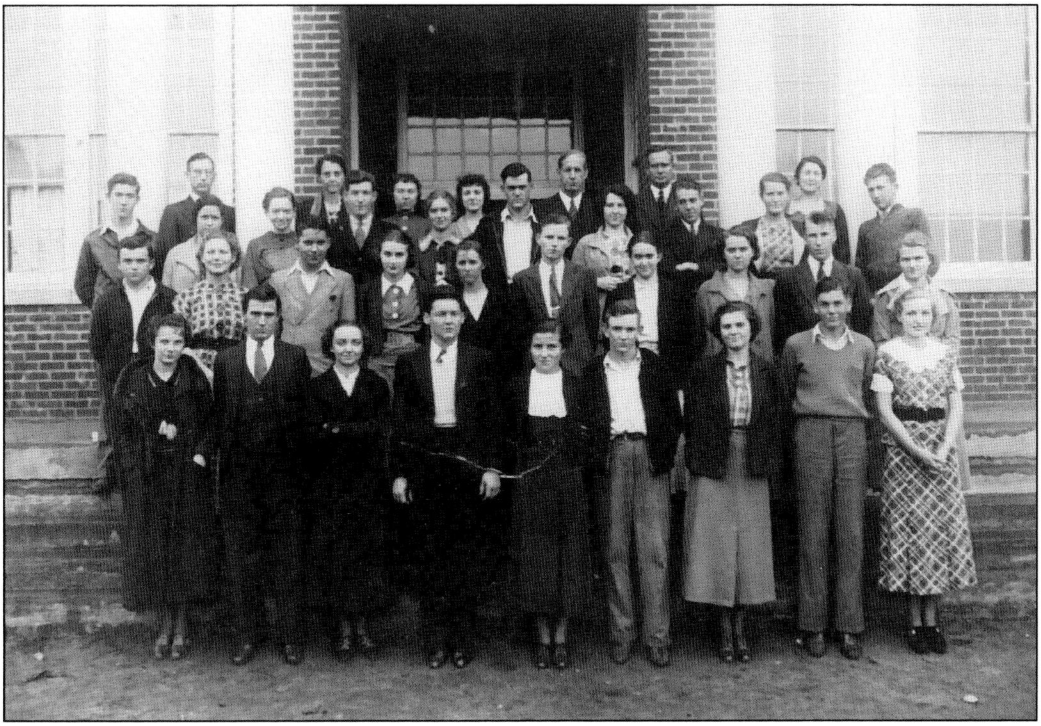

Members of the class of 1936 pictured here are (alphabetically) Mary Burgess, Clarke Causey, George Coble, Mary Coble, Norman Curtis, Berta Fields, Treva Gray, Beulah Hockett, Billy Holton, Ruth Jones, Mearle Kanoy, Mary Wade Kearns, Thomas Kearns, Margaret Kirk, Kate Kirkman, Mae Frances Kirkman, W.C. Marley, Margaret Moser, Lucia Nall, Fay Neese, Bertha Parcell, Clarence Parcell, Cecil Pugh, Wynne Reynolds, Edna Scott, and Wilma Thompson. Faculty pictured are unidentified. (Courtesy of Anne Hice.)

The 1935 Pleasant Garden High School baseball team boasted a 15-2 record. Pictured are, from left to right, (first row) W.B. "Dub" Allred, W.L. Shepherd, Jim Taylor, and Worth Moser; (second row) Raymond Saunders, Rudolph Dunham, Norman Curtis, Wayne Hornaday, Thomas Kearns, and James Vickrey; (third row) E.D. Idol, Daniel Sharpe, Billy Holton, H.L. Holton, and Conrad Hinshaw. After graduation, Vickrey joined the Civilian Conservation Corps. He led a local Boy Scout troop and coached youth baseball. Kearns lettered in baseball at NC State and played semipro baseball in Guilford County. (Courtesy of Anne Hice.)

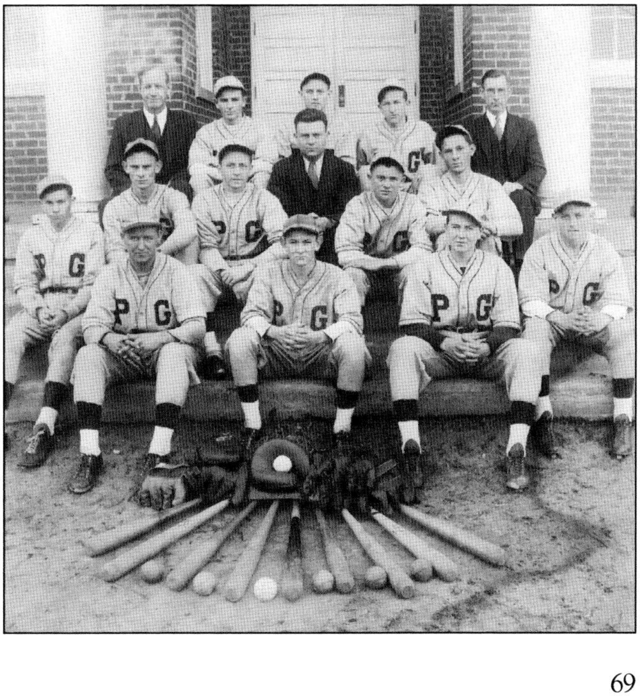

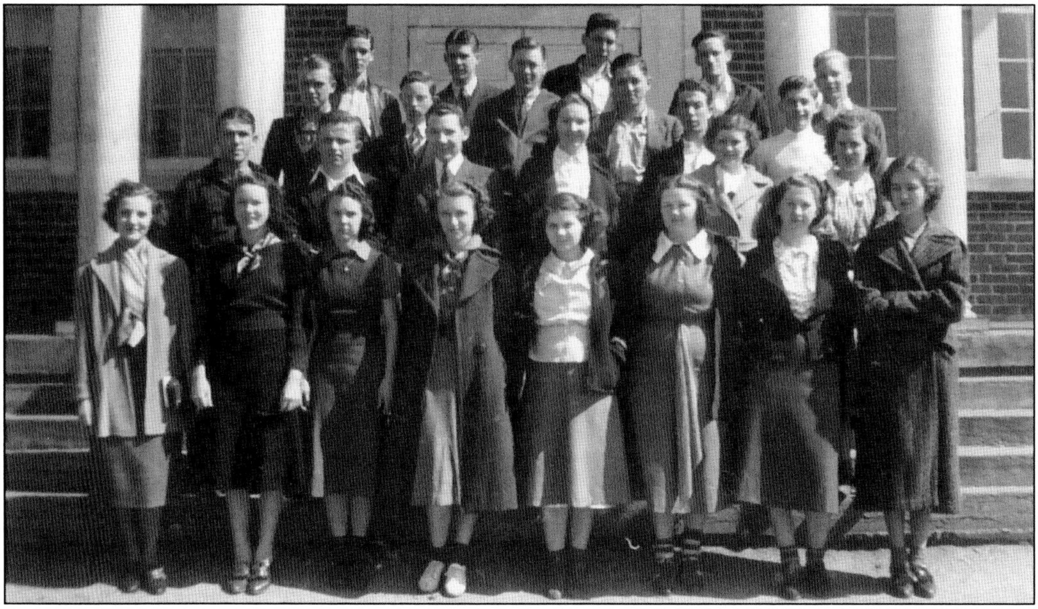

These members of the class of 1938 are (alphabetically) Arthur Coble, Maybelle Coble, Marshall Curtis, Harold Fields, Mary Fay Fruitt, Joe Garrett, Billie Gibbons, Darius Hinshaw, J.W. Hockett, Nancy Idol, W.G. Kirkman, Paula McDaniel, Nana Sue Michael, Evelyn Marion, Mabel Montgomery, Worth Moser, A.W. Otwell, Billy Phibbs, R.B. Samuel, Arthur Lee Teachey, Clay Trotter, Coleman Underwood, Eugenia Ward, and Jane Watlington. Teacher Robbie Dunn is at far left in the front row. (Courtesy of Phillip Way.)

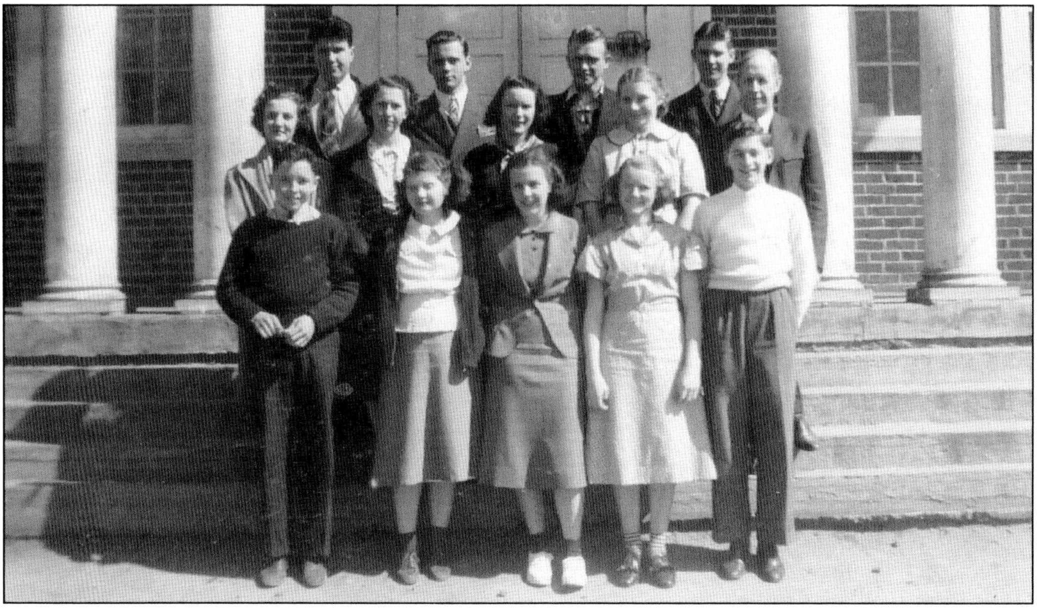

The first school yearbook, *Hi-Lights*, was published in 1938. E.D. Idol was principal; Robbie Dunn, faculty advisor; Nana Sue Michael, editor; Jack Donnell, business manager; and John Smith, art editor. Others on the staff are (alphabetically) Harold Field, Louise Freeman, Nancy Idol, W.C. Kearns, Fagg Nowlan, Mary Frances Orrell, Arthur Lee Teachey, Eugenia Ward, and Kathryn Wood. They were in the 10th and 11th grades (juniors and seniors). (Courtesy of Ellen Osborne.)

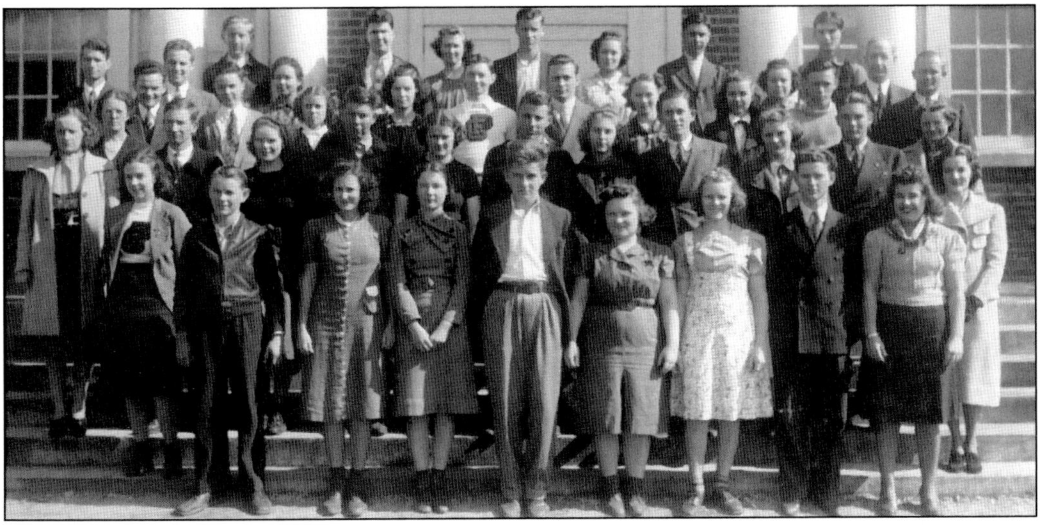

The Pleasant Garden High School class of 1939 were juniors when they assembled in front of the auditorium with faculty members on either side. On the left are Dena Ross, music; Ruth Hockett, mathematics; John Triplett; Mr. ? Howell, science; and Moir Ayers. E.D. Idol, principal; C.J. Deloach, agriculture; Luna Hustpeth, home economics; and Robbie Dunn, English are on the right. Those who went on to graduate in 1939 are (alphabetically) R.C. Allred, N.B. Cheek Jr., Keith Cooper, Virginia Cox, Jack Cranford, Jack L. Donnell, Audrey Earles, Guy Garrett, Hazel Hackett, Anna Lee Hockett, Alfred Horney, Ralph Hulon, Richard Ireland, Dorothy Jones, Ethel Fay Jones, Edith Kirkman, K.N. Kirkman, Howard Lambert, Lois McDonald, Elizabeth Osborne, Kathleen Peele, Reba Rich, Mary Sharpe, C.A. Shoffner, and John Smith, Murphy Westmoreland, and Kathryn Wood. Some in this photograph joined the workforce before graduating and a few completed high school in 1940. (Courtesy of Phillip Way.)

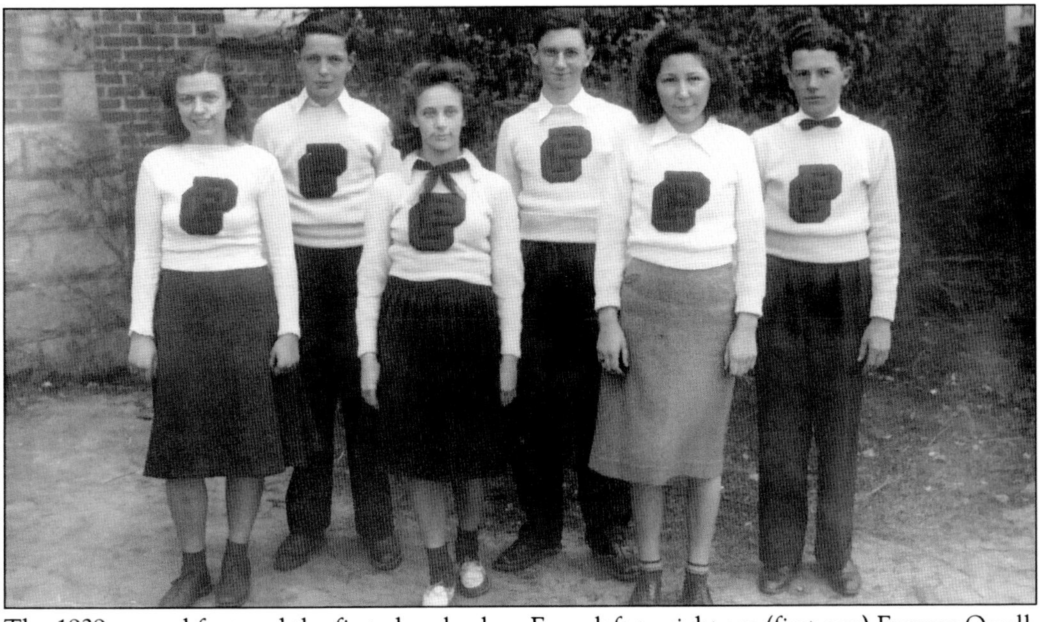

The 1939 annual featured the first cheerleaders. From left to right are (first row) Frances Orrell, Betty Lou Smith, and Margie Samuels; (second row) Rigdon Gibbons, N.B. Cheek Jr., and W.G. Kirkman. In this era, school colors were black and gold. (Courtesy of Phillip Way.)

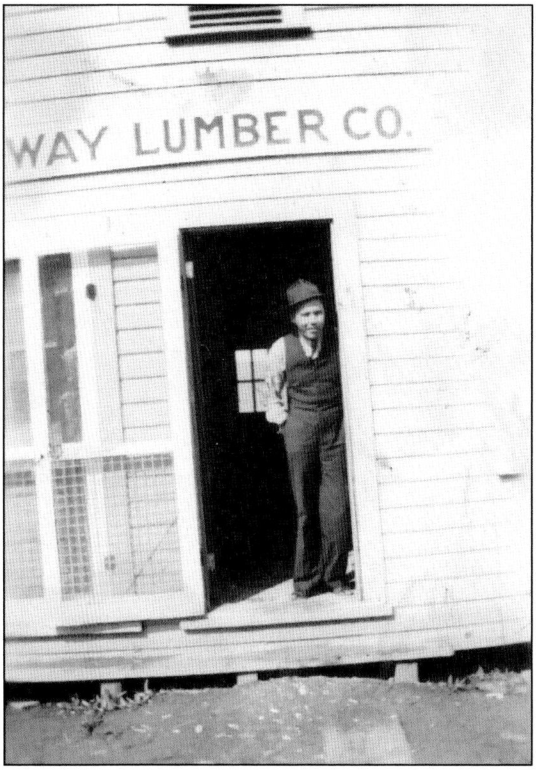

Amos Way was the bookkeeper for a lumber company that he and his father, James Arthur "J.A." Way, owned. During World War II, Way, his wife, Margaret, and their children left Pleasant Garden for a time because all of their employees had gone to work for Uncle Sam. He found employment at a hotel in Sulphur Springs, Florida, where they lived before returning to the village in 1944. (Courtesy of Sue Gregson.)

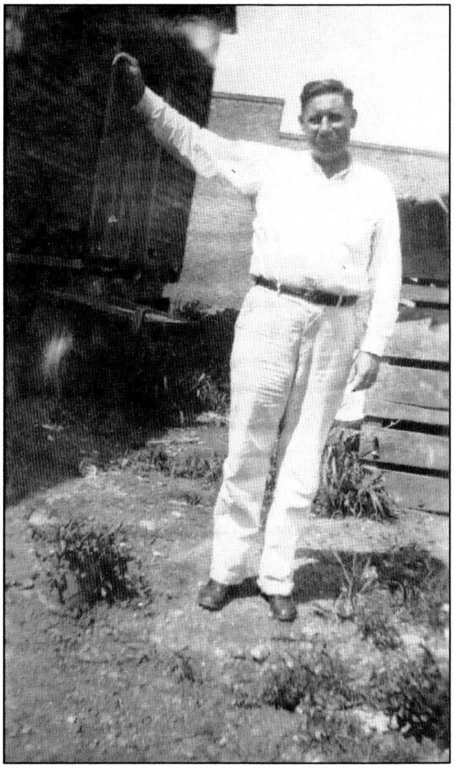

During the 1930s, James Arthur Way built many small houses in the village. Several were bought by sawmill workers who moved from Montgomery County to work for Way Lumber Company. At one time, the workforce was nearly 60 people. (Courtesy of Sue Gregson.)

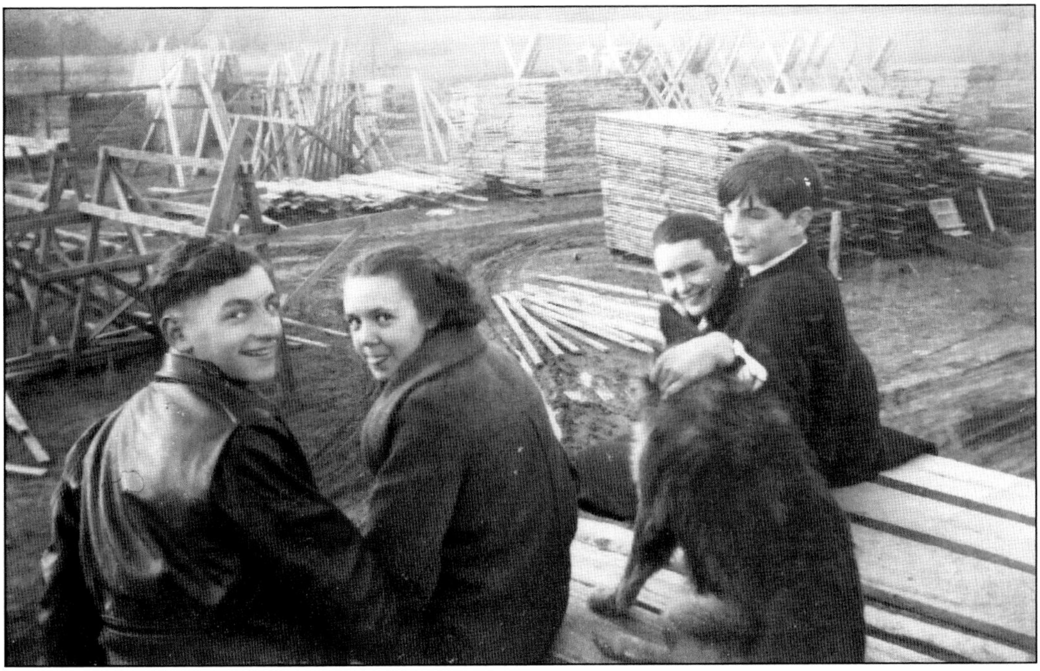

It appears that N.B. Cheek Jr received a camera for Christmas in 1936, according to the date on this photograph. His neighbors were willing subjects. Pictured here, from left to right, are Arthur Lee Teachey Jr., Jane Watlington, Nana Sue Michael, and Ernest Rudd Jr. (Courtesy of Phillip Way.)

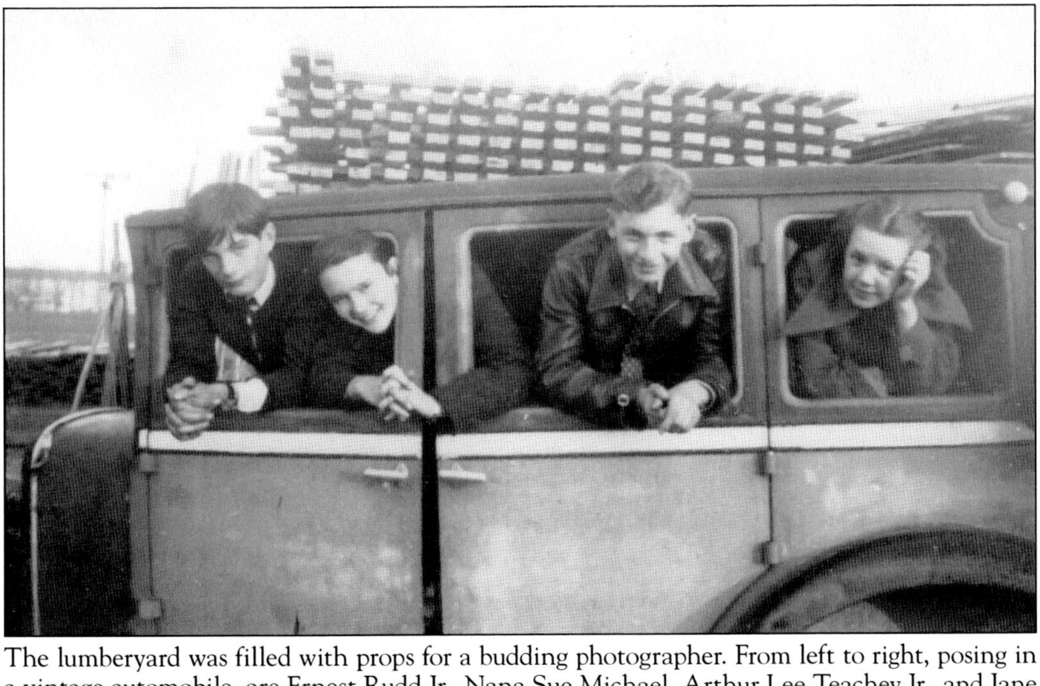

The lumberyard was filled with props for a budding photographer. From left to right, posing in a vintage automobile, are Ernest Rudd Jr., Nana Sue Michael, Arthur Lee Teachey Jr., and Jane Watlington. This car may have been an Essex sold at Pleasant Garden Motors by L.E. Riddick. (Courtesy of Phillip Way.)

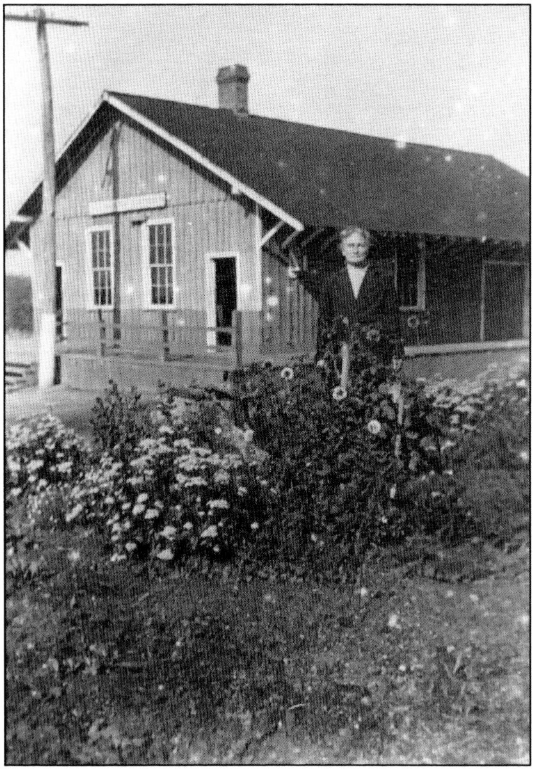

Having a flower garden at her workplace made Annie Neelley's often solitary work more pleasurable. It was located in a sunny spot across the road from the Atlantic and Yadkin Depot and the building that housed the post office around 1918. (Courtesy of Stanley Cichowicz.)

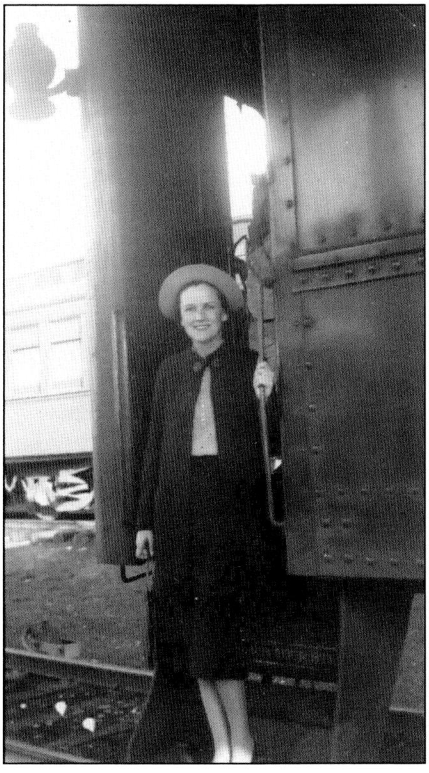

Nana Sue Michael rode on the last Pleasant Garden passenger train on April 30, 1939. She noted on the back of the snapshot that "Vic" (last name unknown) took the photograph. He was once the local stationmaster. (Courtesy of Phillip Way.)

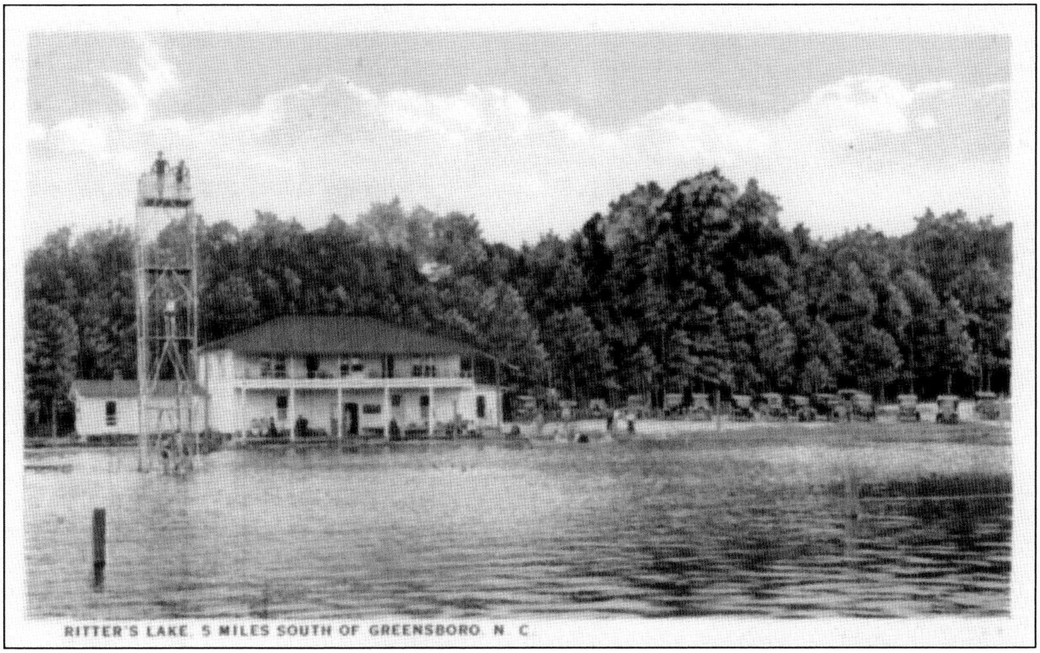

Ritter's Lake was a popular summer recreation destination for many years. Boating and fishing were available, as well as swimming and swan-diving from the 40-foot platform. Square dances were held upstairs in the pavilion. This is one of two postcards available before 1930.

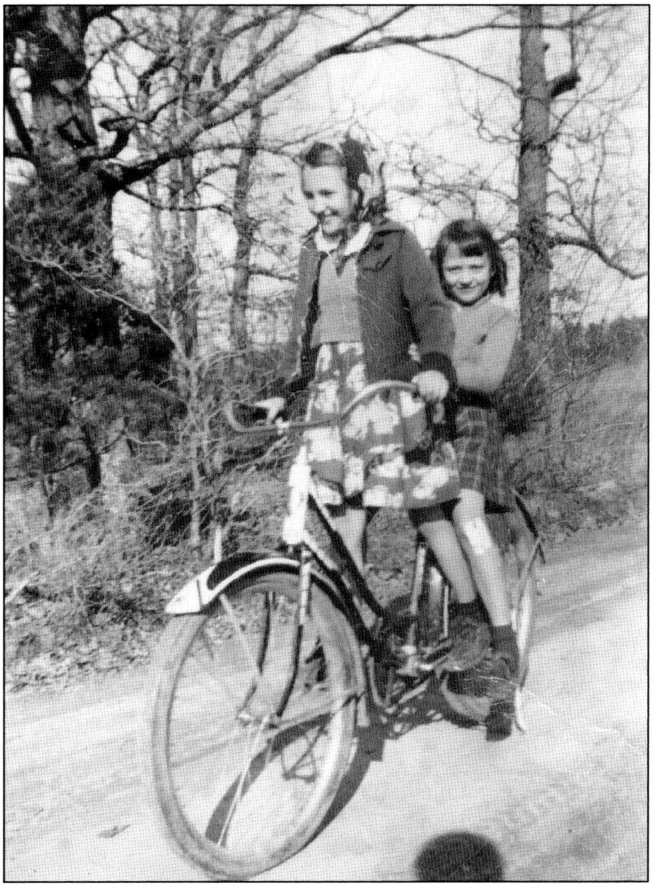

Cousins Frances Hunt (left) and Jane Kirkman explored their neighborhood riding double on a brand-new bike. They lived near each other on Hunt Road and spent many hours together. (Courtesy of Ann Hardin.)

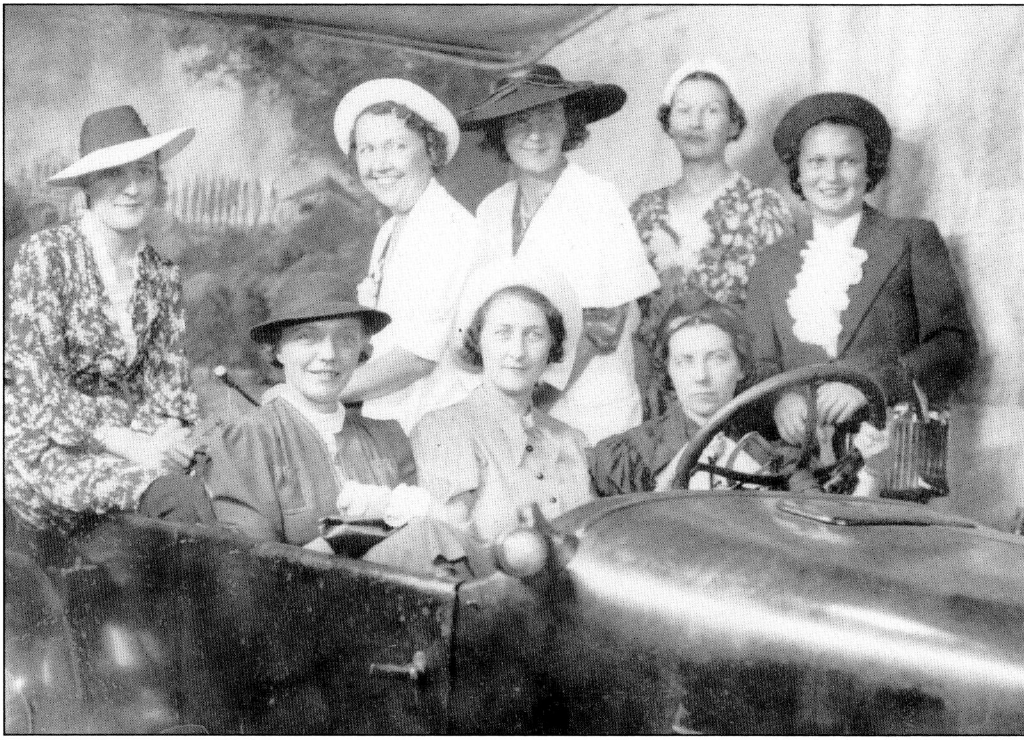

These career women, sometimes called the "Belles of Pleasant Garden," ventured north to visit former residents Margaret Michael and Dorothy Kennett in New York City. Pictured are, from left to right, (first row) Frances Osborne, Nell Kennett, and Ethel Neelley; (second row) Michael, Sarah Neelley, Dorothy Kennett, Helen Shore, and Edith Shore. Michael was a nursing student at Bellevue Hospital in New York City; Kennett had returned to her New York home. (Courtesy of Anne-Marie Kennett.)

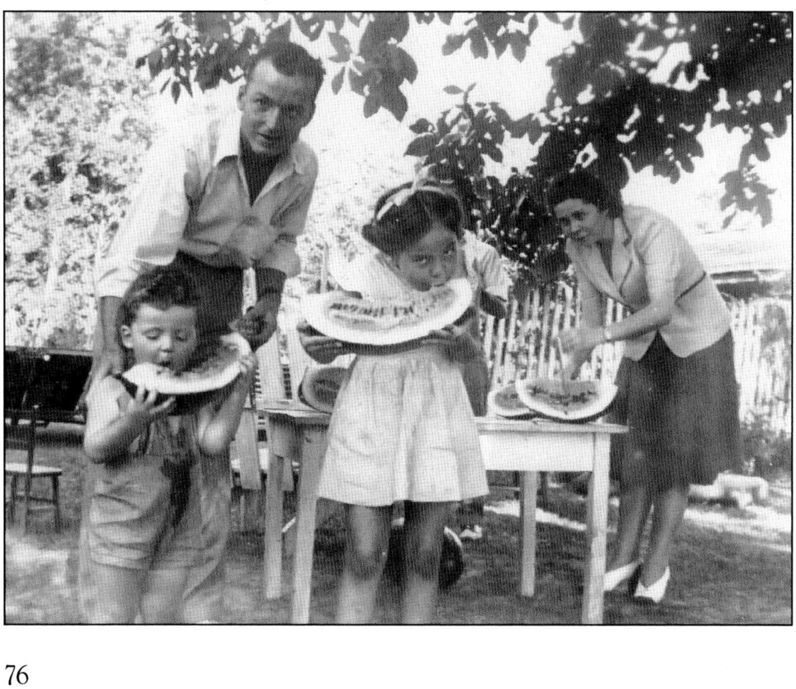

Enjoying a juicy watermelon at the home of John and Lourilla Foust around 1939 are, from left to right, Douglas Foust, J.W. Foust Jr., Sue Britton, and Louise Foust. (Courtesy of Karen Reynolds.)

Four

The 1940s

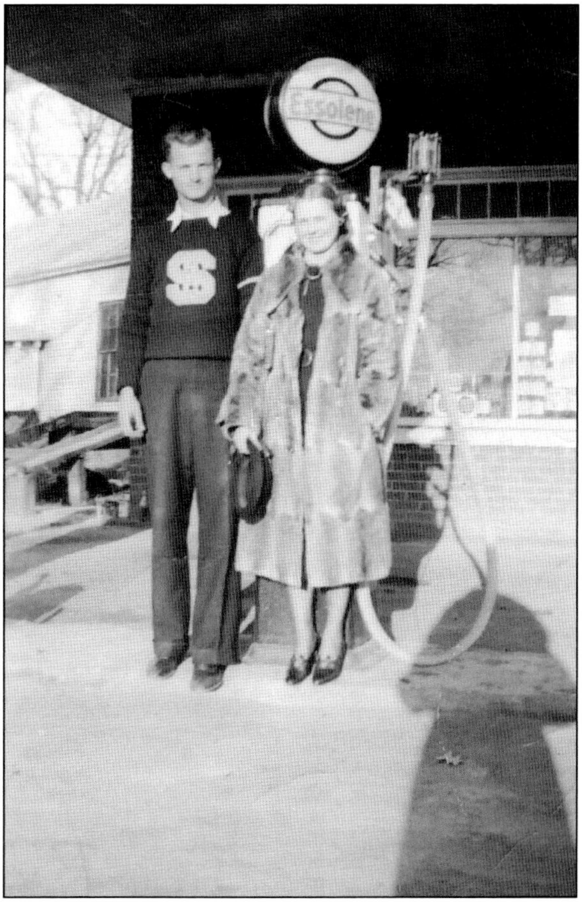

Luna Hudspeth and Charles Riley are pictured on their first date standing in front of the local Esso. A native of Yadkin County, Luna came to teach home economics in the mid-1930s. Charles was a graduate of Pleasant Garden High School and North Carolina State. The Rileys were married in 1942 in Biloxi, Mississippi, and spent the first four years of their married life there while Charles served in the Army Air Corps. (Courtesy of Martha Oakes.)

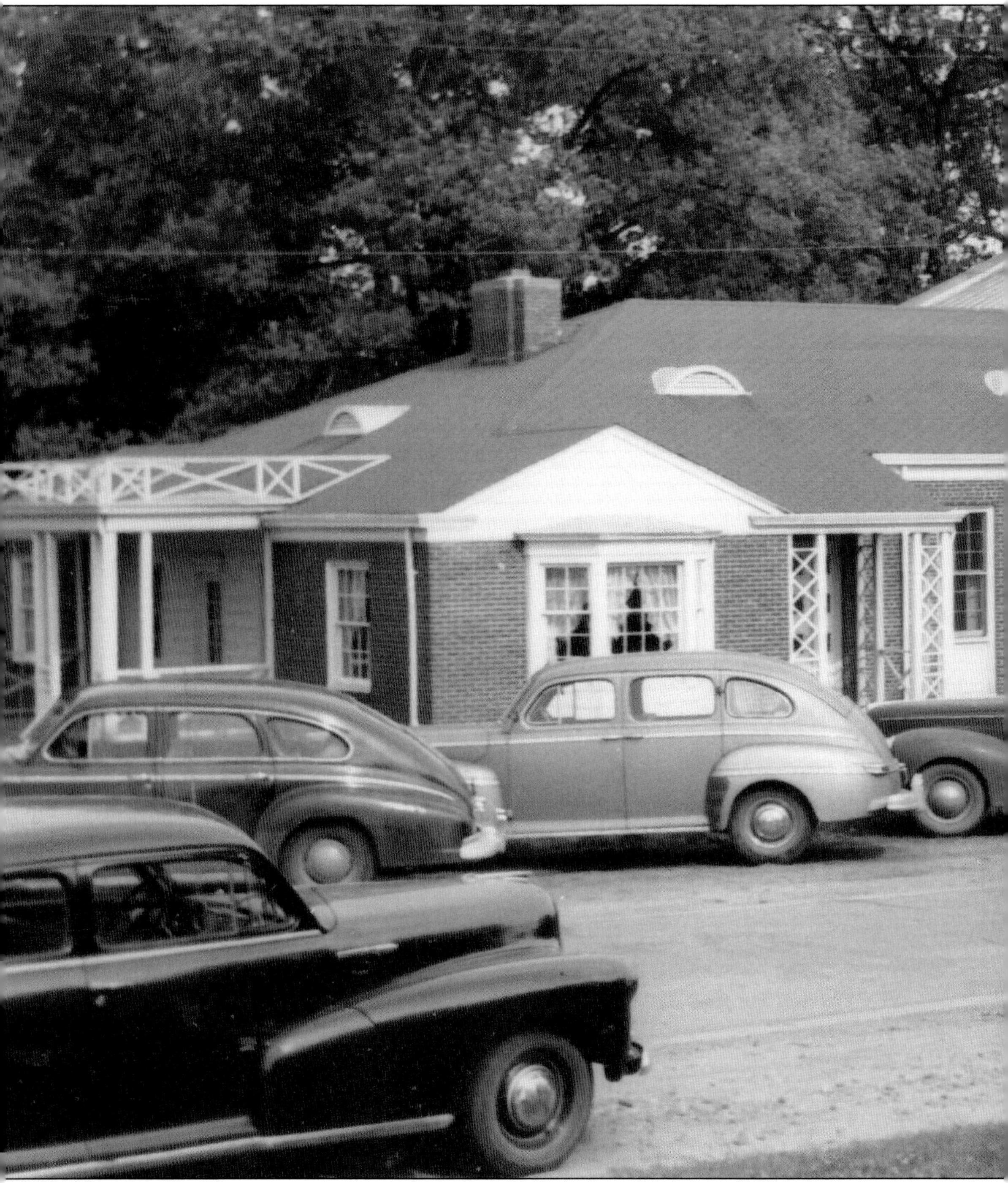

E.D. Idol was principal when this $35,000 building was proposed as a WPA project. The agency lacked $2,300 to build to architect Joseph J. Sawyer's specifications, and the community committed to raise that amount only to learn late in 1940 that because there was no skilled labor available to complete the building, the WPA would abandon the project. When the county took over the project in March 1941, the community scrambled to raise its share. The brick building housed a

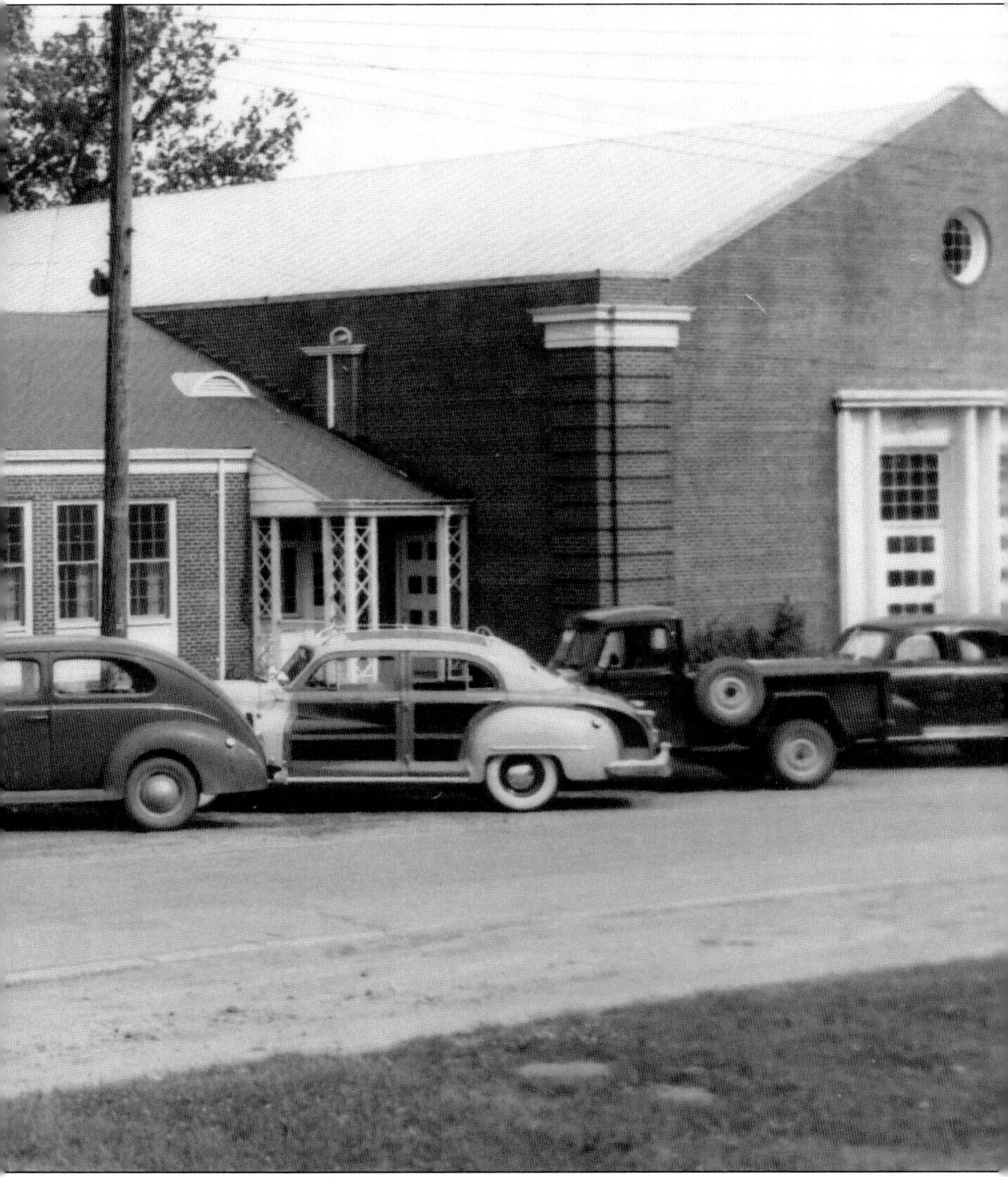

gymnasium with stationary bleachers and dressing rooms. The attached home-economics cottage featured a bedroom and bath, a knotty pine–paneled living room, a dining room that served as a community reception site, and a large laboratory classroom. Since Luna Hudspeth was the teacher, she worked with Idol to select the decor and furnishings. Idol appealed to Charles Riley to canvas the community for financial support.

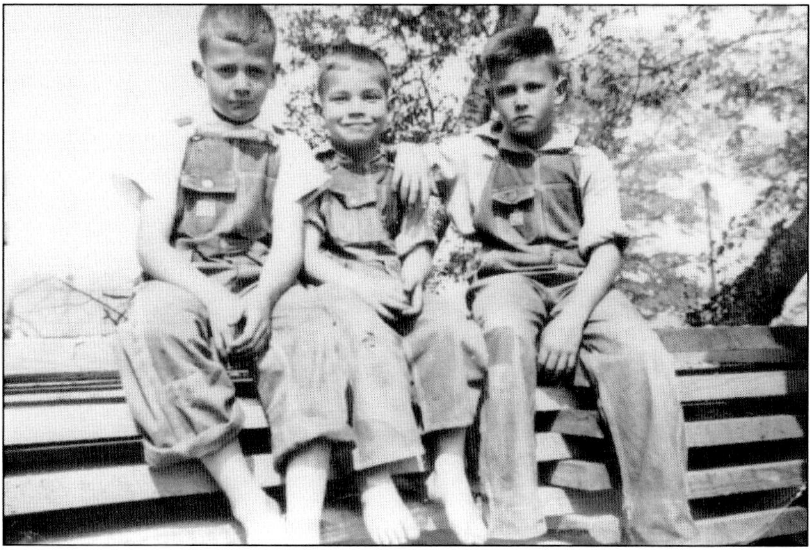

William and Nell Marley Yow's sons Robert (left), Jack (center), and Glenn take advantage of a stack of lumber located just behind the school ball field. It provided a great view of the games. (Courtesy of Ruth Ann Jones.)

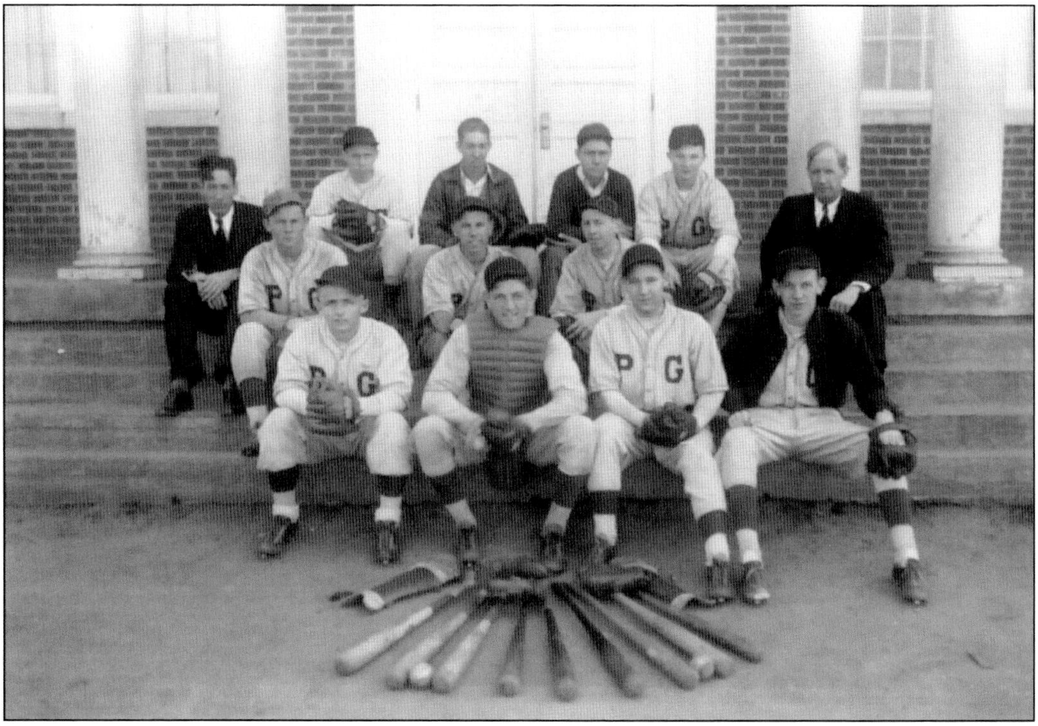

The 1938 Pleasant Garden baseball team came home with the runner-up prize. The school gained renown in the ensuing years because the teams of 1939, 1940, and 1941 won back-to-back state Class C championships—a three-peat before the term was coined. In this photograph are, from left to right, (first row) Bill Gibbons, Worth Moser, R.D. Samuels, and Avery Otwell; (second row) Ed Dunham, Roscoe Taylor, and A.W. Otwell, (third row) coach Conrad Hinshaw and principal E.D. Idol; (fourth row) Kirby Kirkman, Hal Quate, R.C. Allred, and Robert Causey. (Courtesy of Ruth Ann Jones.)

Garden Sass

A Monthly Message To Our Boys In Service

Sponsored by Women's Society of Christian Service

Vol. II. No. 8. Pleasant Garden, N. C. June, 1944.

Rome Falls

As we go to press these news has come to us of the fall of Rome. We rejoice in your victory, for we are sure some of our boys had a part in that victory. We watch your every movement with the keenest of interest and look forward to the day when complete victory will be ours and you will all be home again.

At Home and Abroad

Emmett Tucker writes that he has just had a very pleasant leave, which he spent in a small English town. He says the English are very hospitable and he enjoys them. Flying, he reports, still gives him a thrill, although it has now become a job to be done.

Bud Tucker, Emmett's brother, who is hoping for a chance to come home soon, is learning to become a gunner. He says the desert is still there, still dry, and still hot. For Bud's information, we'd like to say the desert has had no monopoly on hot, dry weather. Our May heat broke all records, even in Pleasant Garden.

Marcus Dunham spent last week-end at home and managed not to have measles, mumps, chicken pox or anything except a swell time.

Therrell Michael is now in New Guinea. He, too, has a weather complaint—too hot and too wet. Our gardens could use some of the wet.

J. W. Hockett has gone into the navy, but we do not yet have an address.

Jack Cranford, with some suntan, is home as we go to pres. He said that he realy goes for Garden Sass in a big way! In fact, while he was on maneuvers everybody in the whole outfit, including his commanding officer, read his G. S.

Jack, out of brotherly affection for Dick, thought he had better check on the latter's girl friend, a beauteous blonde, Julia, with a Powers' model figure and a matching line, a new Orleans gal at W.C. When Jack looked the situation over he issued the edict that Dick was O.K., but a poor topic for a whole evening's conversation. Dick, we are just warning you!

Speaking of Powers' models, Barbara Rudd, home for summer vacation from Mary Washington, has applied for a job with Duke Power company. Some of her friends accused Barbara of Powers' girl ambitions. All we have to say is that Barbara surely has what it takes.

Miss Frances Tucker is visiting relatives and friends in Florida.

D-Day—H-Hour

D-Day and H-Hour have come! Just as the final words of this month's Garden Sass were being written news flashed over the air that the invasion had begun. We know you are there—our own boys. We want you to know that we are there with you in our hearts, our minds, and our prayers. God keep you, dear boys, and give you strength in body, mind and spirit.

From a Soldier To His Dad

Dear Dad, today is your day again,
And, now, I wonder what I could say
To you, my Dad, as from man to man,
To let you know what my thoughts are today.

You don't want poems, silly little lines,
They're futile to tell what I want to say.
I'd like you to know that now our minds
Are as one across the long, long way.

I remember your looks, your words, your smile,
I recall your rebukes, the way you led
To guide my foolish youth and check my guile,
I remember everything you said.

I'm not saying this well, the words won't come,
But, Dad, I understand now, I truly do.
God grant me a chance to just come home,
And be to my boy a Dad like you.

School Library Receives Gift

In honor of his father and mother, Dr. Worth Ross recently gave to the school library nearly 200 books. The "Reading Nook" furnished by the Beta Club is being rearranged into a memorial to the Rosses, who formerly lived in this community. Dr. Ross is also giving a cash donation this summer for the purchase of new books. The school is very appreciative of these gifts.

Early in April Dr. Ross visited the school and library, while spending spring holidays in this vicinity. He owns the farm known as the "Ab Ervin" place, where the Gurley Garretts now live.

Mother's Day Cards

So many of our boys remembered their mothers on Mother's Day. Without exception every mother with whom we talked had received some kind of Mother's Day remembrance from her boy away from home. We are glad you remembered.

Bethlehem Notes

R. C. Allred who was wounded in action, has been sent back to the States. He hopes to be sent to a government hospital in North Carolina.

Guy Reynolds, of Portsmouth, Va., spent the week-end of May 7, at home and with friends here. We are always glad to see Guy back home.

Paul Dunham and Albert Plaster are spending some time at home and with their friends.

Born to Paige and Menzell Fields, May 2, a daughter, Anna Josephine. Menzell and baby daughter are now at home.

Juanita S. McLennan is spending a few weeks in Tennessee. We hope it is cool there.

Mrs. Lee Fields is spending a few days with her brother, Jack Hinshaw, in Baltimore, Md.

James Phillips sends $4.00 to the Staff for Garden Sass. Says he enjoys it so much and always looks forward to receiving his copy.

Roy Curtis sends $1 for Sass. Says it means so much to him and that he hopes the good work will go on 'till it is all over.

Lyon Reynolds flew to California last week to meet Nathan. Lyons' parents in Oxford are keeping the baby while she is away. Lyon was determined to get a reservation because she booked one by both plane and Pullman.

The Glenn Pugh's have moved into the home of Mrs. Annie Neelley. Mrs. Neelley has kept her room and is boarding with the Pugh family.

Higgins' Guests

Mrs. Higgins' brother, Carl B. Hyatt, and his two sons, Lt. Carl B., Jr., and Coleman visited her this month. Carl B., Jr., is home from the Italian battle front, and is due to be sent now to Camp Butner. Colemand reports to the navy the latter part of this month. For the week-end George Ehlhardt joined the group. On Monday George addressed the Lions' club in Greensboro.

Mr. Higgins' mother returned with her son from Asheville, and is spending some time with the Higgins family.

Mrs. Higgins' brother spoke to the people of Bethelehem and Pleasant Garden on a recent Sunday, morning, using for his subject, "I Am An American." This proved to be both interesting and educational

The *Garden Sass* was a newsletter written and distributed by ladies from Pleasant Garden and surrounding communities beginning in November 1942. Every serviceman or woman from the area received this monthly message from home during the remainder of World War II.

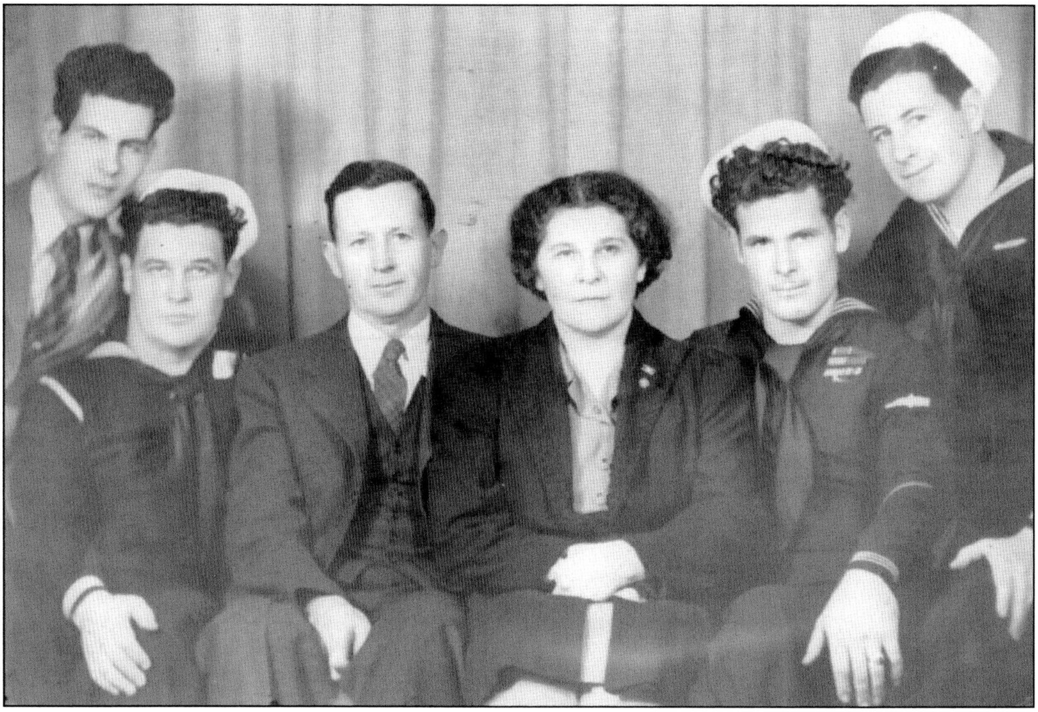

Cecil Marley and Ann Marley reared their four sons in the center of the village, where he operated a garage and she enjoyed sewing for the public. This photograph was made in 1943, when the staff of the Garden Sass honored the family. It had been more than three years since they had all been together. Following are brief biographies of their children, seated on either side of them: Harold Lee (left), called Bobby, who had worked for the war effort in Baltimore, Maryland, was then employed at Vick Chemical Company. The other three (pictured from left to right) had been serving at Pearl Harbor on December 7, 1941. Buford, aboard a ship and uninjured, saw further action in the Southwest Pacific; Thomas was injured while serving as a gunner on the USS *San Francisco* and underwent extensive rehabilitation; William had joined the Navy in 1936 and after three years at sea was stationed on land. (Courtesy of Ruth Ann Jones.)

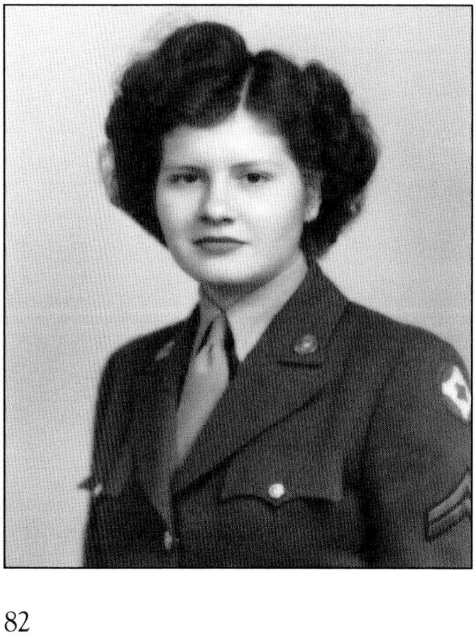

Before she was 21, Nancy Idol had graduated with a bachelor's degree in education from the Woman's College and taught school a year. Then in September 1943, she enlisted in the Women's Army Corps. She was stationed in Boca Raton, Florida, as a classification clerk and attained the rank of sergeant before she was honorably discharged in February 1946. Idol married Benjamin White later that year. Her elder sister Margaret Idol joined the WAVES. (Courtesy of Phillip White.)

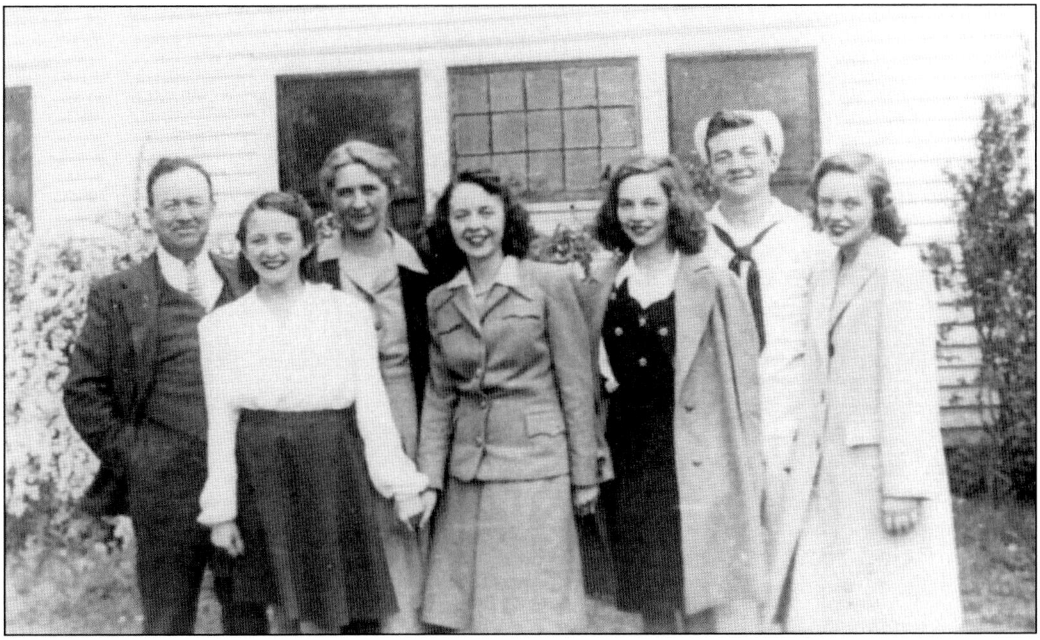

Once David Kirkman enlisted in the Navy following his 1942 high school graduation, family gatherings like these were rare. Pictured here are, from left to right, Bernard W. Kirkman, Jane, Kate Hunt Kirkman, Mary Moling Kirkman, Anna, David, and Rebekah. After the war, David earned an engineering degree from North Carolina State. (Courtesy of Jane Smith.)

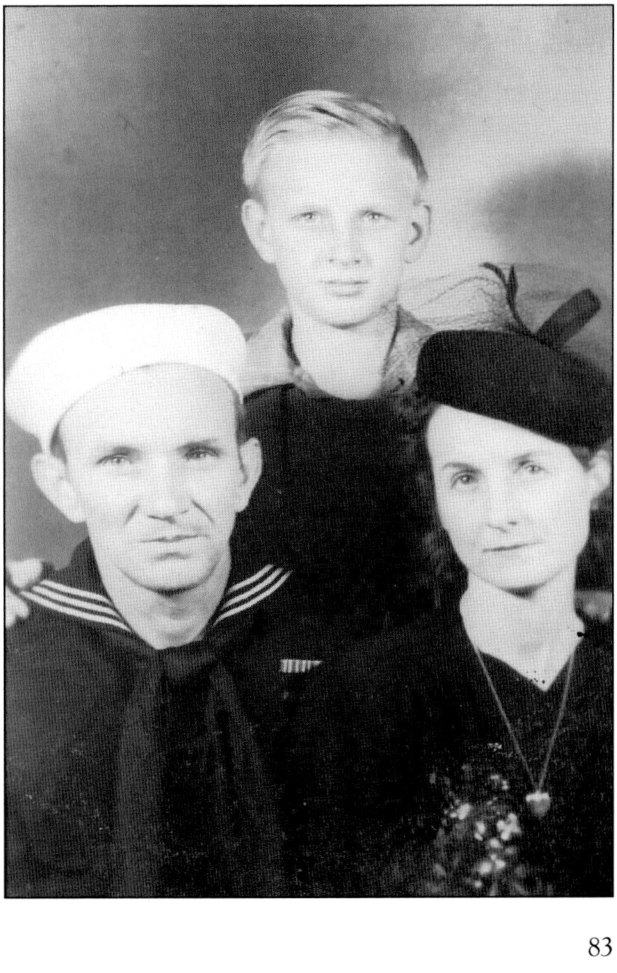

Calvin Ross Berry poses with his wife, Viola Stevens, and their son Wilbur, when he was home on leave from the Navy. Son of John G. and Nettie Fields Berry, Fireman First Class Berry was aboard the USS *Sangamon* near Okinawa when the escort carrier was struck by two kamikazes on May 4, 1945. He was among 11 killed in that attack and buried at sea. (Courtesy of Wilbur Berry.)

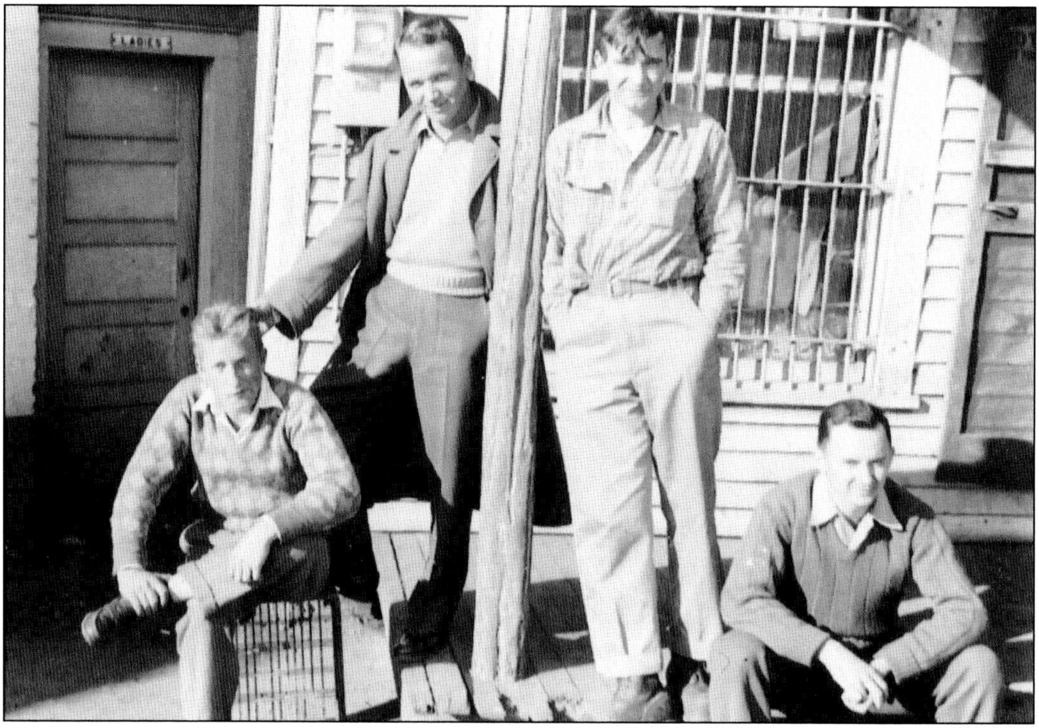

In January 1946, from left to right, Jack Reddick, Robert Ross, Bill Shore, and Howard Foust are at Cheek's Mercantile awaiting Ernest Rudd's arrival by Trailways bus. Pleasant Garden was on the local route from Fayetteville to Greensboro. All had recently returned from serving in World War II, including the photographer, N.B. Cheek Jr. Ross, who served in the South Pacific, opened a Ford dealership in Fayetteville. Foust worked as a bookkeeper at a Greensboro furniture store. (Courtesy of Bill Shore.)

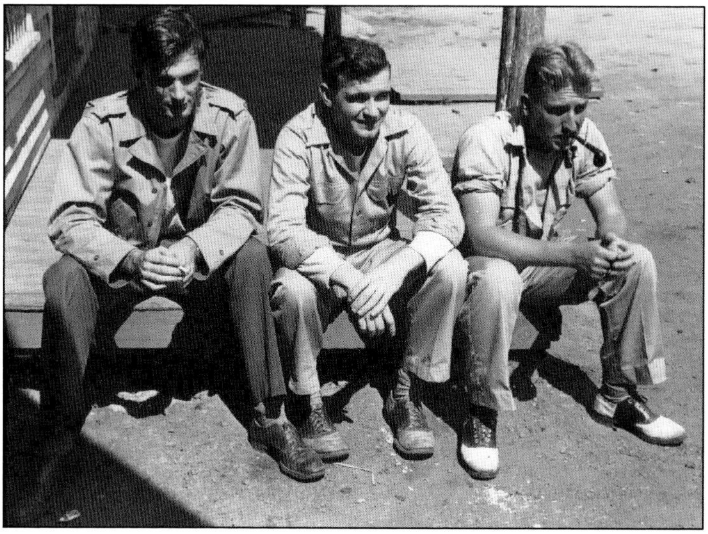

These lifelong friends and neighbors had a lot of catching up to do. Ernest Rudd Jr. (left) made the Air Force his career. Bill Shore (center) walked out of a prisoner-of-war camp in May 1945 and made it across the Atlantic. Jack Reddick (right) was among those storming Omaha Beach. He was injured at the Battle of Huertgen in 1945. Reddick took flying lessons at Routh Airport on Randleman Road and earned his pilot's license. (Courtesy of Bill Shore.)

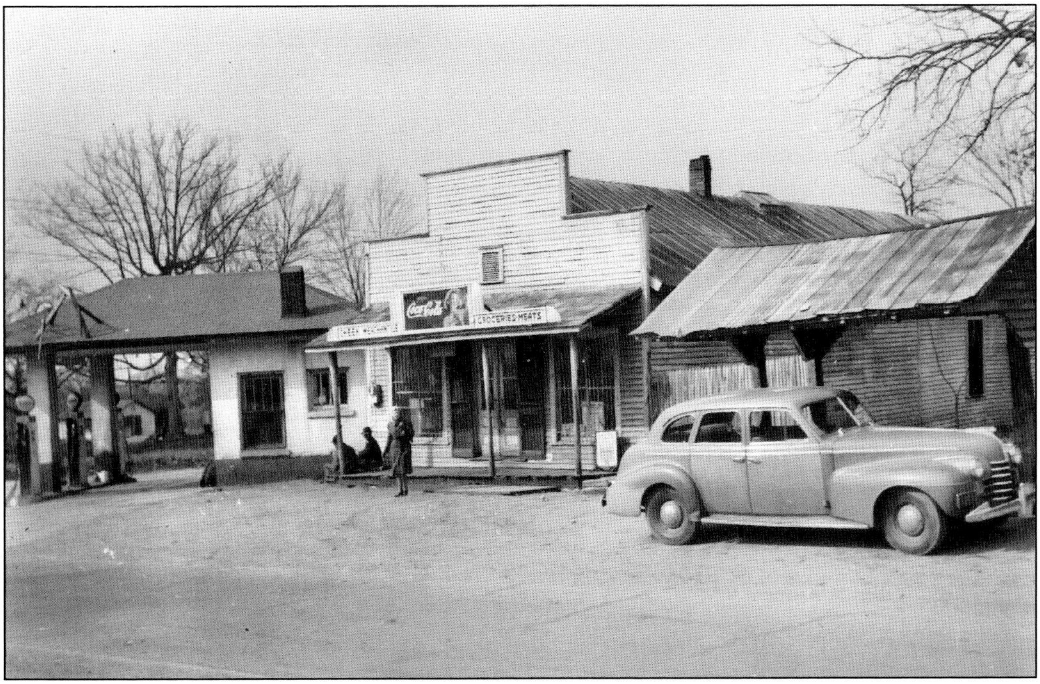

Pleasant Garden Company Store was later operated by N.B. Cheek and underwent a name change to Cheek's Mercantile. The shed alongside the general store served as the bus stop for the passengers awaiting the Trailways to ride to Greensboro. In the evenings, the bus headed south to Fayetteville. (Courtesy of Phillip Way.)

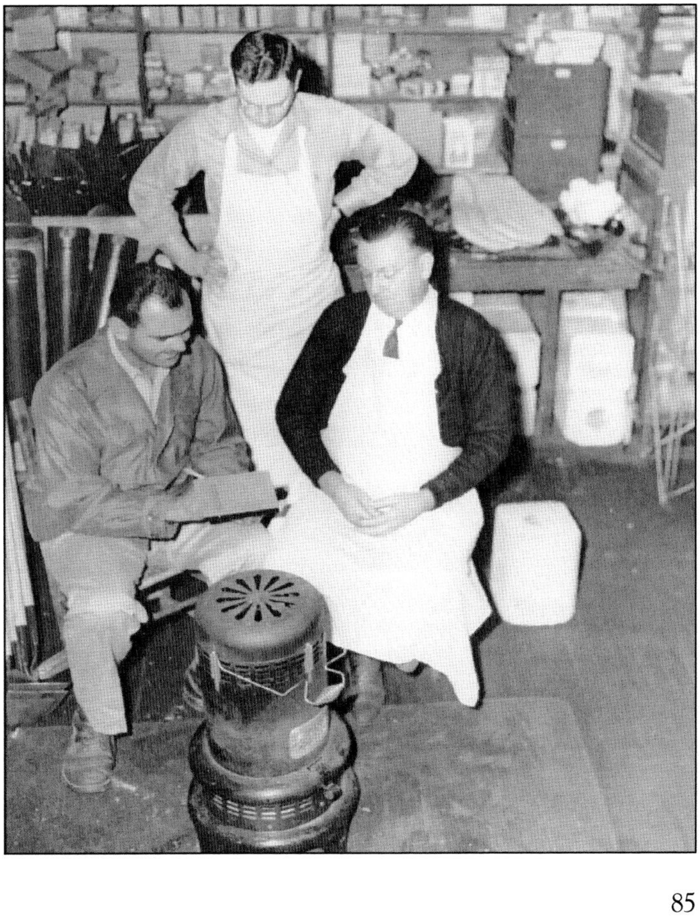

N.B. Cheek Sr. is seated (in the apron) consulting with an unidentified salesman. N.B. Jr. is standing behind them. The old store housed a variety of merchandise that included hardware, from hoes to stovepipes. (Courtesy of Phillip Way.)

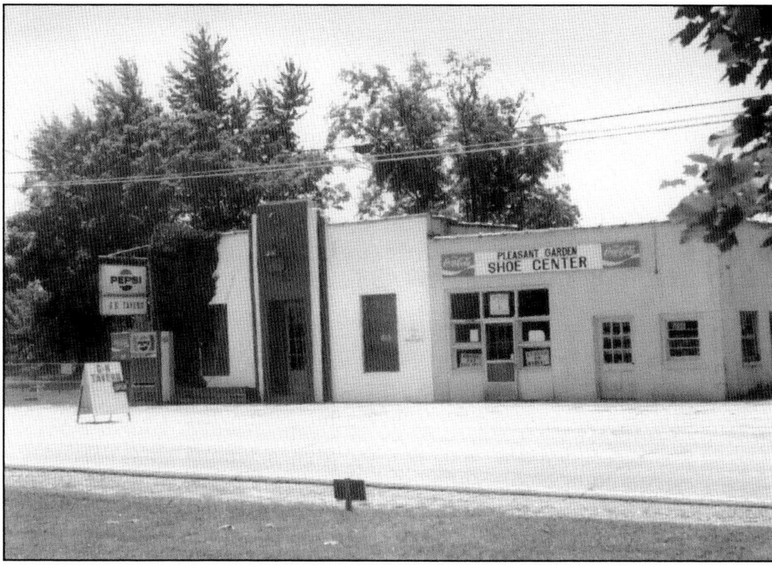

When fire destroyed a wooden store/garage building in 1941, Arthur Lee Teachey rebuilt in brick and block. Tucker's Grocery was on the left; in the center was a lube rack for the service station on the right. The building was modified in the mid-1950s and saw many different businesses. (Courtesy of Phillip Way.)

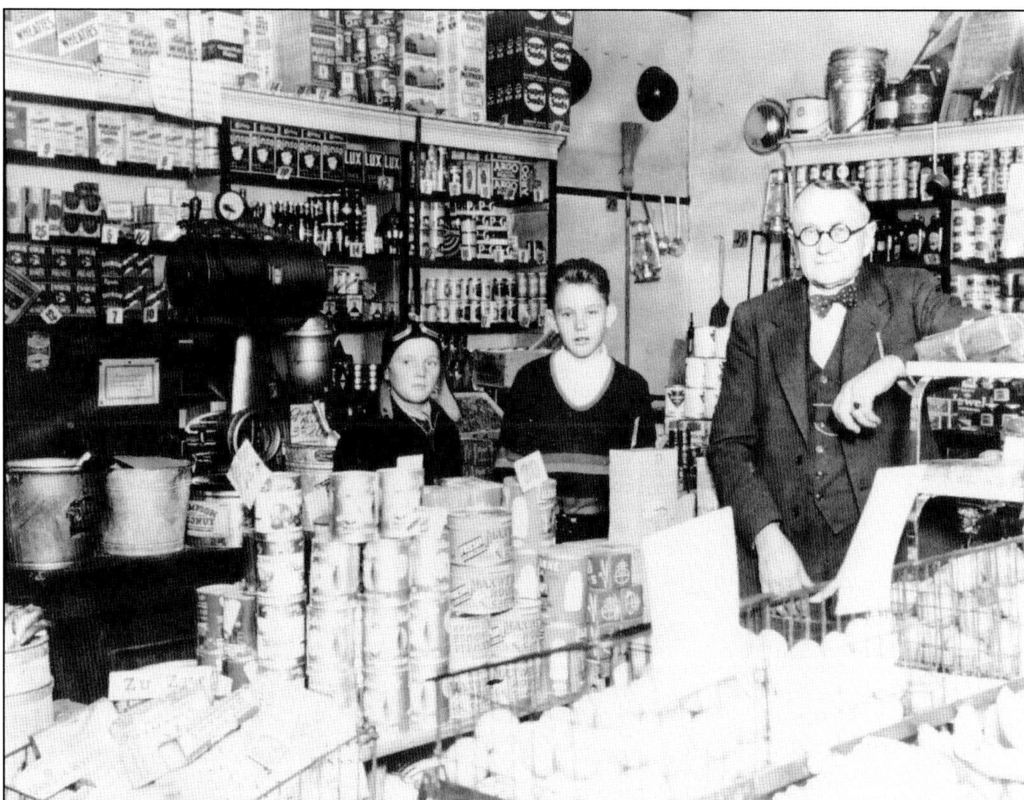

Edgar Tucker became a grocer at the turn of the 20th century. This photograph was made in the 1940s, and the business bears a strong resemblance to his old store in Greensboro. (Courtesy of Phillip Way.)

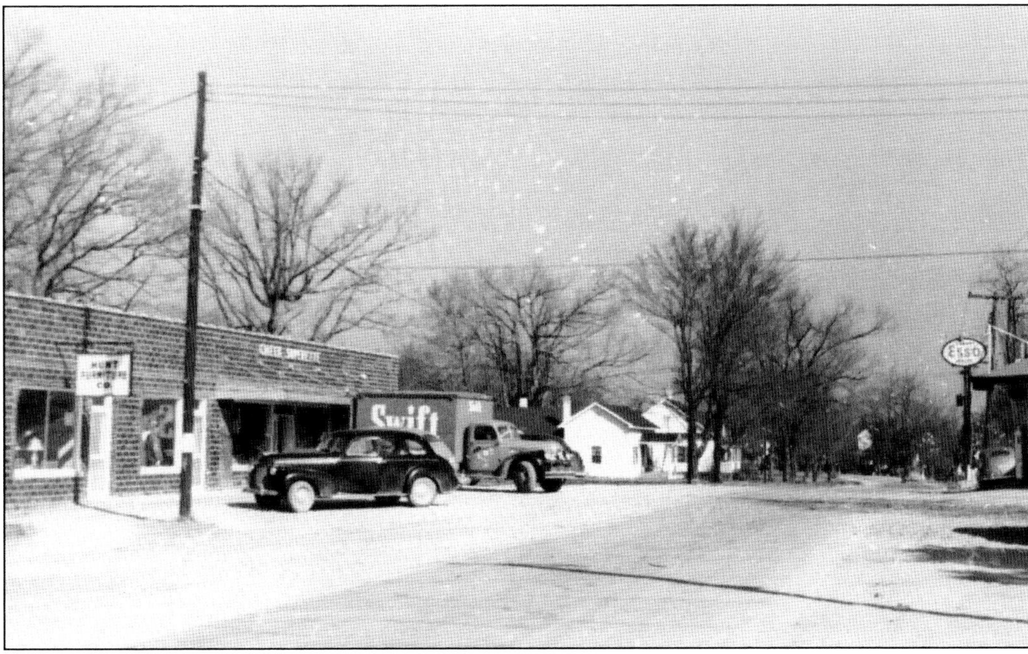

Today, Cheek's Superette would be referred to as the anchor store, housed in the glazed tile and brick building constructed by Gage Kirkpatrick. There was space for five more businesses beside the modern self-service grocery. Roy Curtis opened a soda shop and Ruby Turner, a beauty shop. (Courtesy of Phillip Way.)

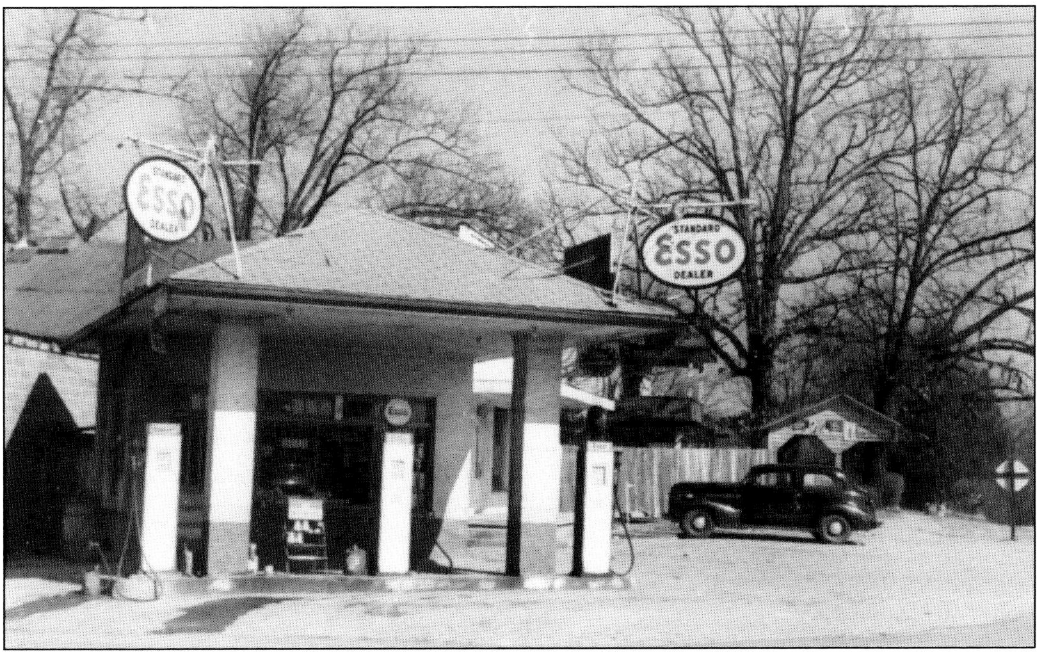

The Pleasant Garden Company successor Carolina Warehouse dissolved in 1929. Wade B. Kearns bought the corner and became the Esso dealer. The 1940 agreement with Standard Oil stated that each month he would pay 1¢ per gallon of gasoline with a $35 per month minimum. (Courtesy of Phillip Way.)

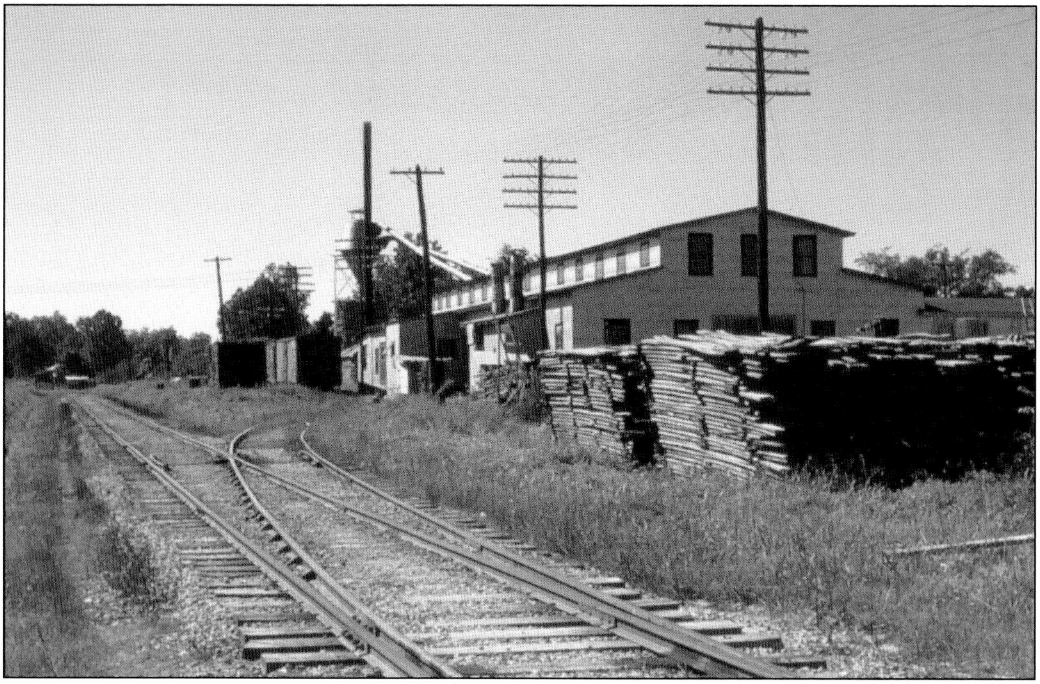

Pleasant Garden had two manufacturing businesses near the railroad tracks. Robbins Millwork Company (show here), operated by C.E. Robbins, was a sash and door plant, and PG Novelty Works, owned by B.W. Kirkman, J.W. Foust, and L.R. Hunt, made small tables and store fixtures. Elliott Wood, a High Point furniture executive, and John Miller, a Greensboro furniture retailer, formed a partnership and bought both around 1946. After a short time, Ed Thrower, an employee Wood had trained, was brought in to be superintendent. Within the span of a few years, Founders Furniture was incorporated, and Thrower owned the majority of the stock. Wayne Davis joined the corporation in 1950 as chief engineer; designer Jack Cartwright, in 1956. Used as assembly room, it was the hub of the modernized plant. A fire wall protected the rest of the facility when the assembly room was destroyed by a massive fire in 1963.

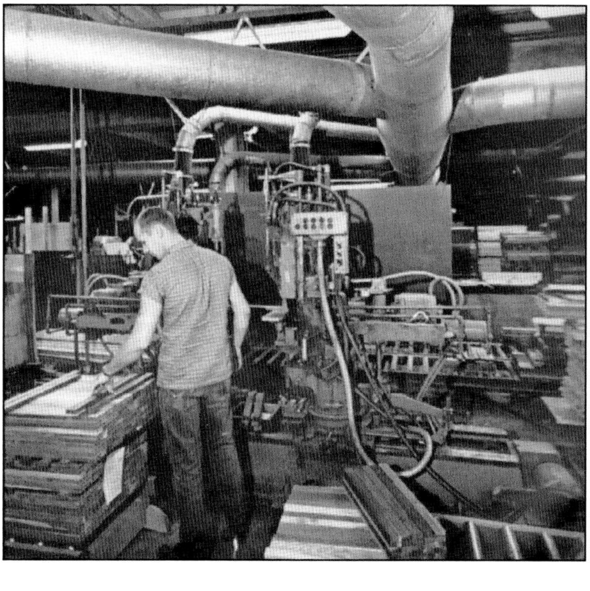

William Jones shared an article from *Furniture Design and Manufacturing* in December 1960. He is featured operating a Bell mitering and boring machine. Jones was one of more than 200 local men and women who crafted modern walnut furniture finished with boiled linseed oil. He retired from Founders after 30 years. (Courtesy of William Jones.)

As the result of being chosen to exhibit in trade shows in Istanbul, Barcelona, and Moscow, Founders Furniture was shipped around the globe. Jack Cartwright's clean contemporary designs were extremely popular in metropolitan locales such as New York City, Chicago, and Los Angeles. Bobby Prevo (pictured) made regular deliveries to trendy Northern department stores from the Pleasant Garden factory. (Courtesy of Phillip Way.)

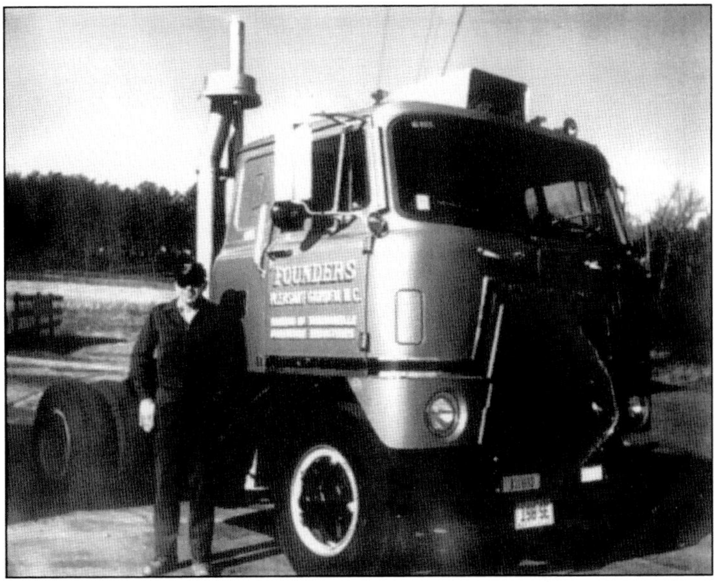

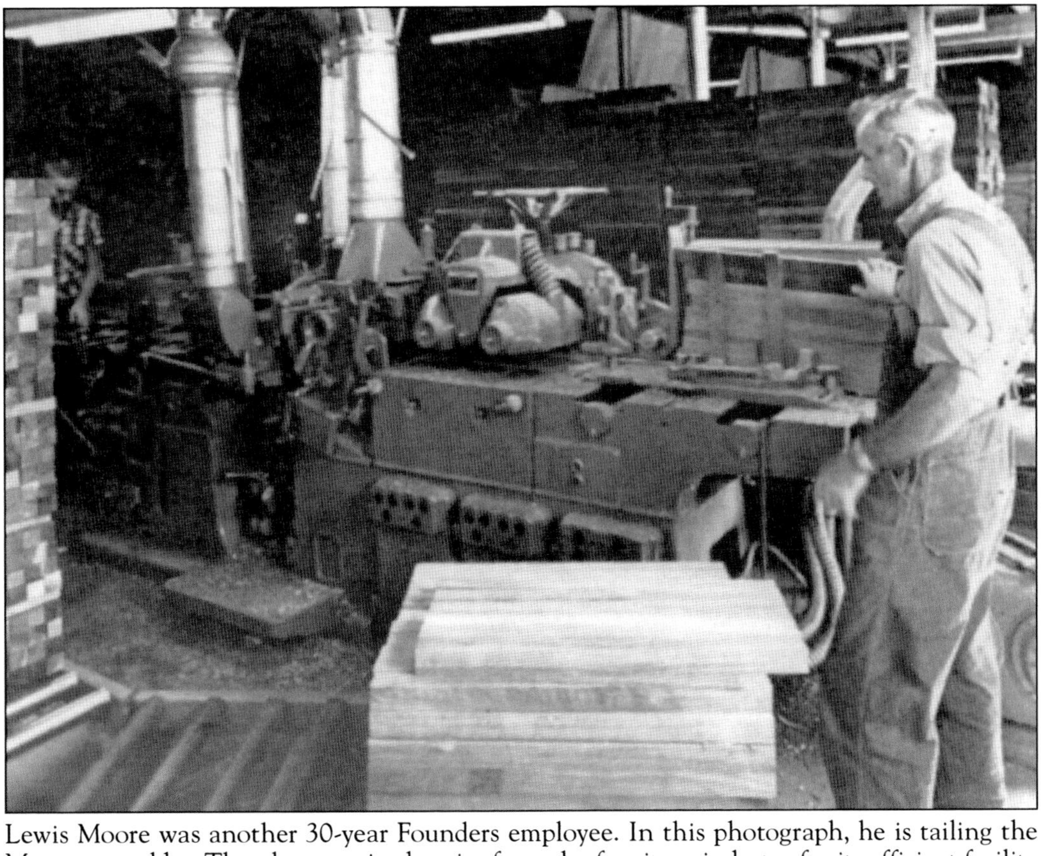

Lewis Moore was another 30-year Founders employee. In this photograph, he is tailing the Matteson molder. The plant received praise from the furniture industry for its efficient facility that enhanced production utilizing an innovative conveyor system. Magazines also featured the furniture that was sold through decorators. (Courtesy of William Jones.)

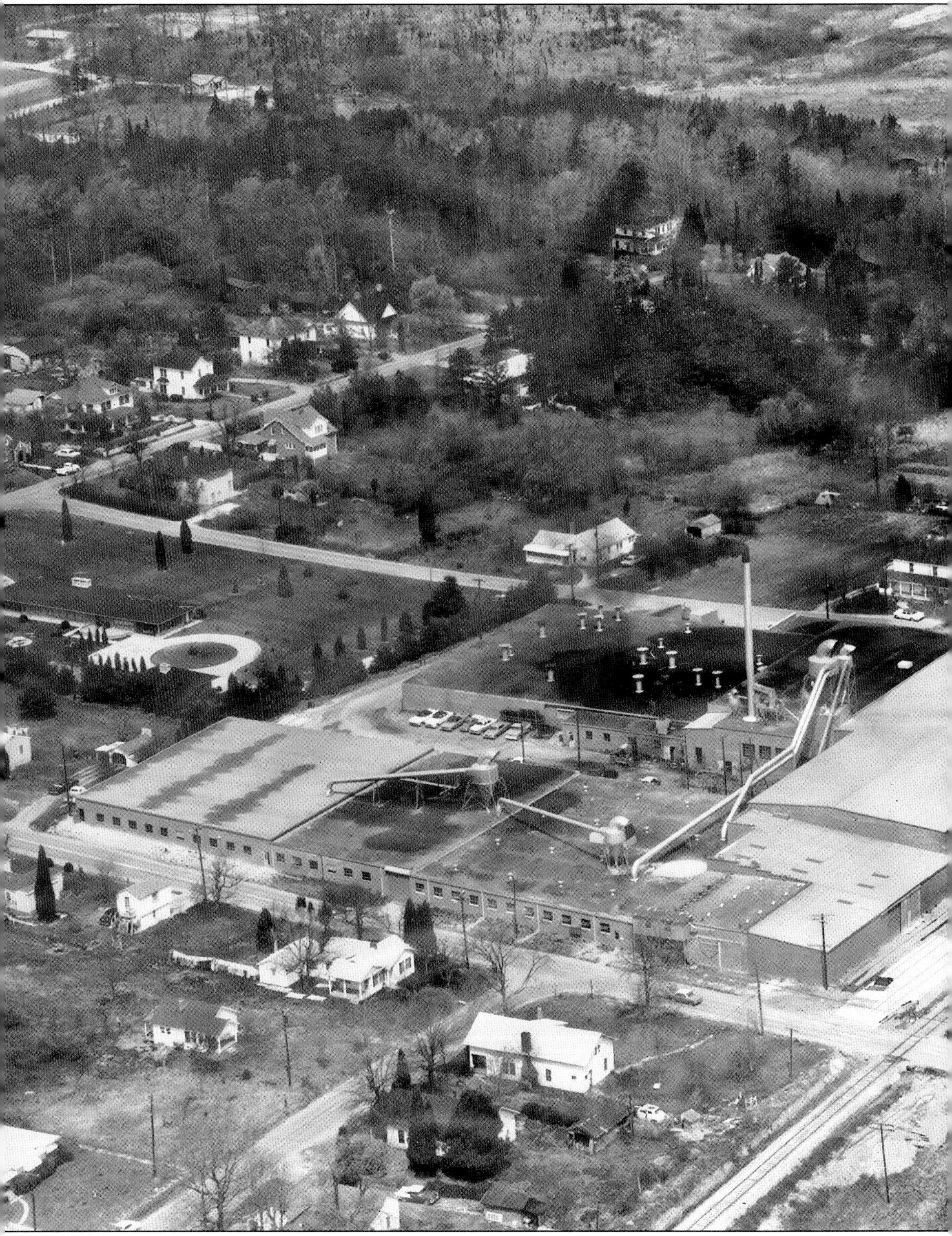

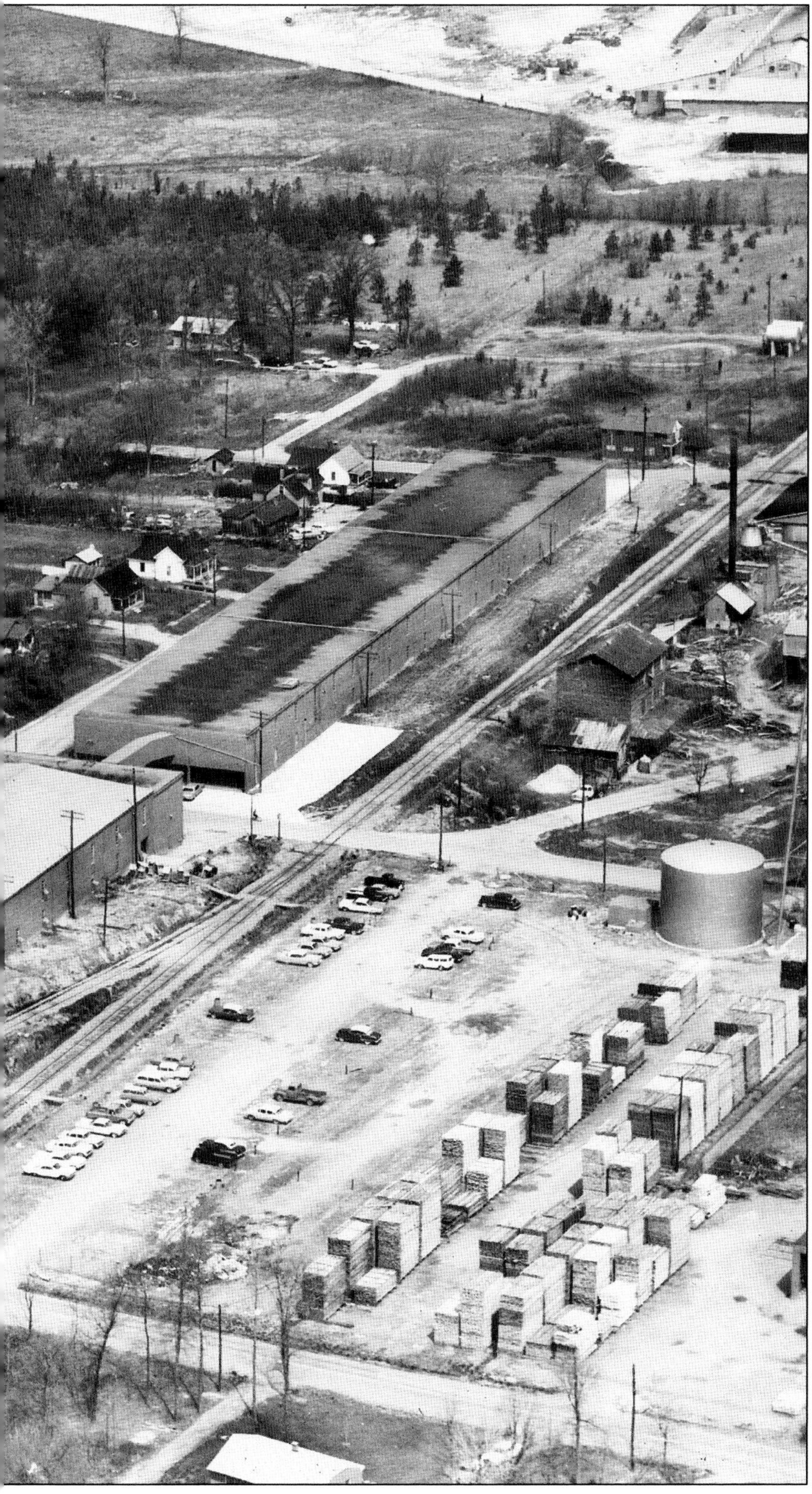

This photograph was made by Harold Cooke, a Founders Furniture salesman. The furniture plant is located left of the railroad tracks. A row of factory houses in the middle of the photograph was bought and demolished when the company expanded from 12,000 to 100,000 square feet to become one of the largest case-goods factory in the country. (Courtesy of the Pleasant Garden Fire Department.)

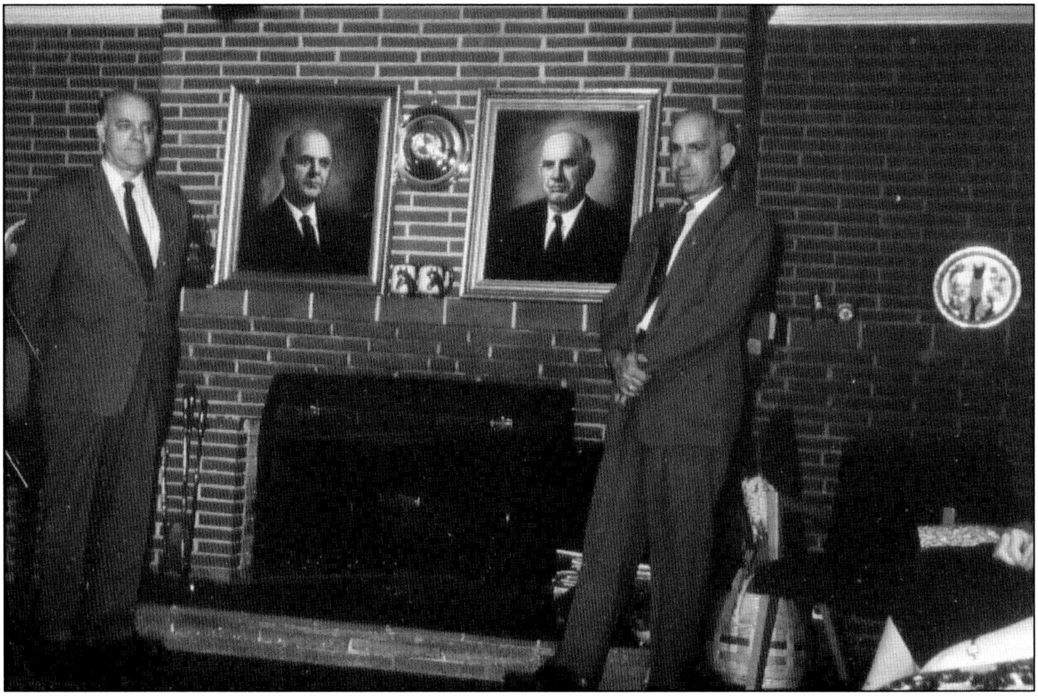

After working more than 25 years at Pomona Terra-Cotta, a company owned by their uncle, brothers Orton Boren and Cecil Addison Boren Jr. left to found Boren Brick and Tile in Pleasant Garden in 1947. Orton (left) was named president and treasurer. Addison (right) was vice president and superintendent of the plant that was built by local contractors Vickery and Kirkpatrick. He and other supervisory personnel bought property and built homes near the plant. This photograph was made in the brick and tile home Addison and his wife, Nanalyn Fuller Boren, completed in 1952. Some 23,000 Norman bricks were used for the exterior. Wood was only used for the roof, paneling, and cabinets. (Courtesy of Cecil Boren III.)

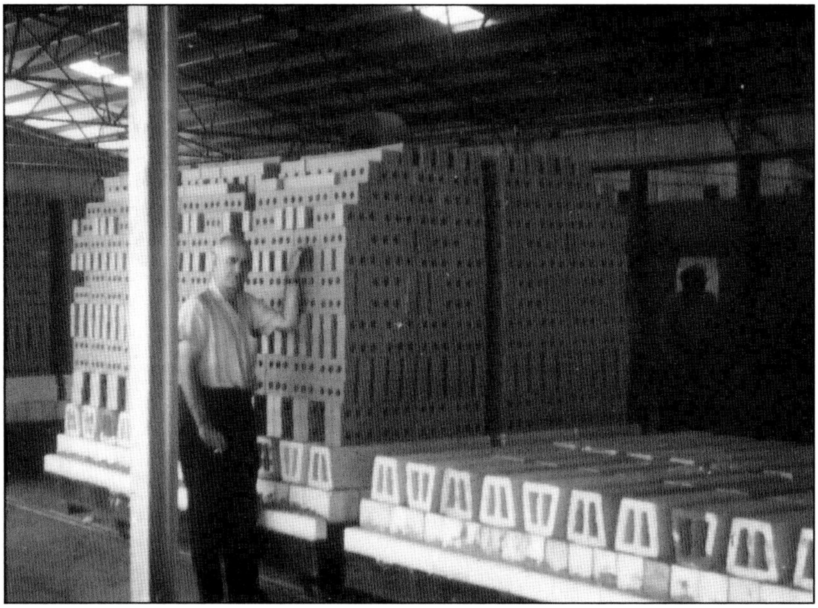

The Boren Brick plant was built on a 42-acre tract fronting the railroad in Pleasant Garden. Supt. Addison Boren poses beside the first bricks fired in the tunnel kiln. The company also molded bricks the old-fashioned way. Wynne H. Ross designed those special bricks. (Courtesy of Cecil Boren III.)

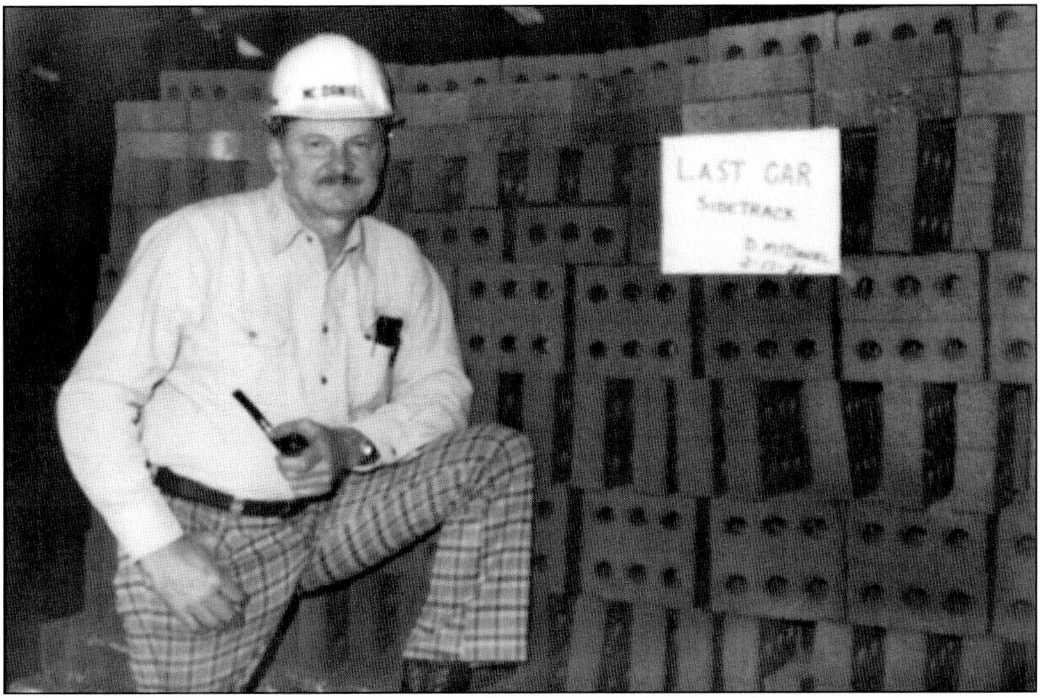

Donald E. McDaniel joined Boren Brick shortly after it was organized. In 1964, when he was named superintendent, the company employed 240 persons in North and South Carolina. McDaniel poses next to the last car of brick made in a kiln that fired brick for 33 years. A more modern Plant One opened in 1981. (Courtesy of Donald E. McDaniel Jr.)

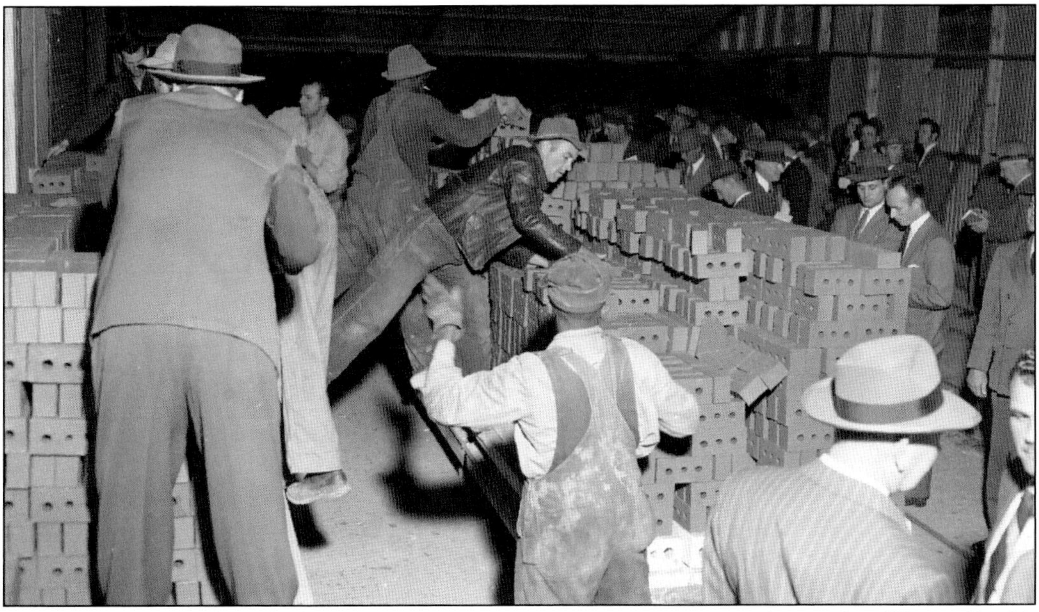

In March 1949, brick- and tile-industry representatives came to inspect the results of Boren Brick's innovative car-conveyor system that moved brick through oil-fired (later, natural gas) kilns, shortening the normal production time from 10 days to 36 hours. Antique, the company's first product line, was created when bricks from three kilns were intermixed after being fired. (Courtesy of CWM.)

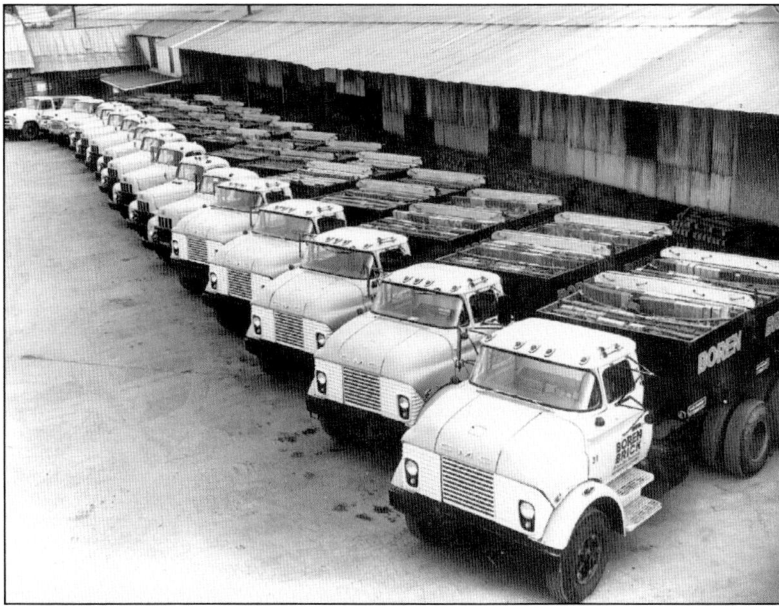

Many local residents were hired to deliver brick across the piedmont. Marvin and Thurman Holt owned and operated a fleet that grew over the years. The convenience of being located in central North Carolina provided a steady flow of brick and tile along the East Coast. (Courtesy of an anonymous source.)

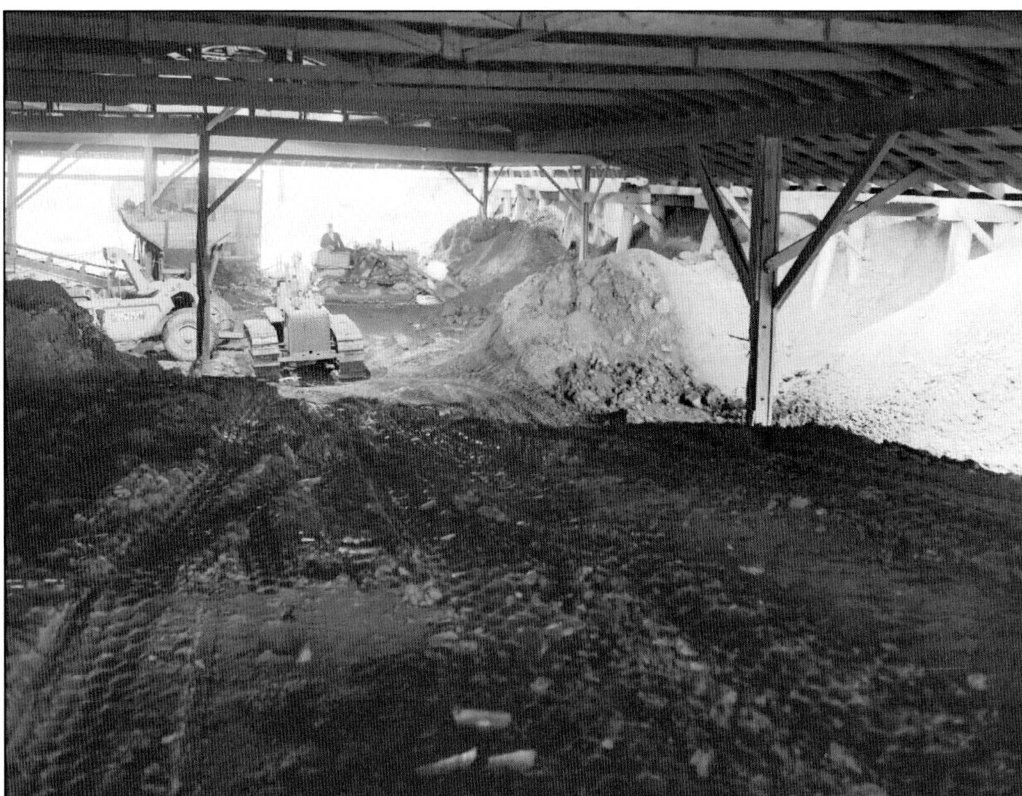

E.L. Rummage Grading owned and operated the earthmoving equipment used for mining local clay and Chatham County shale. Bulldozer operators prepared a 50-50 mixture of the two raw products before it is ground in a huge mixer. After screening, it was mixed with water, extruded, and cut, then transported through the tunnel kilns for drying and burning. (Courtesy of CWM.)

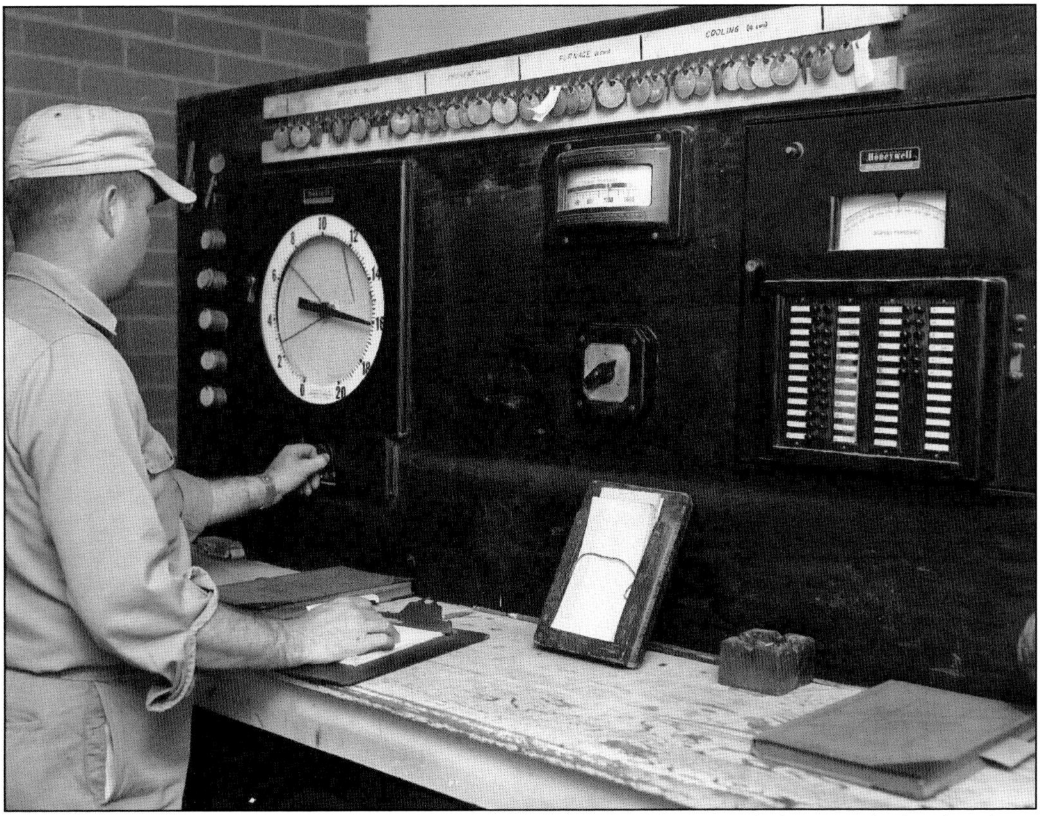

Philip Pearce designed Plant Two. It opened in 1960. In this photograph, he is in the brickmaking room. Located on a 150-acre tract just south of central Pleasant Garden, it was capable of producing 175,000 brick a day. (Courtesy of CWM.)

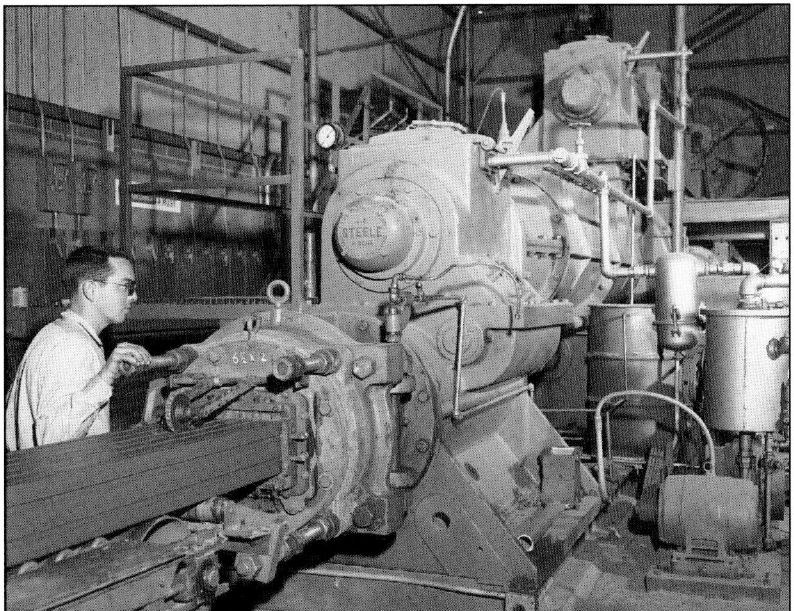

Martin Coble joined the company as a young man. He is operating the brick machine in the new Plant One. It was built in 1981 behind the original location. (Courtesy of CWM.)

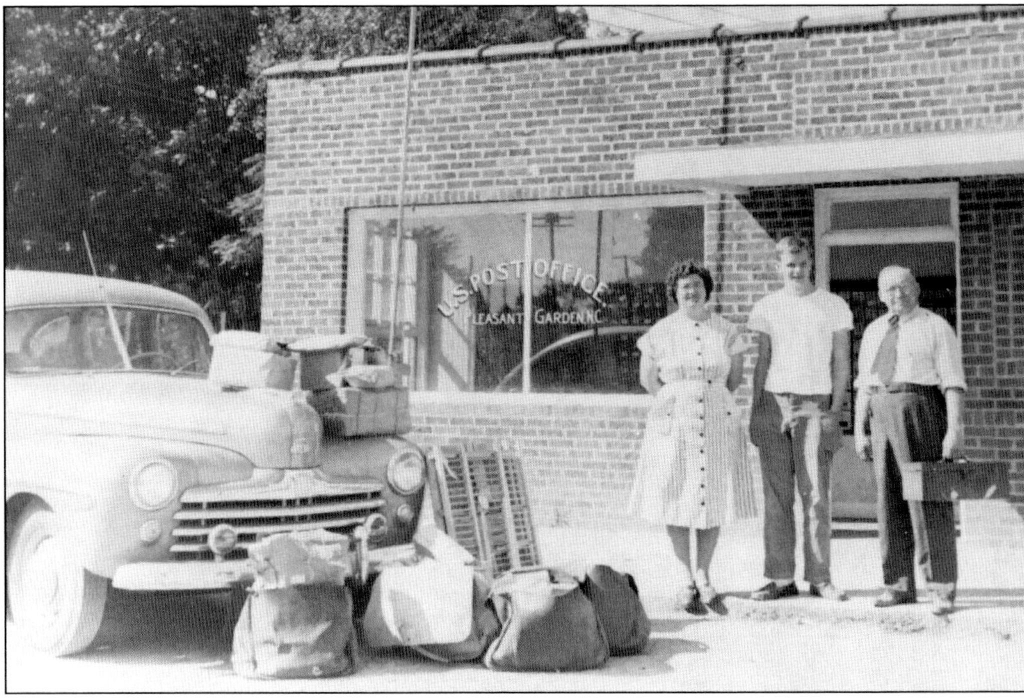

Worth Fields (right) pauses while loading the mail for delivery to residents along Route 1 in Pleasant Garden. He retired in 1961, having served those patrons for 42 years and five months. Beatrice Richardson and her son Billie E. Richardson are also shown in this photograph, taken in front of the new post office around 1947. She was postmaster for 30 years, during which time she was president of the North Carolina Postmasters and honored nationally. (Compliments of Phillip Way.)

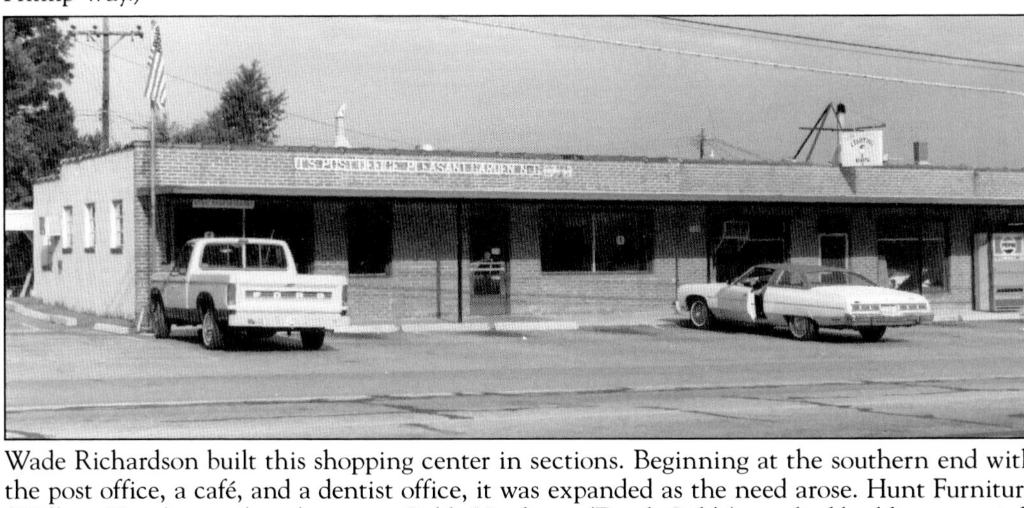

Wade Richardson built this shopping center in sections. Beginning at the southern end with the post office, a café, and a dentist office, it was expanded as the need arose. Hunt Furniture (William Hunt) moved up the street; Coble Hardware (Frank Coble) supplied building materials and a gathering spot for local workers. George's Trading Post (George Gibbs) was followed by Nova Fields's Pleasant Garden Department Store. Gray Jewelry may have been 10 feet wide, just enough space to showcase watches and rings and a workspace for Ben Gray to repair watches. It may have been 1950 before a space was added for Dr. Fagg Nowlan to set up practice and Gilmer Jones to establish Pleasant Garden Barber Shop. (Courtesy of Phillip Way.)

Beatrice Coltrane and Wade Ross Richardson are pictured here around 1965. She operated a lunch service called Bea's Soup Bowl before there was a school cafeteria. He worked as a mason and made his own cement blocks that he used to build the shopping center. (Courtesy of Wayne Richardson.)

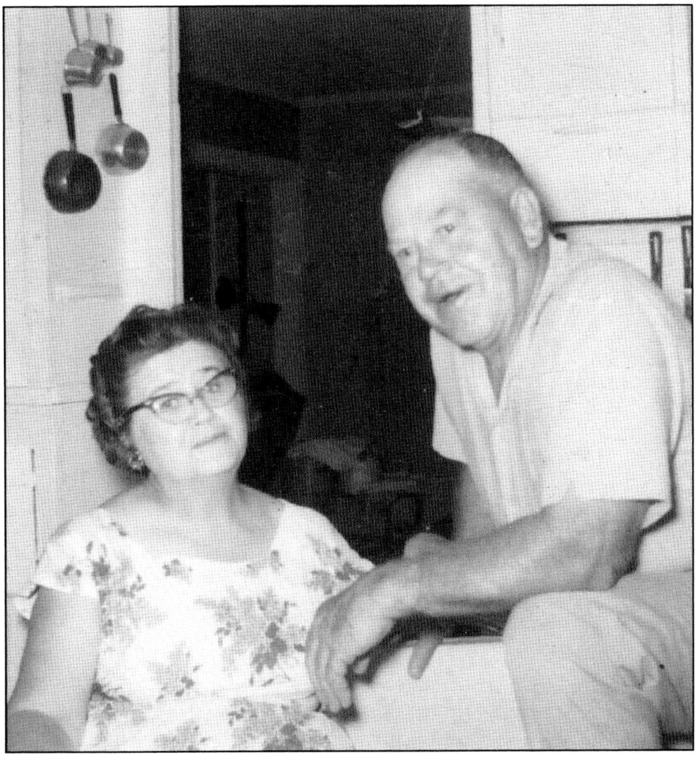

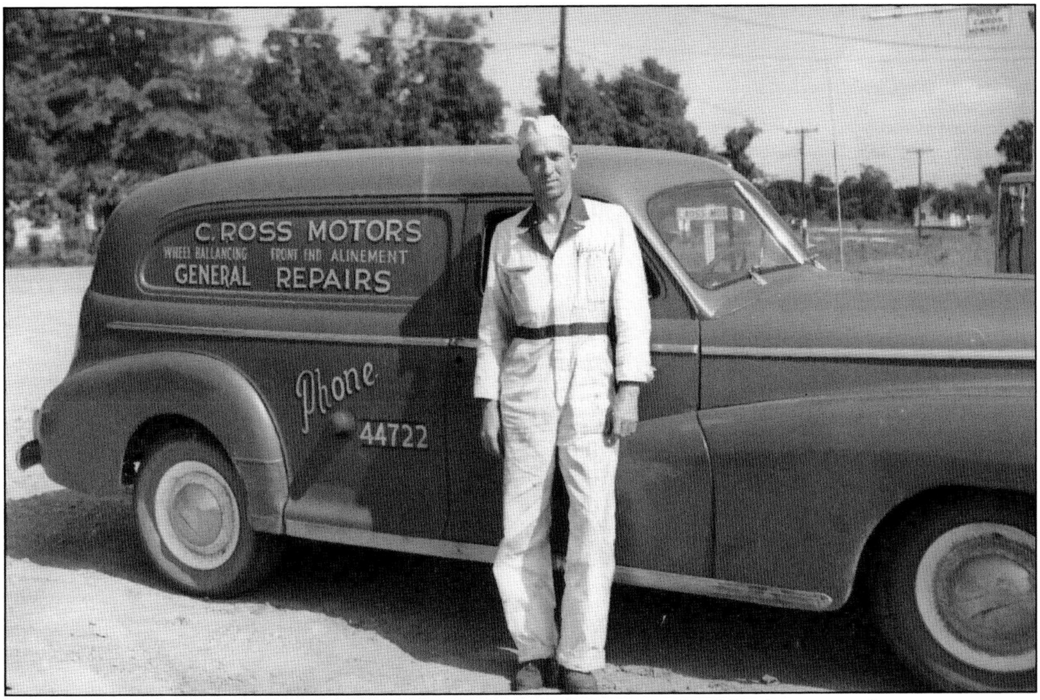

Charles C. Ross returned to his hometown after the war to build a home and open a garage across the road in 1947. C. Ross Motors operated a wrecker service and sold Gulf gasoline when it opened. (Courtesy of Tom Ross.)

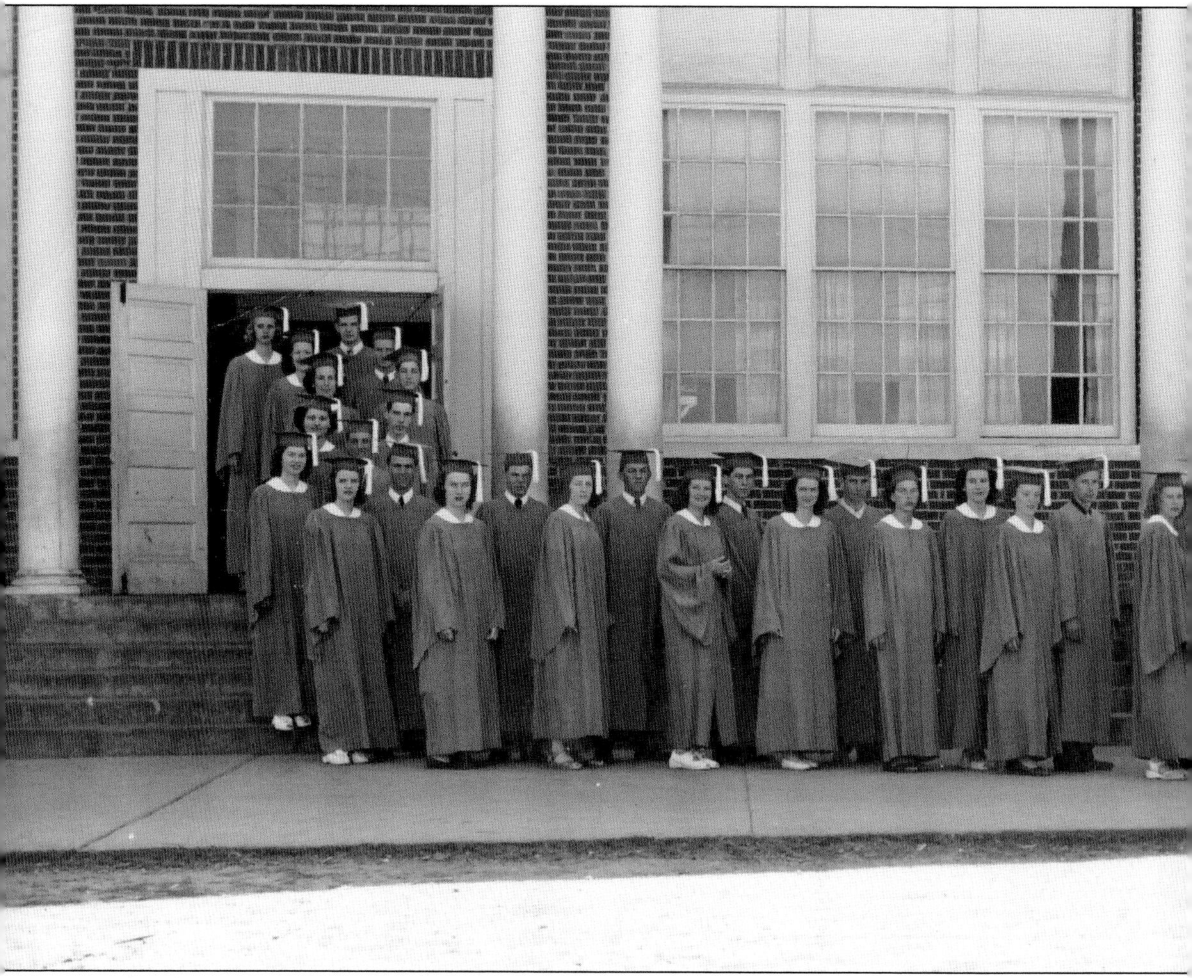

The class of 1948 was touted as being the largest when it began high school in 1944. The graduates pictured as they exit the auditorium are, from left to right, (first/top row) Jane Hockett and Billie Richardson; (second row) Margie Garrett and Bobby Pugh; (third row) Lucinda Jones and Paul Allred; (fourth row) Martha Ann Coble and Billy Hunter; (fifth row) Sally Osborne and Johnny Rich; (sixth row) Betty Ross, Clayton Gardner, Emily Neese, Clarence McClintock, Annie Alice

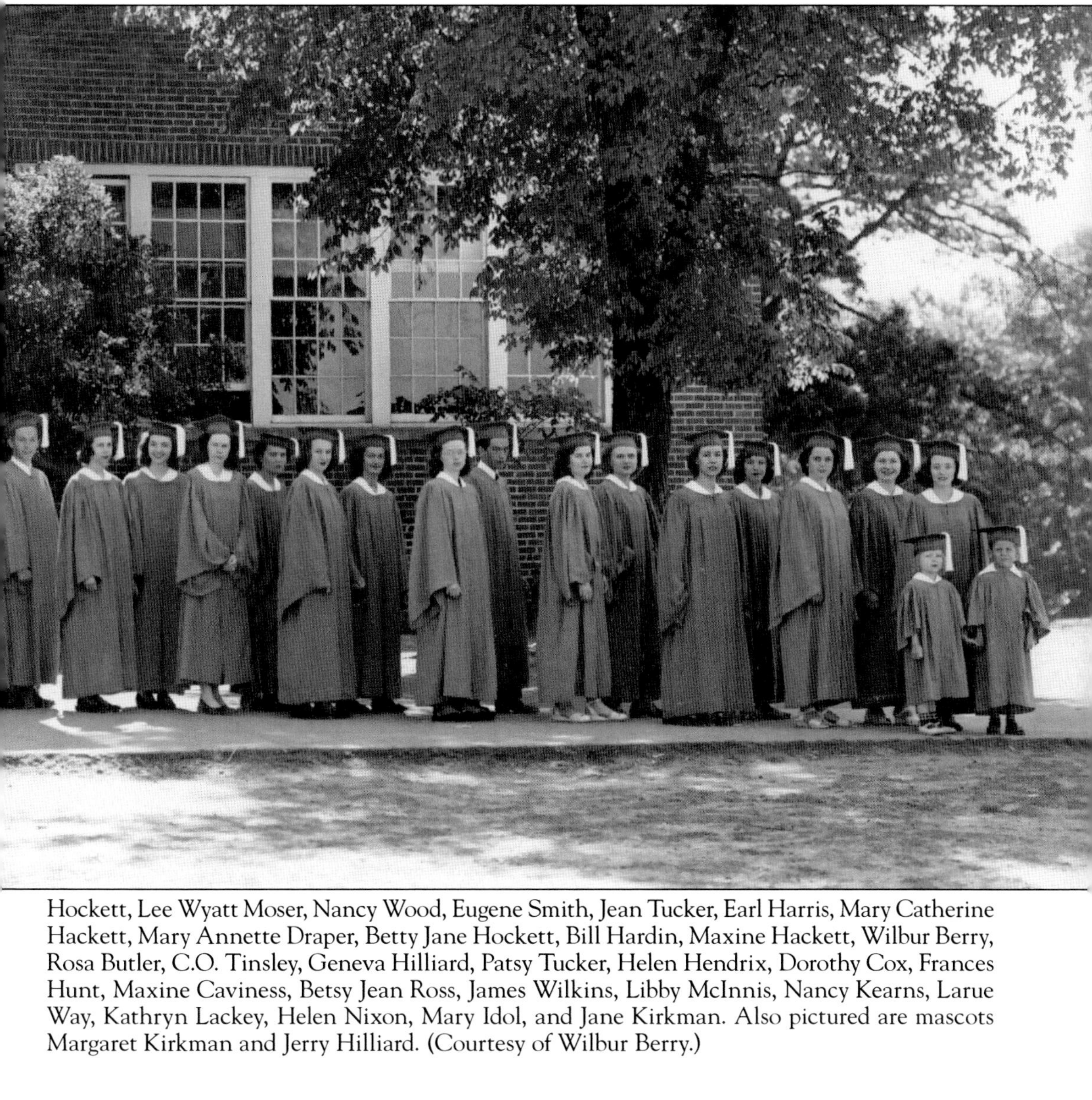

Hockett, Lee Wyatt Moser, Nancy Wood, Eugene Smith, Jean Tucker, Earl Harris, Mary Catherine Hackett, Mary Annette Draper, Betty Jane Hockett, Bill Hardin, Maxine Hackett, Wilbur Berry, Rosa Butler, C.O. Tinsley, Geneva Hilliard, Patsy Tucker, Helen Hendrix, Dorothy Cox, Frances Hunt, Maxine Caviness, Betsy Jean Ross, James Wilkins, Libby McInnis, Nancy Kearns, Larue Way, Kathryn Lackey, Helen Nixon, Mary Idol, and Jane Kirkman. Also pictured are mascots Margaret Kirkman and Jerry Hilliard. (Courtesy of Wilbur Berry.)

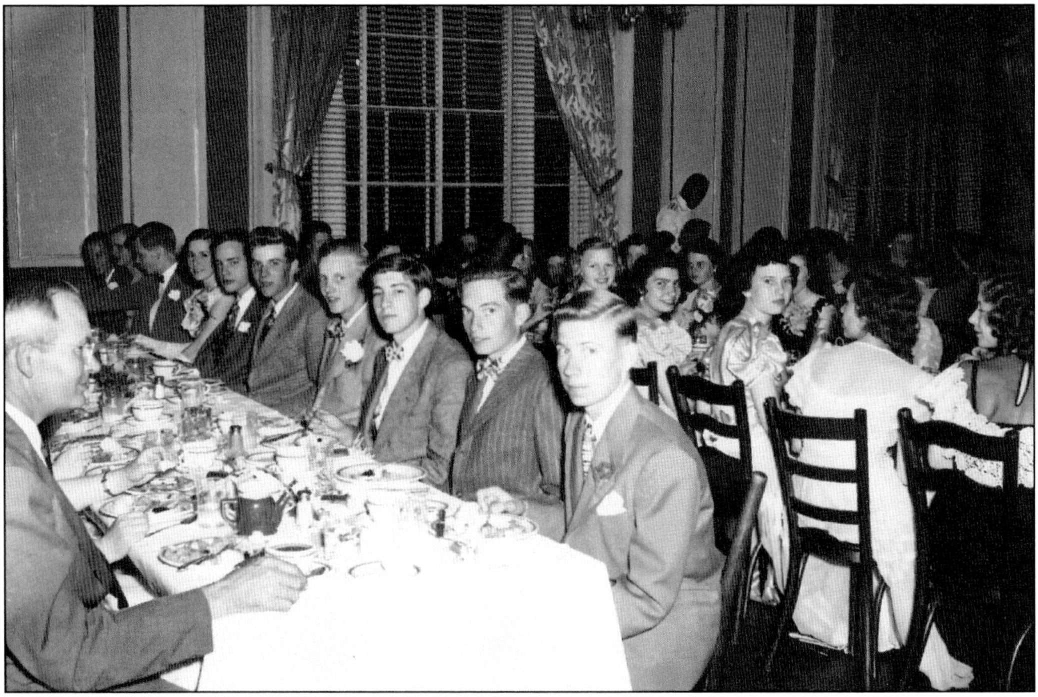

The junior-senior banquet was an anticipated event that climaxed the high school career of the graduating students. The class of 1949 hosted this formal affair at the O.Henry Hotel in Greensboro. (Courtesy of Wilbur Berry.)

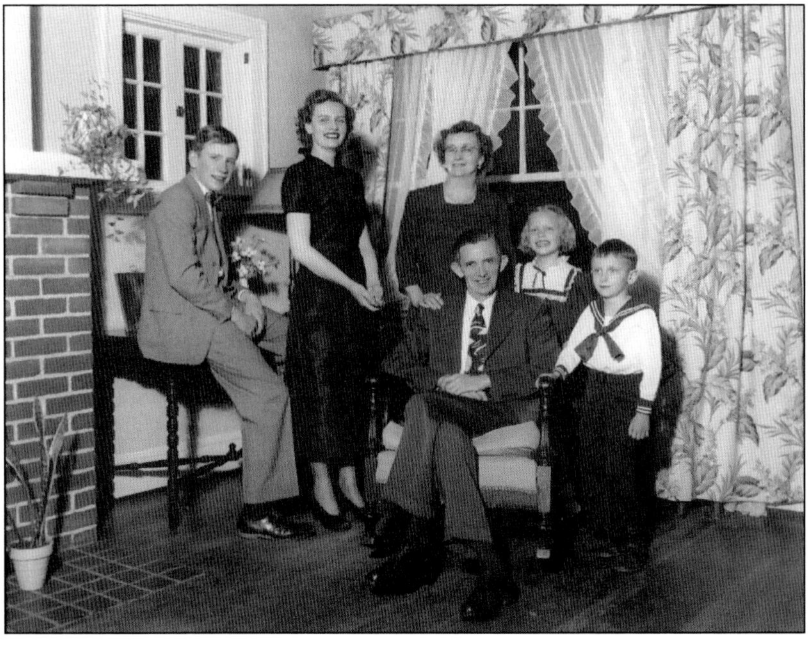

Guy and Nancy Coleman Ross lived in the center of Pleasant Garden in a home they completed in 1929. The family is circled around Ross in this 1949 photograph; from left to right are Guy Jr., Betty, Nancy, Nancy Jo, and Coleman.

Five

THE 1950s

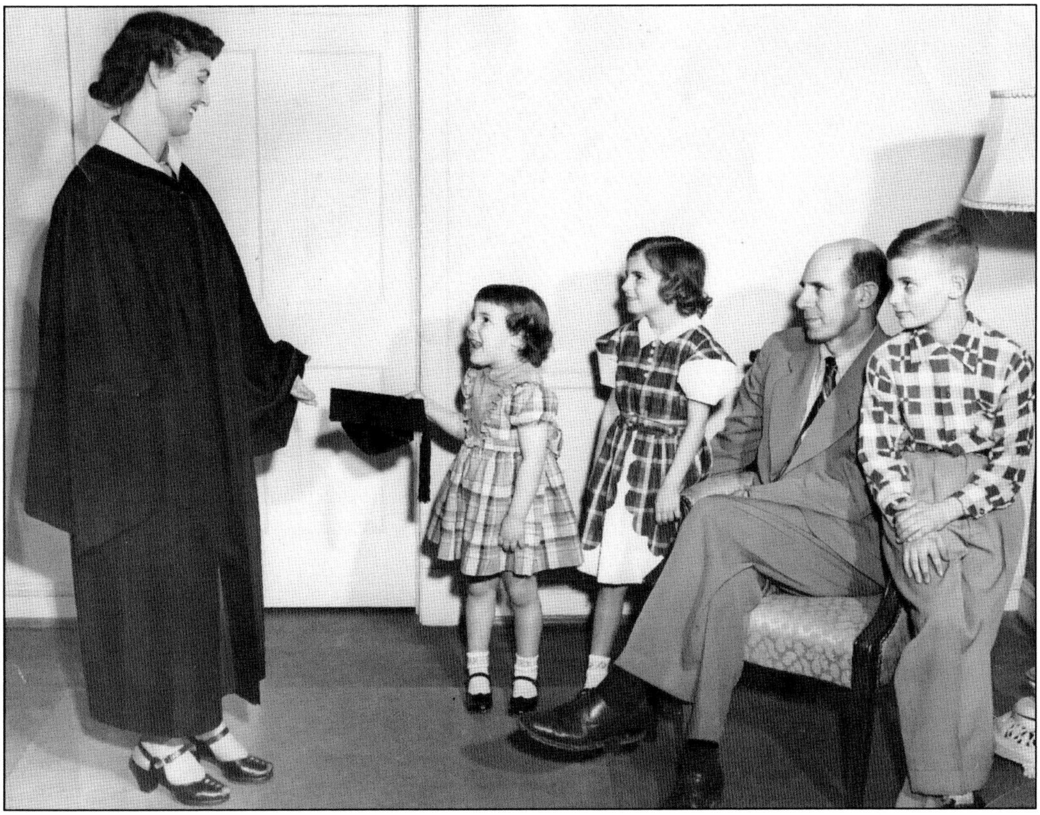

Greensboro College announced that Glenn Crowder Ayers was its first married-with-children graduate when she returned to receive her bachelor's degree in 1952. She had only completed two years when she married Robert Ayers in 1939. He was principal of Pleasant Garden High School for 28 years. Pictured here are, from left to right, Glenn, Sylvia, Ellen, Robert, and Dick Ayers. (Courtesy of Ellen Osborne.)

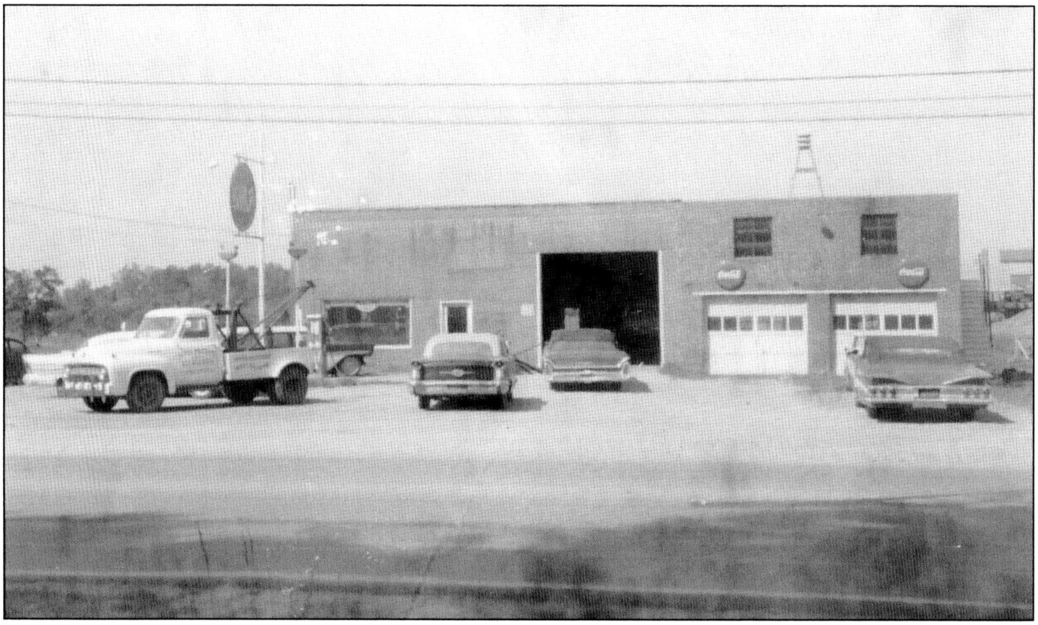

Pleasant Garden residents Patrick Winston and Frank Plunkett incorporated the Pleasant Garden Fire Department in 1948; however, organization did not materialize until 1952 when Pleasant Garden Baptist pastor Dewey Armstong led a successful effort. The first station was housed in the two-bay addition to C. Ross Motors. (Courtesy of Tom Ross.)

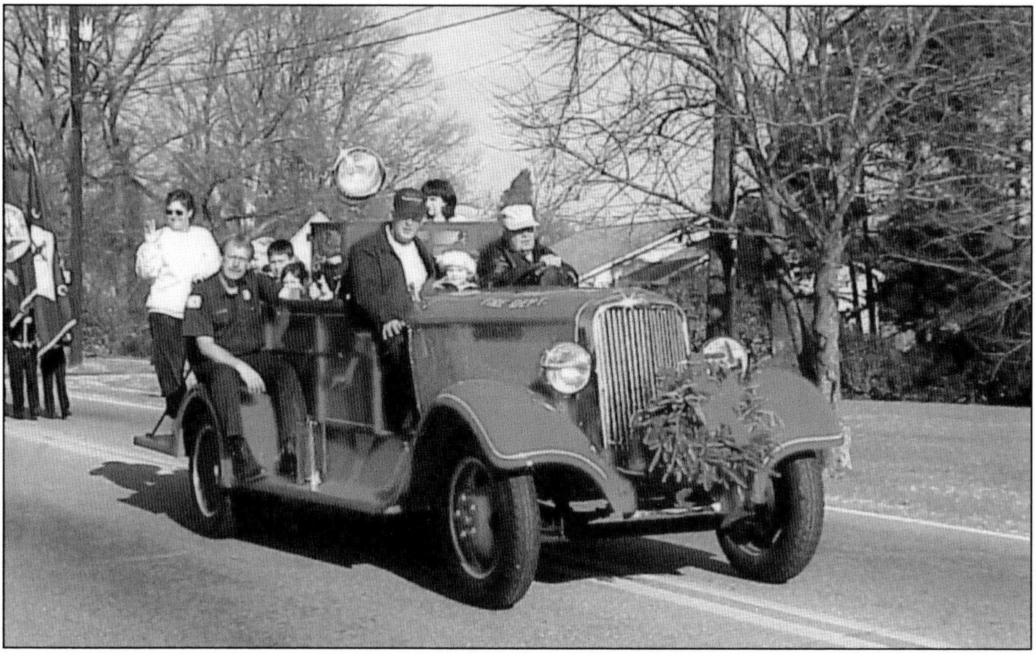

With fire chief J.D. Long, W.E. Yow drove this open fire truck from Mayodan to Pleasant Garden on a very cold winter day. It was the first piece of equipment for the new fire department. He is also at the wheel of the restored pumper in this Pleasant Garden Christmas parade. Those along for the ride on this trip are, from left to right, Susan Marley, Jeff McNabb, and Dale Marley. (Courtesy of Billie Kay Hall.)

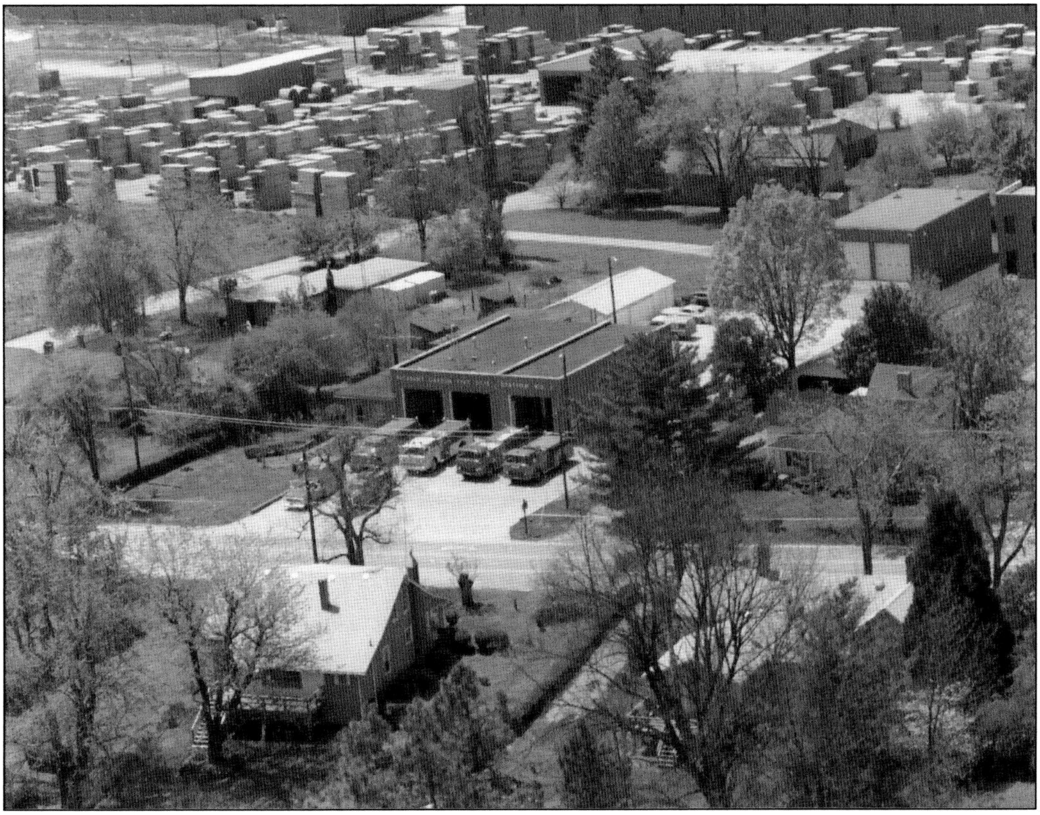

Jack Reddick was at the controls when Phillip Way made this aerial photograph of the second firehouse, built by Vickery Brothers in 1962. It consisted of a 30-by-60-foot bay that housed four pieces of equipment and a kitchen, bedroom, bath, and office. Although there were 28 firemen, the station was unmanned with the exception of the 24-hour period beginning at 6:00 p.m. Saturday night. Emergency calls to the firehouse also notified eight additional locations. The roof-mounted siren alerted volunteers, who sped to the station in their personal vehicles to drive the trucks. (Courtesy of the Pleasant Garden Fire Department.)

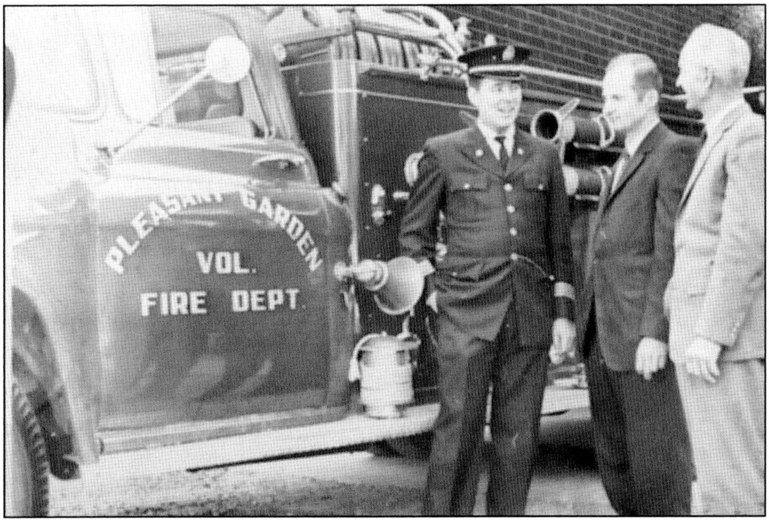

County fire marshal Robert Grant (left) attended the dedication of the second fire station. Fire chief Donald McDaniel (center) oversaw the construction of the $19,000 building. Guilford County commissioner Charles J. Hunt (right) was one of the 10,000 residents of the district. (Courtesy of Donald McDaniel Jr.)

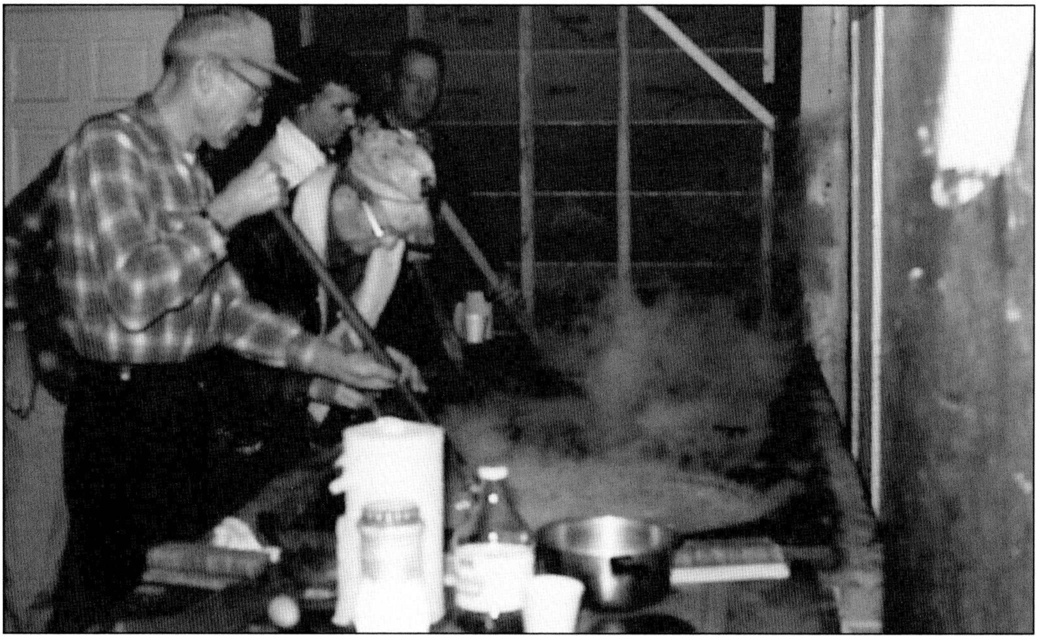

Although the department was supported by taxes from residents within a three-mile radius, the all-volunteer group raised additional funds with Brunswick stew sales. The men stirring the stew are Charles T. Ross (left), Charles Vickery (second from left), and two unidentified volunteer firemen. (Courtesy of the Pleasant Garden Fire Department.)

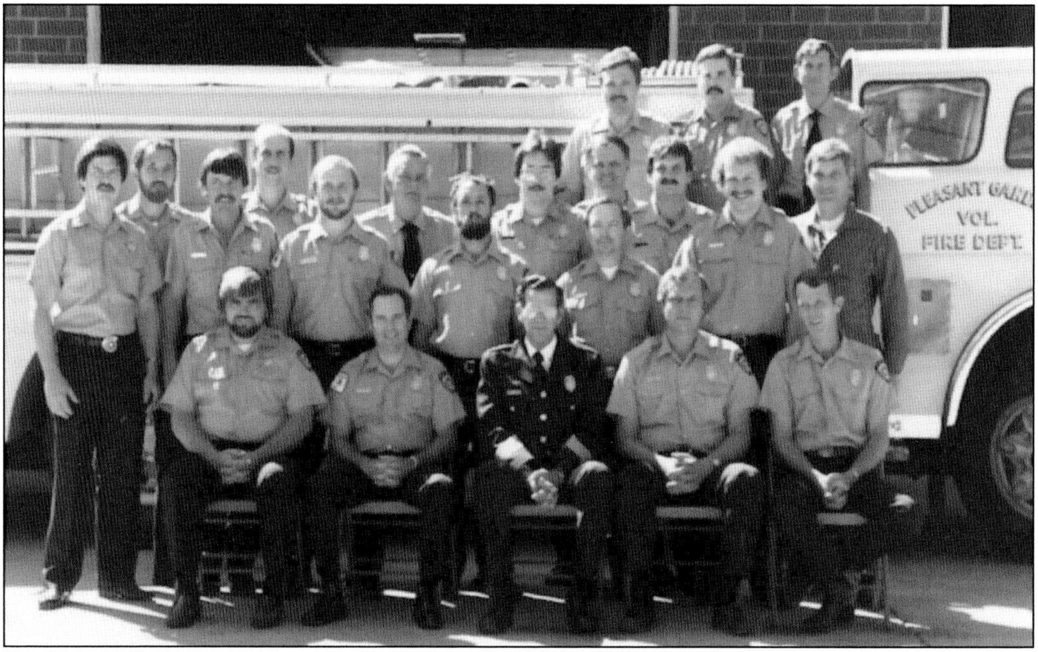

Fire chief Cletus Surratt is seated in the center of the front row. He served in that capacity for nearly 30 years, from 1958 to 1988. John L. "Jake" Phillips (third row, third from left) and Robert O'Conner (fourth row, right) served in various leadership capacities. (Courtesy of the Pleasant Garden Fire Department.)

While Leonard Oliver, better known as "Gus," was working in a hosiery mill, he envisioned his family's future Bonnie Kay's Seafood sitting on the family farm. In 1957, he erected a plain brick building that initially seated 78. He was also the chief cook, frying fresh fish in peanut oil five nights a week. (Courtesy of Tina Oliver.)

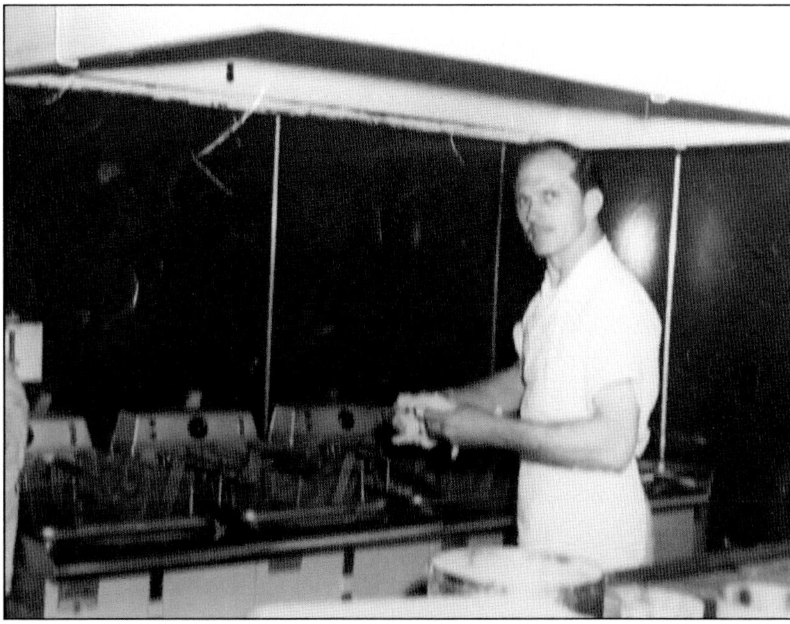

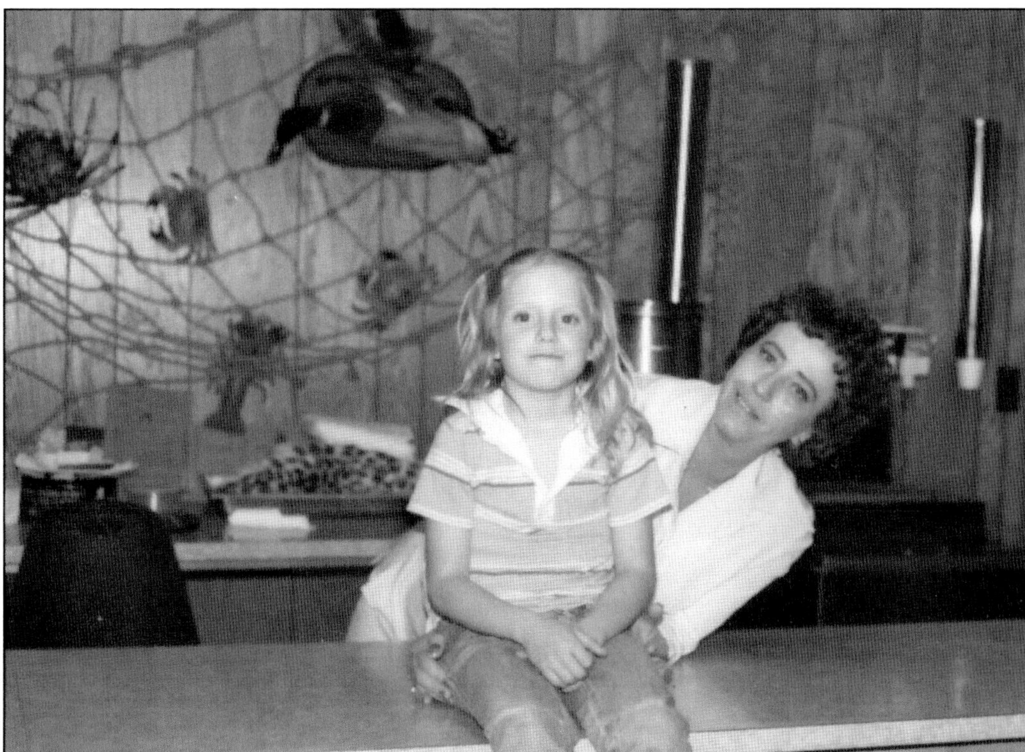

Bonnie Kay's Seafood was a family restaurant in more ways than one. Ann Oliver presided over the front; daughters Bonnie, Kay, and Tina, born after the restaurant was opened, have all worked there. Bonnie's daughter DeAna Voss poses with her grandmother. Voss also worked there when she grew up. (Courtesy of Tina Oliver.)

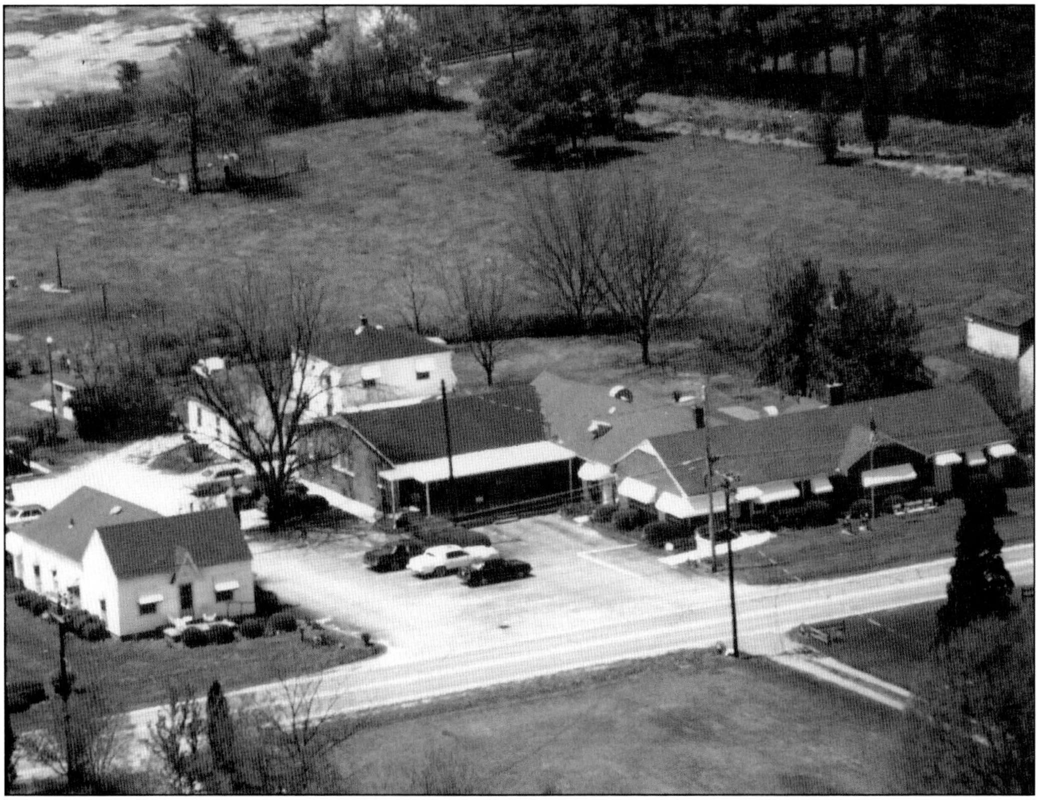

Clapp's Nursing Home, the oldest privately owned nursing home in Guilford County, has the motto "A family caring for families," because that was the way it all began in 1952 when Mary Riley Clapp started caring for her aged mother. Within three years, she and her husband, Wilson Clapp, expanded their home to become the large brick building shown in this aerial photograph. The facility eventually had a capacity of 42 beds before becoming an assisted-living facility with 25 employees to care for 30 patients. Sons Riley and Donald Clapp and their respective wives, Laura and Libby, also became administrators. When stricter government regulations required that caregivers have training to administer medications, Mary Clapp, second from the right in the photograph below, and Ruhama Causey Maness took classes and became licensed practical nurses in 1955. (Above, courtesy of Phillip Way; below, courtesy of Laura Gwen Clapp.)

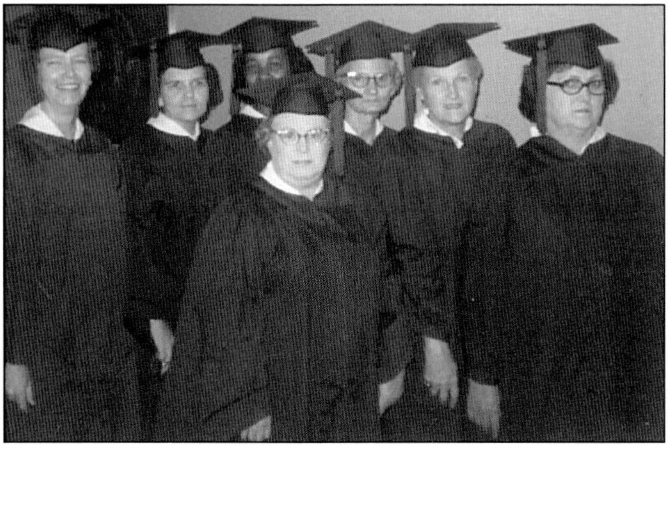

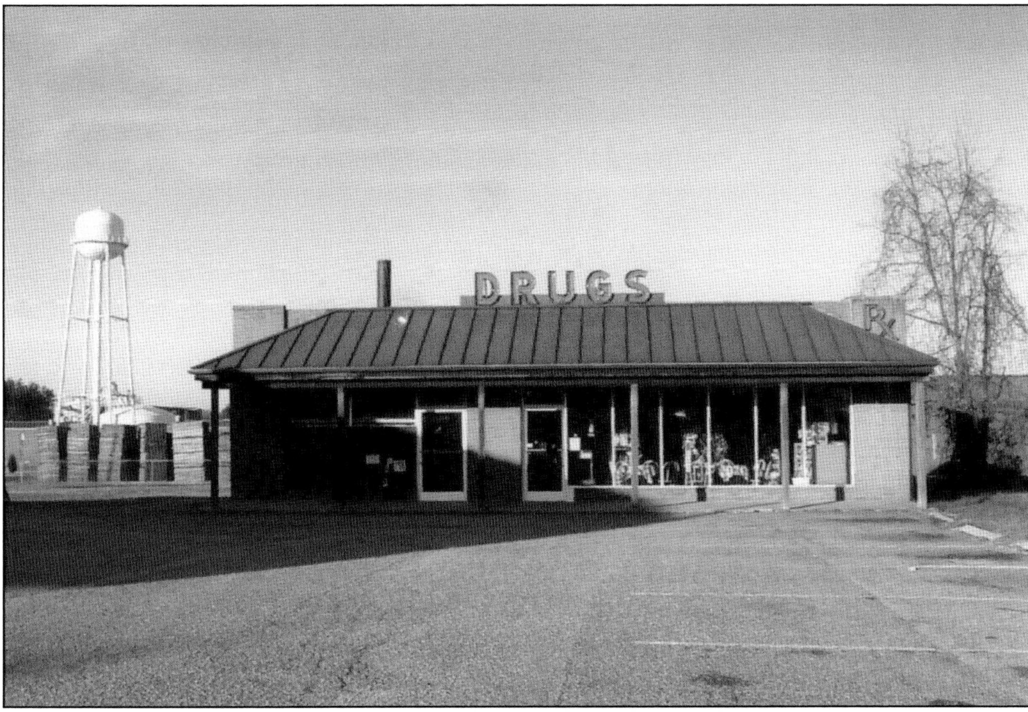

The first Pleasant Garden Drugstore was located beside Cheek's Superette in the spot vacated by the soda shop. Pharmacist William H. Barton had been joined by Verner H. Smith by the time this building was constructed around 1959. Later, Barton partnered with Joe Davis to operate the independently owned pharmacy. Ronald Langdon followed Davis around 1969. (Courtesy of Ronald Langdon.)

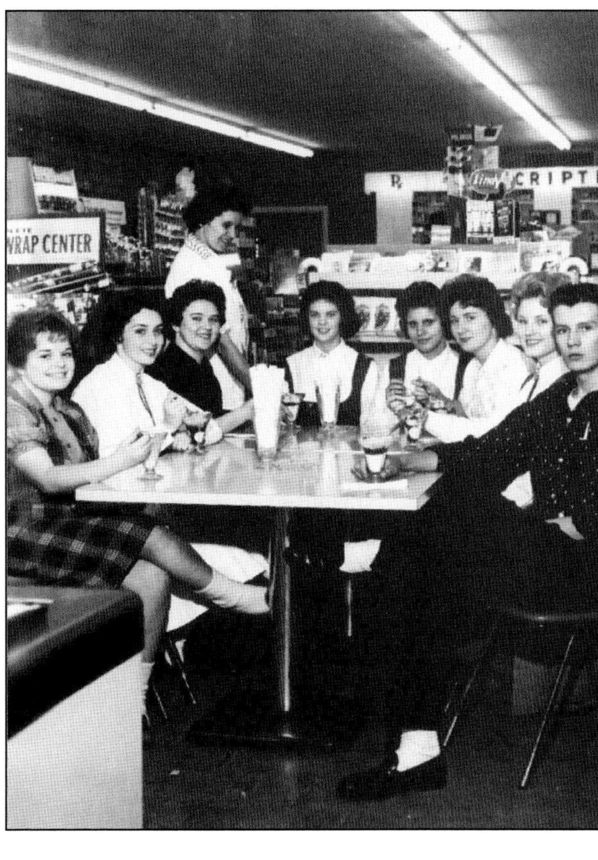

Pleasant Garden Drugstore became a popular place to drop in for a cup of coffee or a milk shake and to catch up on the local news. These students comprise the annual staff for the last *Hi-Lights*, published in 1962. Pictured are, from left to right, Anne Hice, Rebecca Vickery, Joyce Fields, Ola Mae McGinnis (drugstore employee), Jo Ann Carter (editor), Janet Vernon, Carolyn Curtis, Linda Rumley, and Jim Vickery. (Courtesy of Anne Hice.)

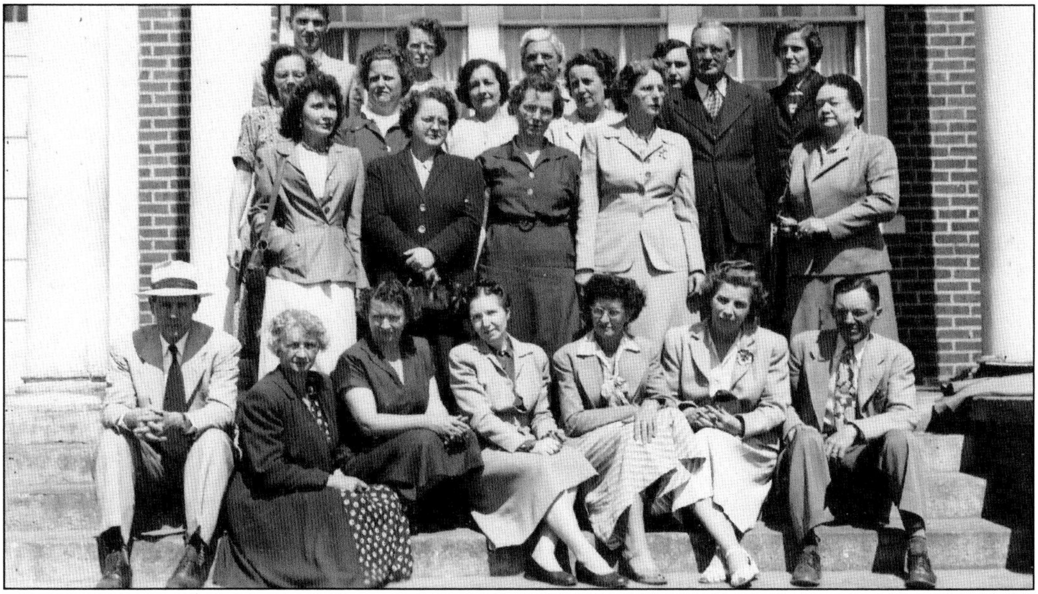

The 1951 Pleasant Garden School faculty assembled for this photograph. From left to right are (first row) Robert Ayers, Kate Hunt Kirkman, Edna DeLoach, Ruth H. Hunt, Mary Lee McLeod, Pherlie Siske Lambeth, and J. Leroy Dawson; (second row) Mrs. Marion Luther, Esther Jones, Nell Kirkman, Mary Bess Coleman, and Blanche Burgess; (third row) Susan Gray, Belle Coble, Nell Sillmon, Elizabeth Fields, and C.J. DeLoach; (fourth row) unidentified, Ruth Hockett, Anna Mae McCulloch, Mary Lou Kiger, and Ethel Fields.

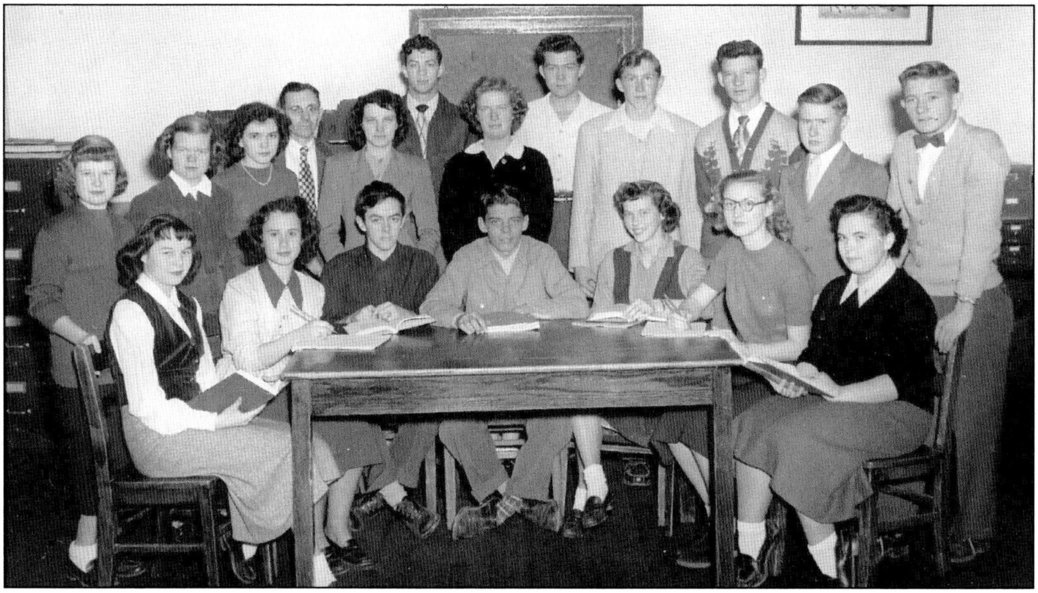

J. Leroy Dawson was the teacher/advisor for this group of Distributive Education students. They usually went to school in the mornings and worked in the afternoons. Pictured in 1950 are, from left to right, (first row) Jo Ann Gray, Nancy Nixon, Clay McInnis, Jack Monnett, Betsy Brown, Tessa Weatherly, and Rosa Neelley; (second row) Lois Smith, Peggy Thompson, Margaret Still, Dorothy Mowery, Velvie Steinback, Tommy Kirkman, Lester Davis, Garland Ingold, and Ray Caudle; (third row) Dawson, John Watson, and Bill Marley. (Courtesy of Phillip Way.)

Heading into the conference tournament, the 1951 basketball team was undefeated. Pictured from left to right, Reggie Raper, Pete Taylor, Doug Curtis, Guy Ross Jr., and Bernie Garner all played to win. Coach Hebron Coble was in his second year at Pleasant Garden. Suffice it to say all were shocked when the team did not win the championship.

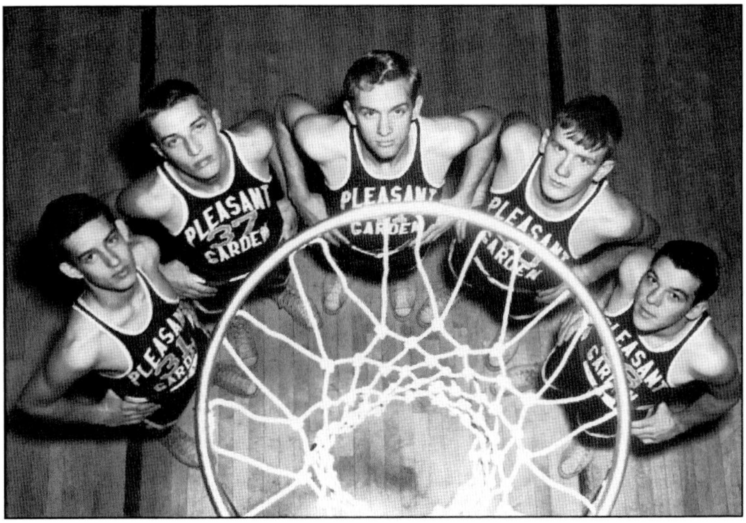

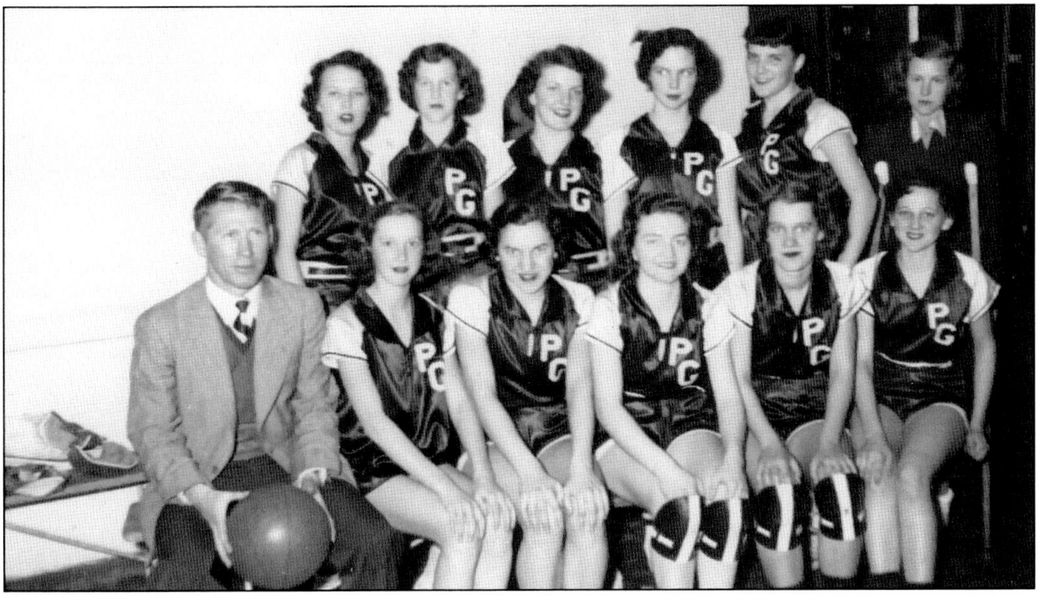

Wilma Surratt scored the game-winning points when the 1952 Pleasant Garden girls' team was declared Guilford County champions after a hard-played game in the Guilford College Gymnasium. Coach Hebron Coble holds the basketball, with Surratt at his right. The other players are, from left to right, (first row) Mary Catherine Neese, Louise Frye, Ruth Ann Marley, and Betty Fields; (second row) Betty Brown, Jane Kirkman, Margaret Kirkpatrick, Lucy Bowman, Betty Thompson, and Judy Coble, who suffered a leg injury at the end of the regular season. Coble continued to play basketball after graduating in 1955, representing the United States in the 1963 Pan American Games. She was the first woman in the state of Tennessee to referee a boys' basketball game. (Courtesy of Ruth Ann Jones.)

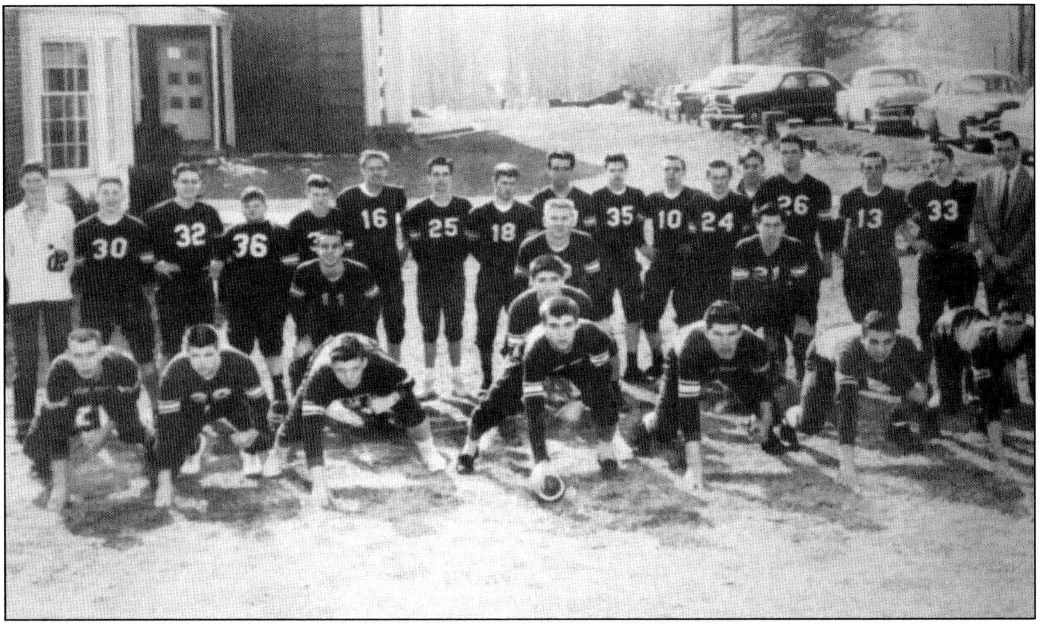

Football was the last sport added to the Pleasant Garden High School athletics program. Home games were played during the day on an unlighted field behind the gym. The 1956 team is pictured here lined up on the front lawn. Milton Reece was the coach.

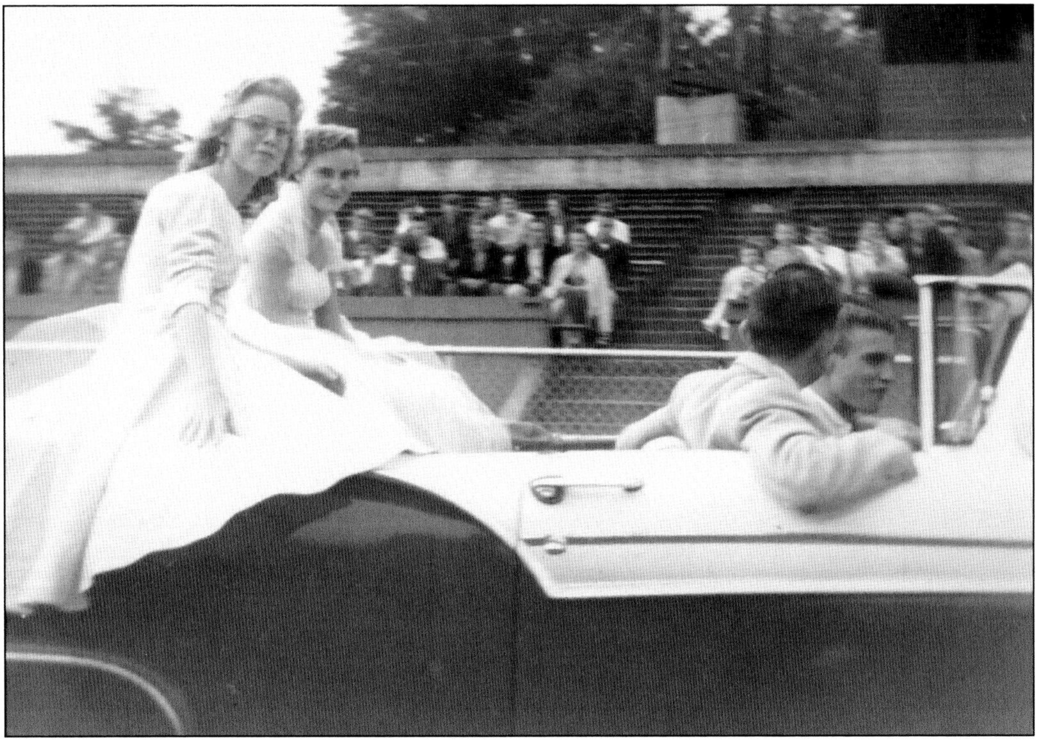

The 1957 homecoming football game was held at Greensboro's War Memorial Stadium. As members of the homecoming court, Patricia (left) and Judy Greeson make their entrance at halftime riding in a convertible. (Courtesy of Brenda Boyce.)

Nell Kirkman taught her fourth graders how to perform a grand flag march that became a PTA program. Here, each student is dressed in a costume representing the country whose flag he or she carried. Shown are, from left to right, (first row) Harold Gray, Barry Vickery, Charles W. Fields, and Norman Carroll; (second row) Mike North, Herbert Crymes, Jane Frye, Patricia Oliver, and Mary E. May; (third row) Nancy Jo Smith, Dick Ayers, Carol Kirkman, Frieda Ross, and Jeanette Sasser.

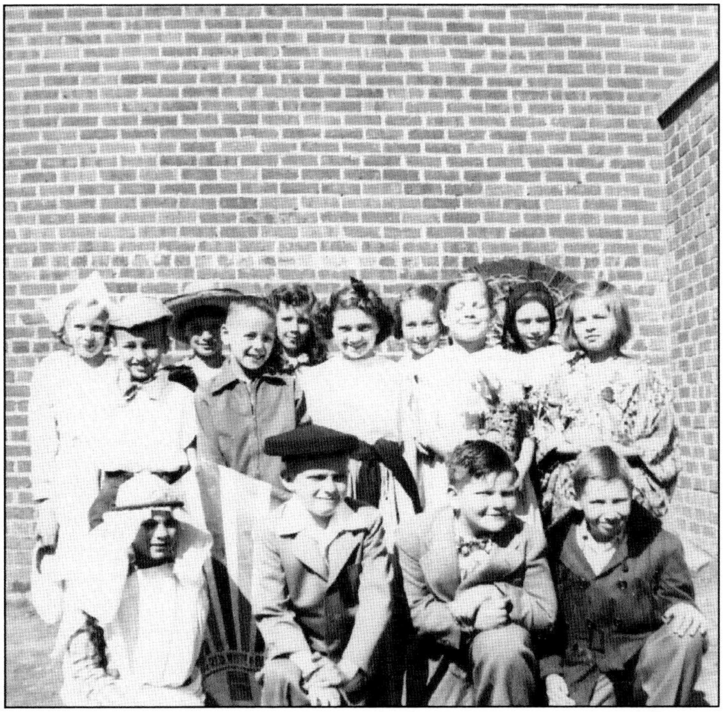

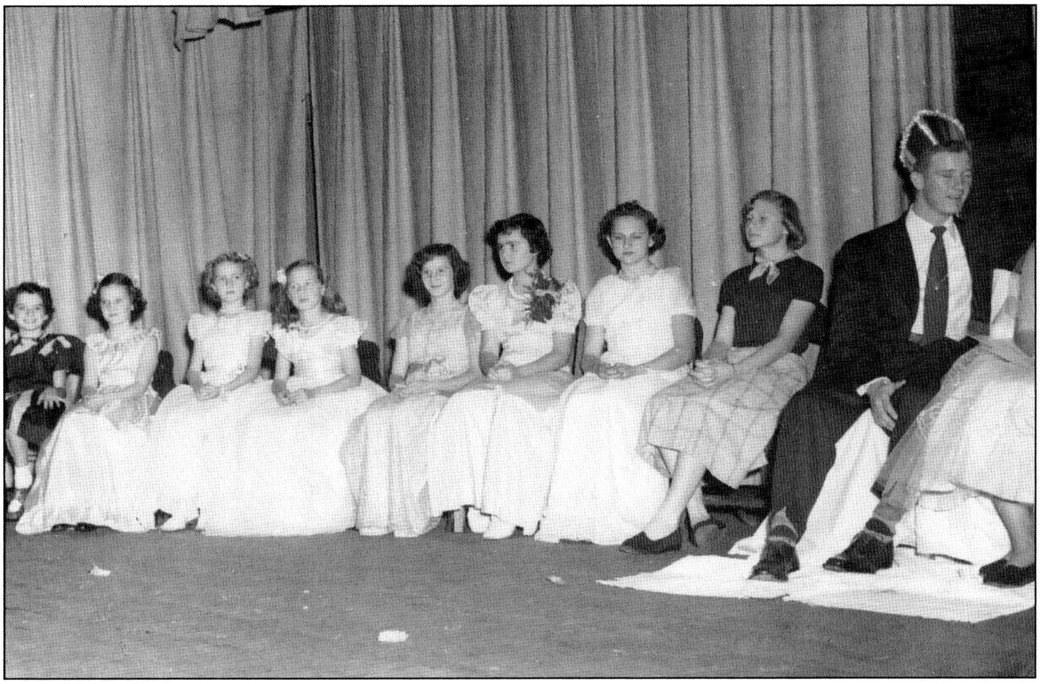

The main PTA fundraiser, a harvest festival, was held each fall. There was a Brunswick stew supper, and each room had a child friendly activity. The grand finale was the crowning of the Harvest Queen and King. Pictured here in 1952 are, from left to right, Nancy Allred, Brenda Smith, Brenda Shipman, Sandra Oliver, Sharmel White, Geraldine Harris, Hazel Denny, Betty Pratt, and Ray Caudle. (Courtesy of Brenda Boyce.)

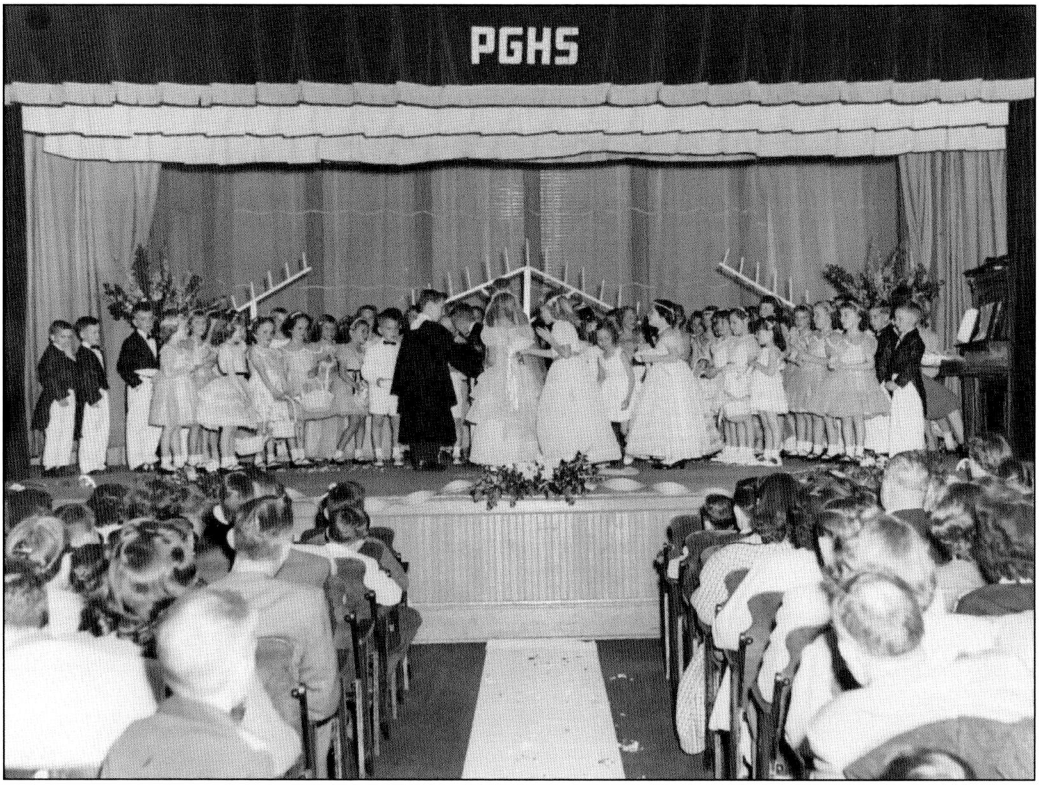

A Tom Thumb wedding was held to raise funds for a new piano. The bride and groom were second graders Mary Ross and Douglas Curtis, and soloists Sylvia Ayers, Linda Cheek, and Judy Jackson were accompanied by music teacher Ruth Hunt. Mary Lee McLeod's and Kate Kirkman's first graders were flower girls, train bearers, and junior ushers. Mary Bess Coleman's and Nell Sillmon's second graders were senior bridesmaids and ushers. This 1955 event raised $241.50.

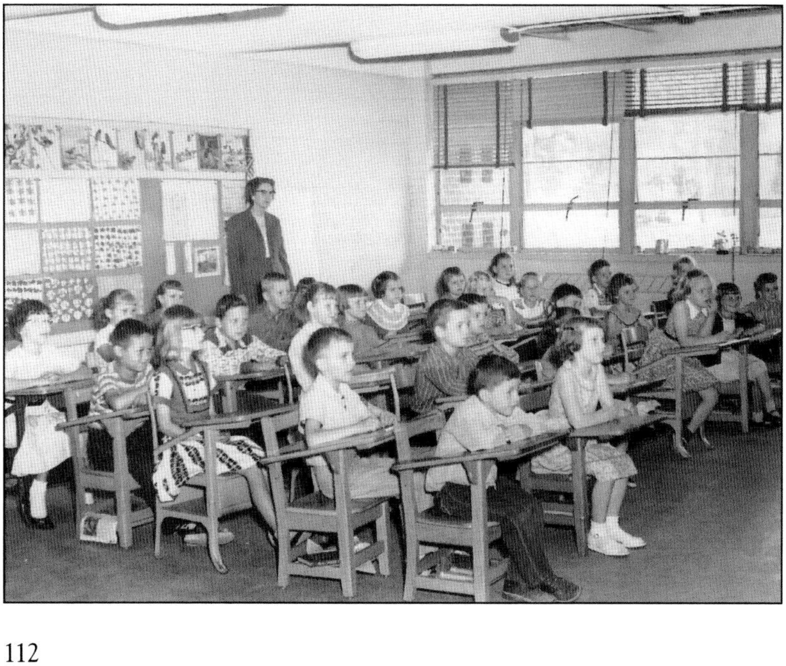

In 1954, the teacherage was moved in sections a couple of miles away. The new building housed first, second, and third grades on the upper level. A modern cafeteria and recreation room were located in the walk-in lower level. Mary Bess Coleman's second-grade classroom (pictured) was in the middle on the north side of the building.

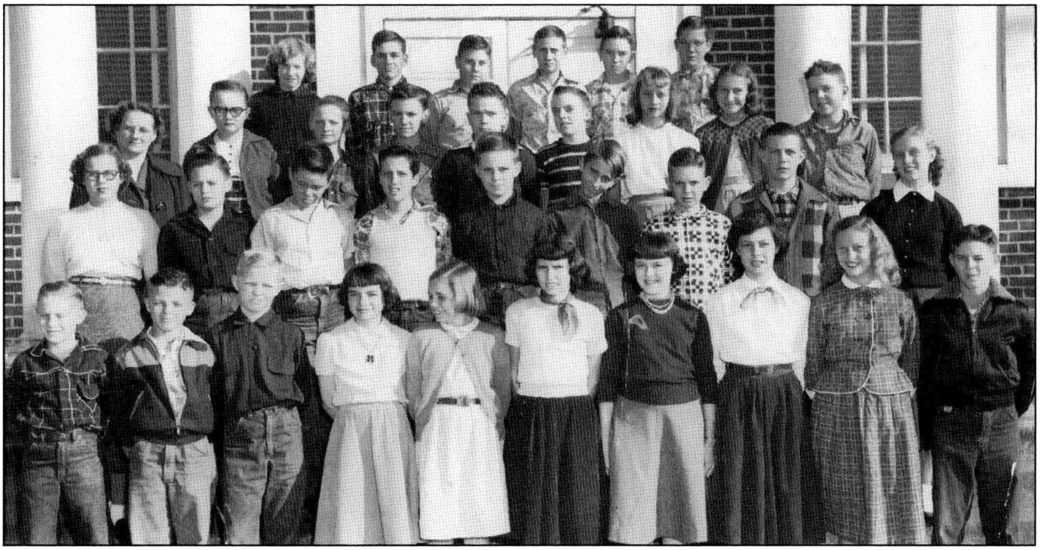

The class of 1959 was always divided into two groups. This photograph of one group in the seventh grade includes, from left to right, (first row) Tommy Ross, Tommy Kirkman, Jimmy Garrett, Nancy Allred, Mary Virginia Tullock, Peggy Beal, Eutha Alexander, Judy Tucker, Lydia Woodard, and Edward Moser; (second row) Libby Routh, Charles Herndon, Roger Smith, Craig Emerson, Branson Coltrane, Don Cockerham, Phil Way, Francis Snow, and Sarah Farlow; (third row) Roberta Barrow (teacher), Mary Florence Hockett, Ferrell Weatherly, Doug Jones, John Beal, Bill Venable, Carolyn Chandler, Georgia Simmons, and Dan Lewis; (fourth row) Peggy Mowery, Grady Highfill, Grady Hockett, Dalton Fields, Tom Wright, and Ray Maness. (Courtesy of Phillip Way.)

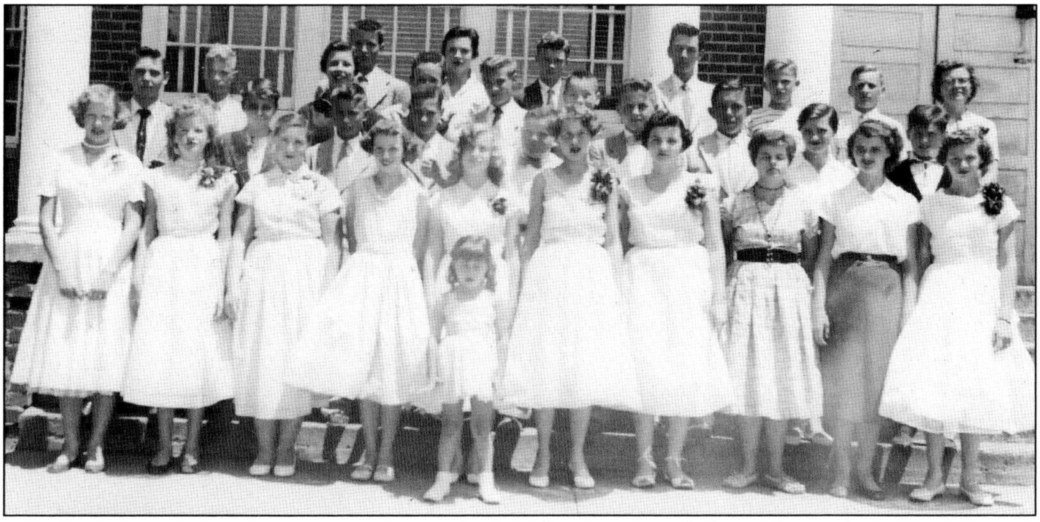

Members of the class of 1959 are pictured after their 1955 eighth-grade graduation ceremony. The photograph includes, from left to right, (first row) Nancy Jo Ross, Sue Clapp, Annie Mae Cross, Jeanette Sasser, Patricia Greeson, Glenda Surratt (mascot), Frieda Ross, Jonaleen Lasley, Mary E. May, Mary Kirkman, and Tula Osborne; (second row) Luther McCravey, Wayne Hall, Robert Nichols, Ralph Tart, Charles W. Fields, Jerry Drake, Charles Cox, Jane Frye, and Charles Saunders; (third row) Dick Ayers, Carol Kirkman, John Waugh, Herbert Crymes, Barry Vickery, J.W. Surratt, and Mary Dunn Kearns (teacher); (fourth row) Hoke Hahn, Faye Smith, Larry McCluskey, and Eugene Brady.

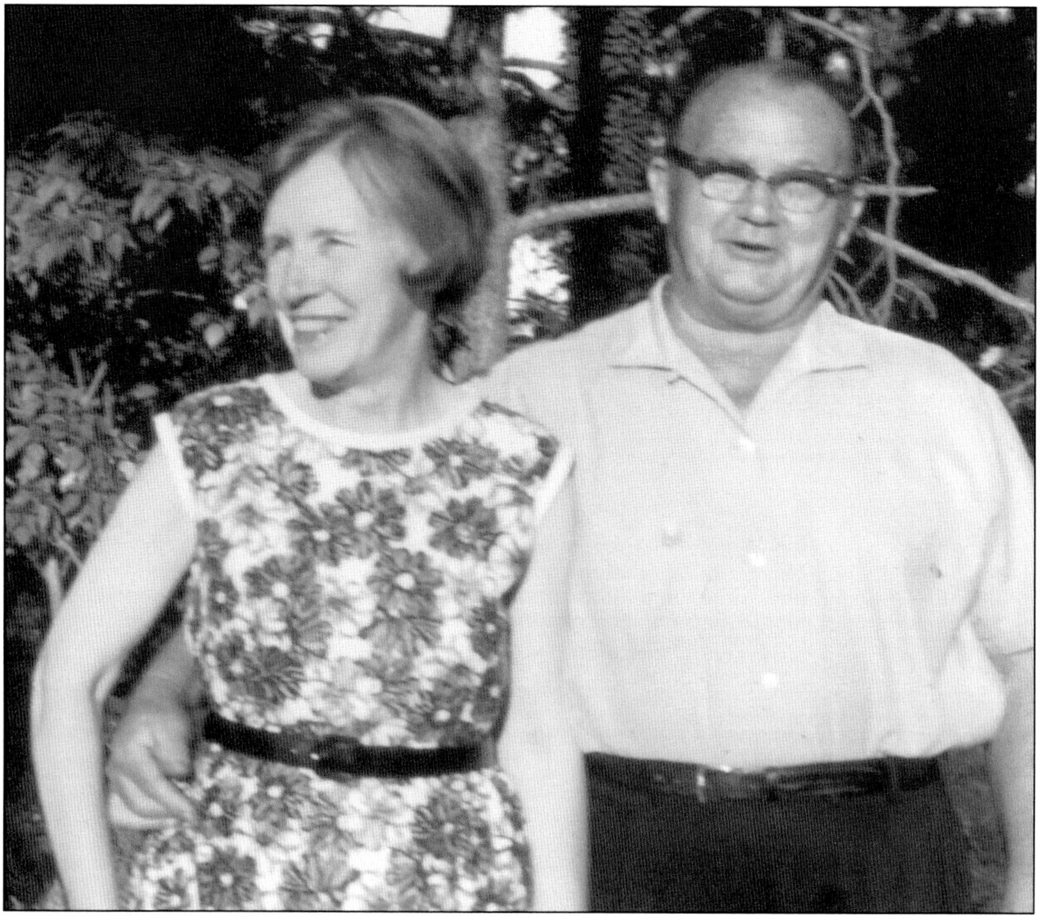

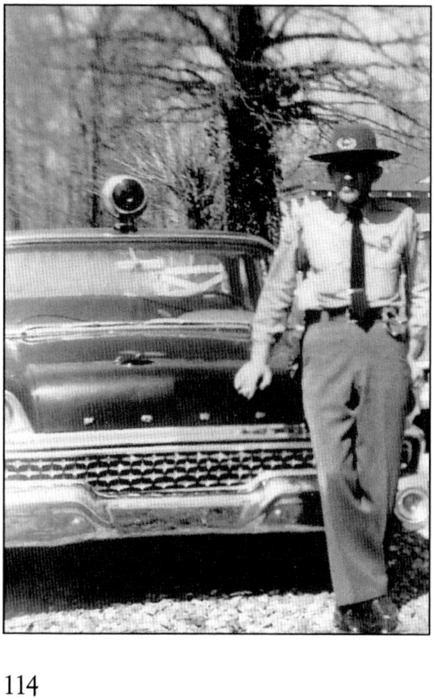

The Lionel Dane Melvin family moved to Pleasant Garden in 1950. He became a well-known North Carolina nurseryman who was one of the first to promote the use of native plants in home landscapes. A founding member of the North Carolina Wildflower Preservation Society, Melvin propagated and distributed a number of unusual forms of the state's native trees, shrubs, and wildflowers. Lucy Lambeth Melvin taught piano students in their home. This photograph was made around 1969. (Courtesy of Sandra Gray.)

The affable Alvis Bailey was respected by all. He was a barber when he came to the village; then he worked at the new Texaco before signing up as a deputy sheriff in the late 1950s. Posing by a squad car, he presents the image of a local Barney Fife. (Courtesy of Phillip Way.)

Six

The 1960s

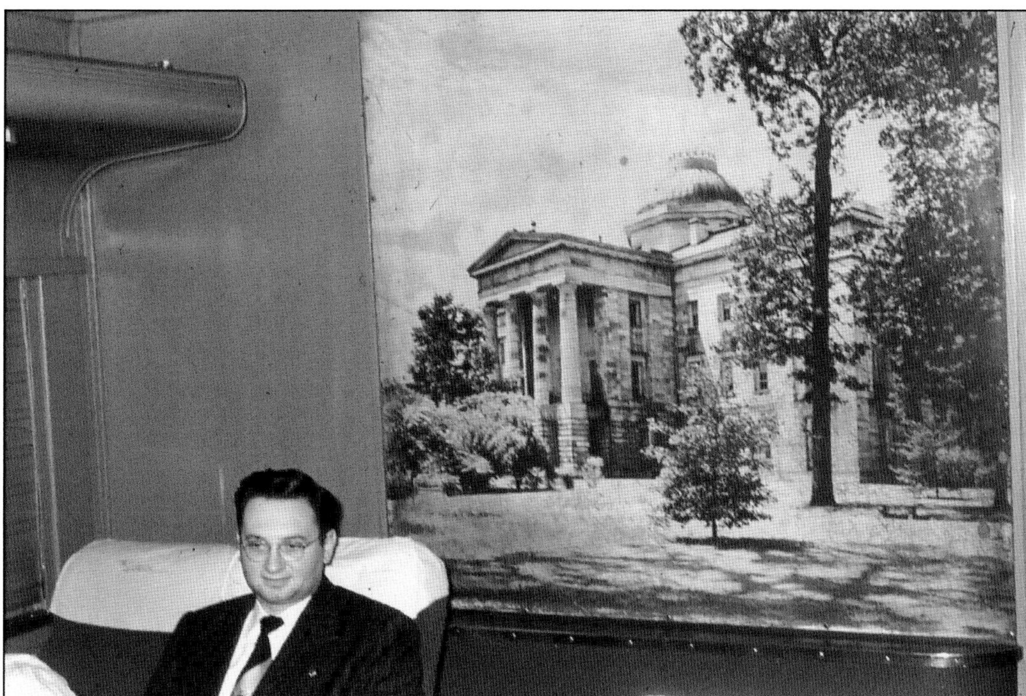

N.B. Cheek Jr. graduated from Pleasant Garden High School and Brevard Junior College. A student at the University of North Carolina when he entered the Army, Cheek served in a field hospital in England. When he returned home, he was at work in Cheek's Mercantile the next day. Cheek loved to travel and take photographs of daily life around the village. Many of his photographs that were passed on to others are in this book. He married Alma York and they operated two Bi-Rite Supermarkets.

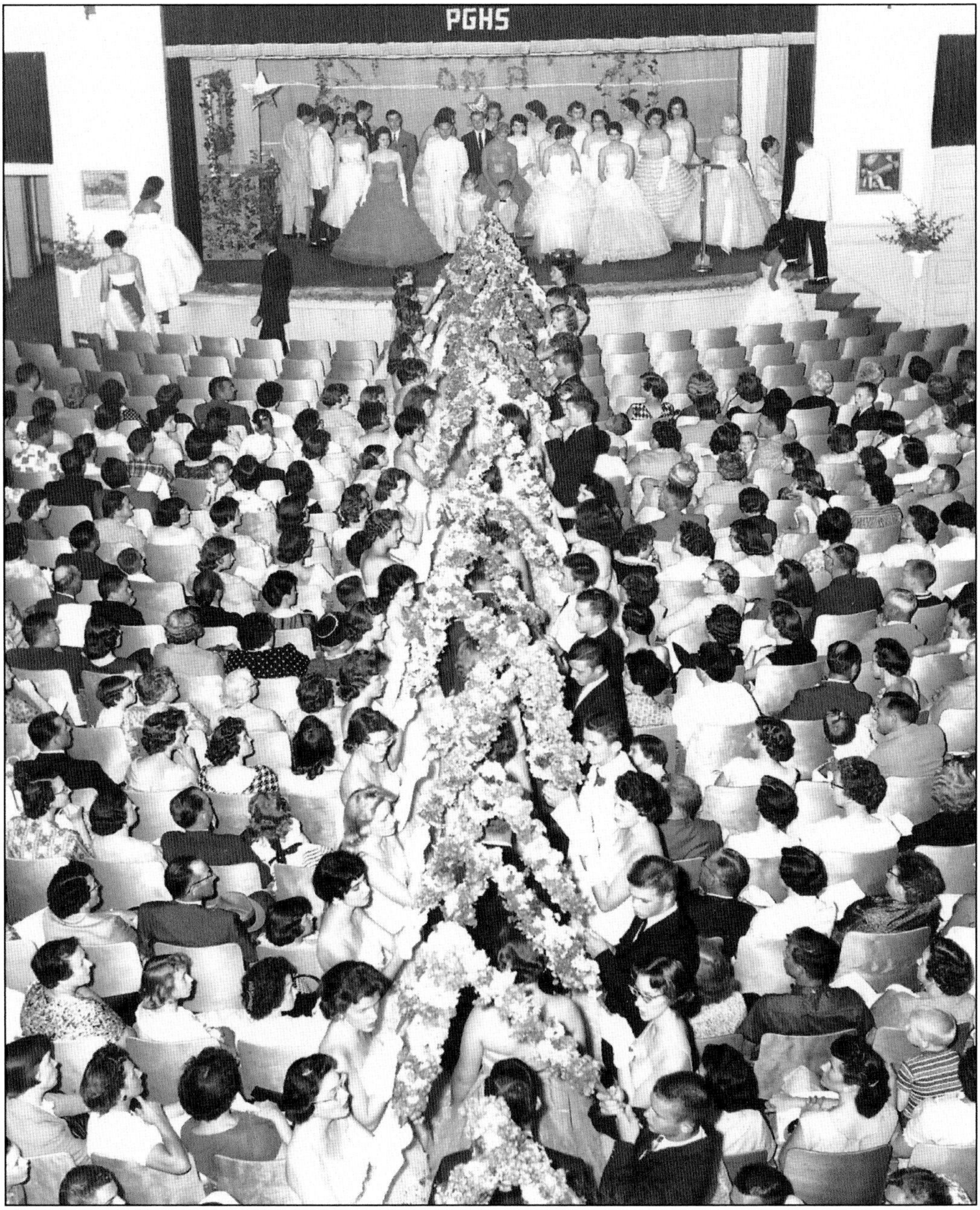

Presenting the graduating class with a daisy chain for Class Night was a long-standing tradition. The class of 1960 entered the auditorium under arches of flowers as juniors sang, "We love you dear Seniors." It took the underclassmen all day to gather assorted wildflowers to fashion garlands twice the length of the aisle. (Photograph by Worth Reynolds, courtesy of Judy Fields.)

Class Night was another occasion to wear the formal attire purchased for the junior-senior banquet. It was the seniors' night to shine. They performed skits and shared the class history, prophecy, and last wills and testaments. Clever token-gifts were presented to each class member. (Photograph by Worth Reynolds, courtesy of Judy Fields.)

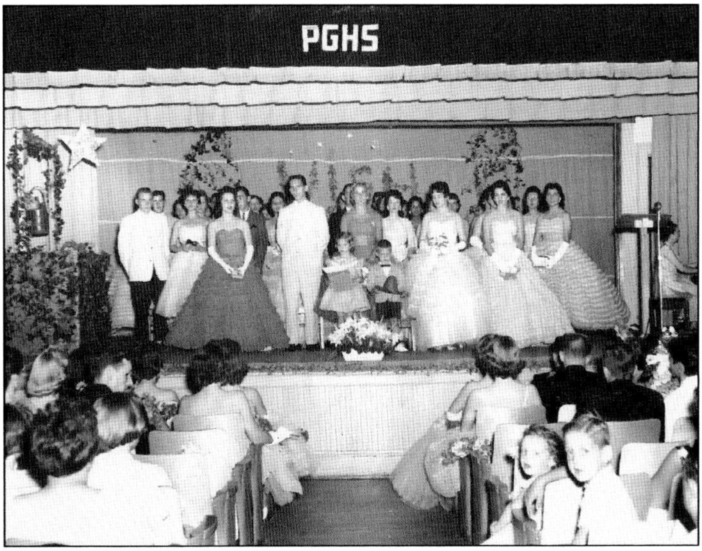

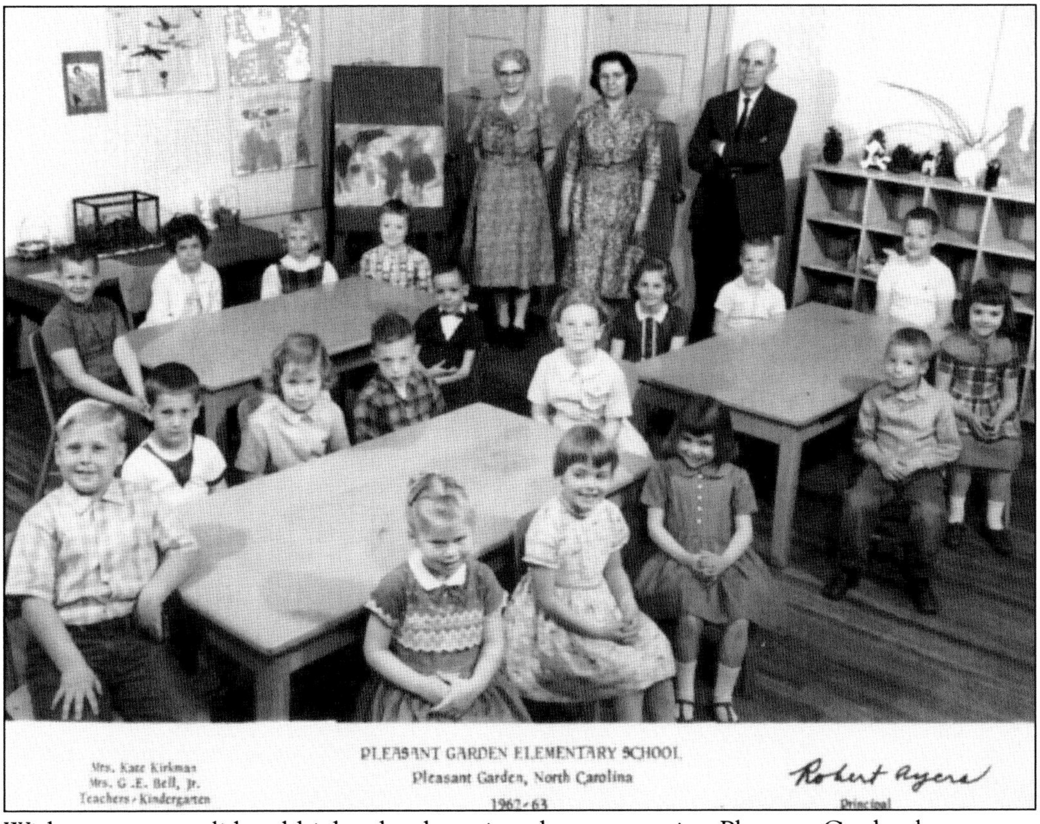

With a new consolidated high school serving the community, Pleasant Garden became an elementary school in the fall of 1962. A group of active parents found a way to use a vacant classroom and opened Pleasant Garden Kindergarten. It was an unprecedented collaboration, a private kindergarten in a public school. Shown standing in the back are Kate Hunt Kirkman (left), who came out of retirement to serve as the first teacher; Marie Bell, teaching assistant; and principal Robert Ayers.

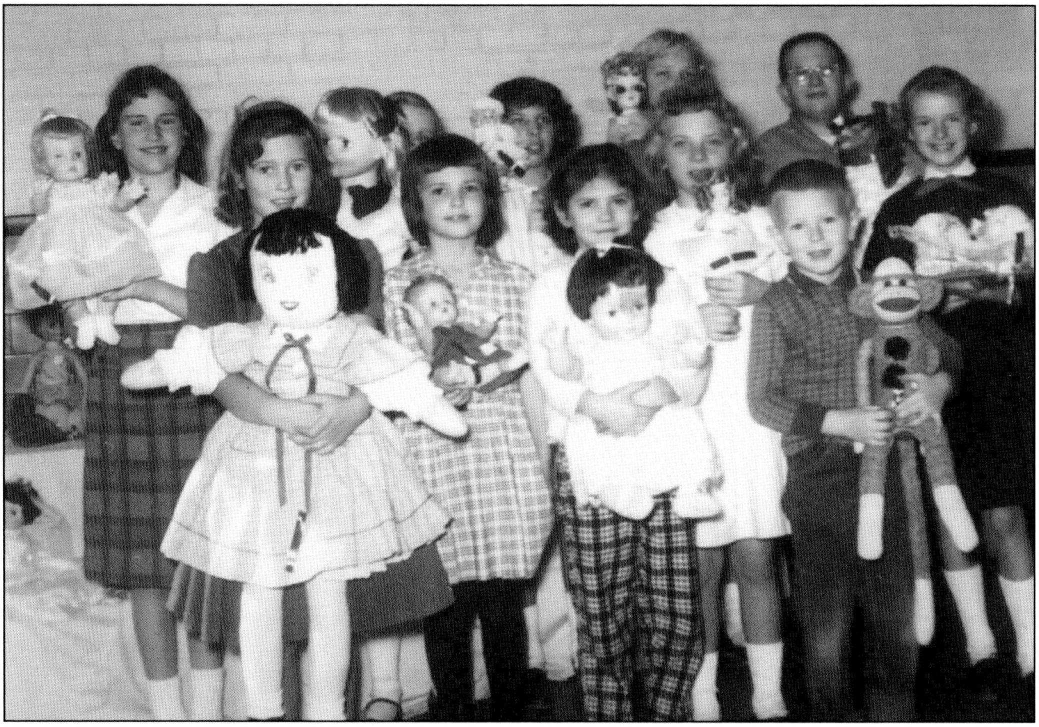

First-grade teachers at Pleasant Garden School were known for their innovative way to raise extra funds for school supplies. In the early 1960s, Della Dick, Mary Lee McLeod, and Kate Kirkman established the doll shows that became a January tradition. There were 250 entries, with blue ribbons awarded in 16 categories. Brenda Gardner had the oldest doll; Emily Ross, the smallest; and Billie Kay Yow, the largest.

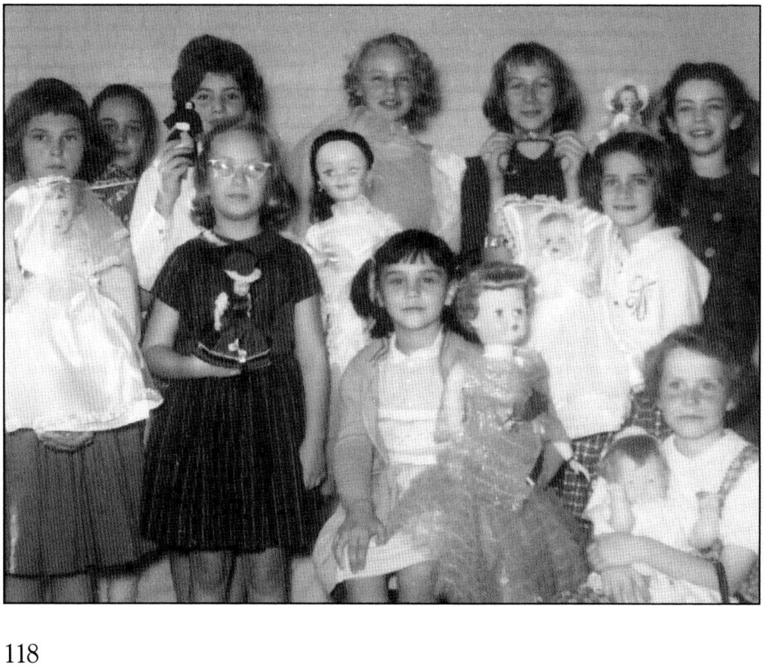

Some of the other winners were Cindy Haas for the prettiest character doll, Lindley Smith and Donna Smith for the prettiest stuffed animals, and Shirley Highfill and Suzanne Gray for the prettiest bride dolls. Amy Hecht was recognized for the most unusual doll clothes, and Doris Harris and Karen Harris had the prettiest handmade doll clothes. Margie Taylor is holding the prettiest big girl doll.

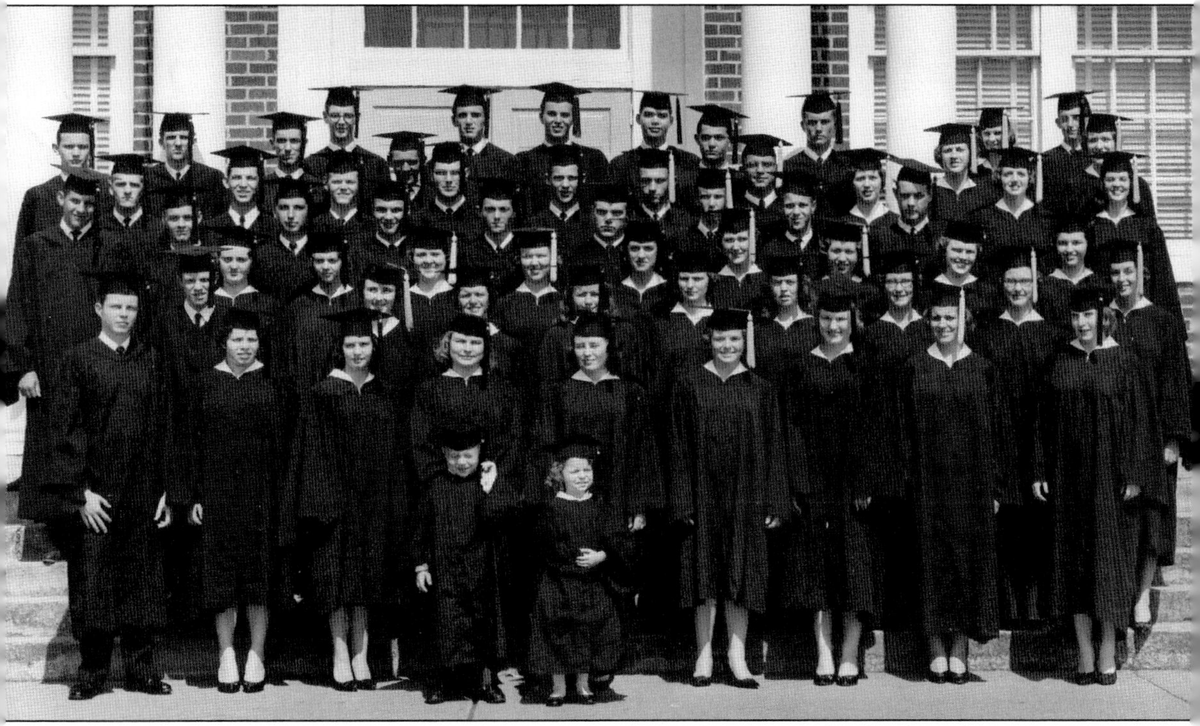

The class of 1962 was the last to graduate from Pleasant Garden High School. The following year, a consolidated Southeast Guilford High School welcomed grades 9 through 12. Pictured here, from left to right, are (first row) mascots Rodney Golden and Kathy Edwards; (second row) Douglas Graham, Carolyn Coble, Faye Norris, Gay Hinton, Nancy McCraw, Anne Kearns, Linda Rumley, Janet Vernon, and Ellen Wilson; (third row) Billy Coble, Linda Greene, Mary Knight, Margie Capps, Ellen Osborne, Katrine Marley, Marilyn Smith, Carolyn Smith, and Rebecca Vickery; (fourth row) Frances Fields, Margaret Allred, Joyce Fields, Brenda Baynes, Gail Wyrick, Carolyn Curtis, Linda Creed, Brenda Tucker, and Diane Garrett; (fifth row) Mike Edwards, John Gray, Ben Shaw, Robert Pine, Ronald Knight, Don Venable, Vinnon Williams, Keefer Pine, and Wesley Hall; (sixth row) Edwin Meyers, W.C. Shaw, Dan West, Joseph Kirkman, Gary Dunham, Randal Underwood, Roger Knight, Phyllis Ross, Barbara Coble, and Joann Carter; (seventh row) Marvin Taylor, Steve Vickery, Ronald Redding, Earl Fields, Vance Davis, Barbara Ross, and Anna Fields; (eighth row) Charles Collins, Ken McGinnis, Charles Smith, Steve Herndon, James Vickery, Kay Drake, and Erwin Underwood. (Courtesy of Anne Hice.)

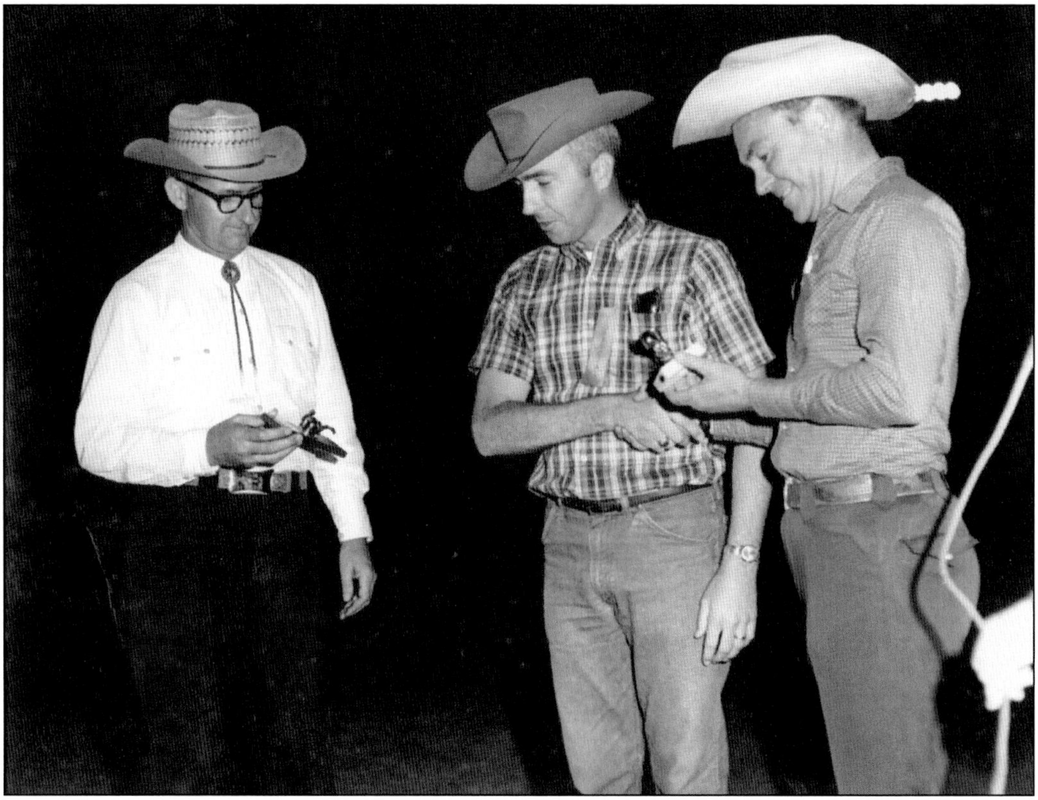

With plans to build a community center, John Hall suggested hosting a horse show to raise funds. By the second year (1964), this event had over 300 entries and was the largest single-day show in the state. The show was held at the school and the community center in 1965 and continued to be a revenue source for 14 years. That was the year Wayne Davis (left), Joe Davis (center), and Hall served as cochairmen of the Pleasant Garden Horse and Pony Show. (Courtesy of JoAnn Davis.)

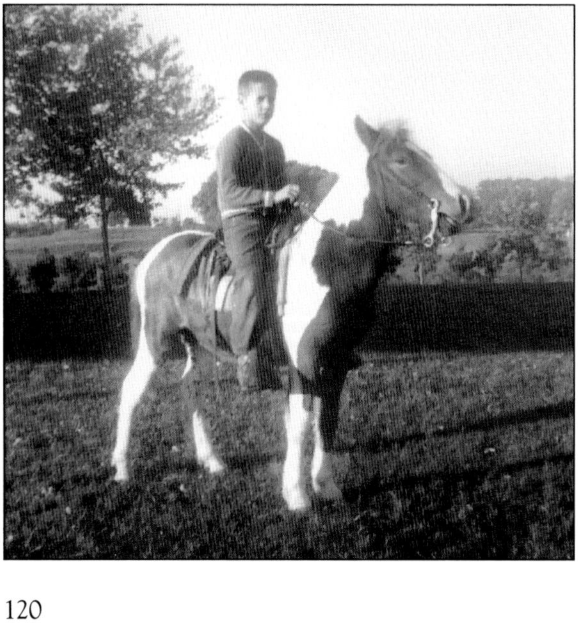

Mitchell Jones entered in the pony class. Now working as a farrier, Jones continues to spend his days around horses and works the show circuit in a different capacity. (Courtesy of Ruth Ann Jones.)

Drew Boren proudly displays the trophy he won in 1965. He was entered in the lead-line class that was open to children younger than six years old. (Courtesy of Martha Boren.)

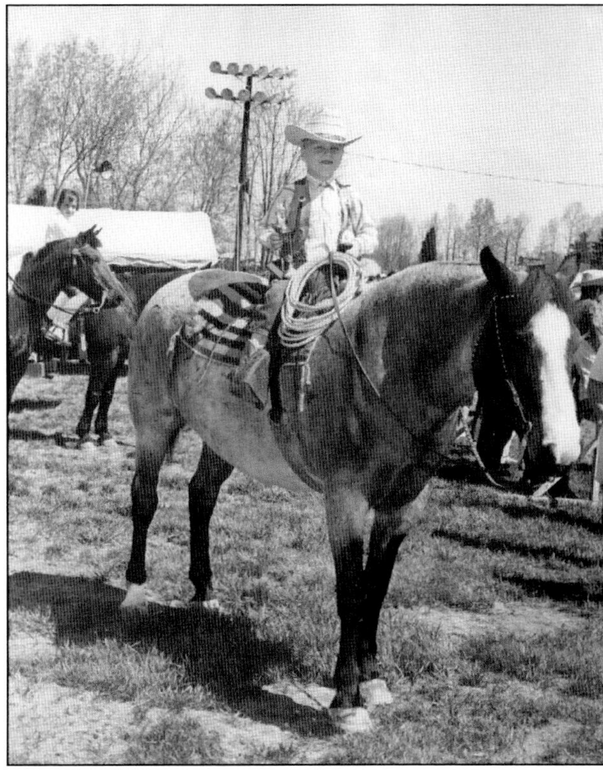

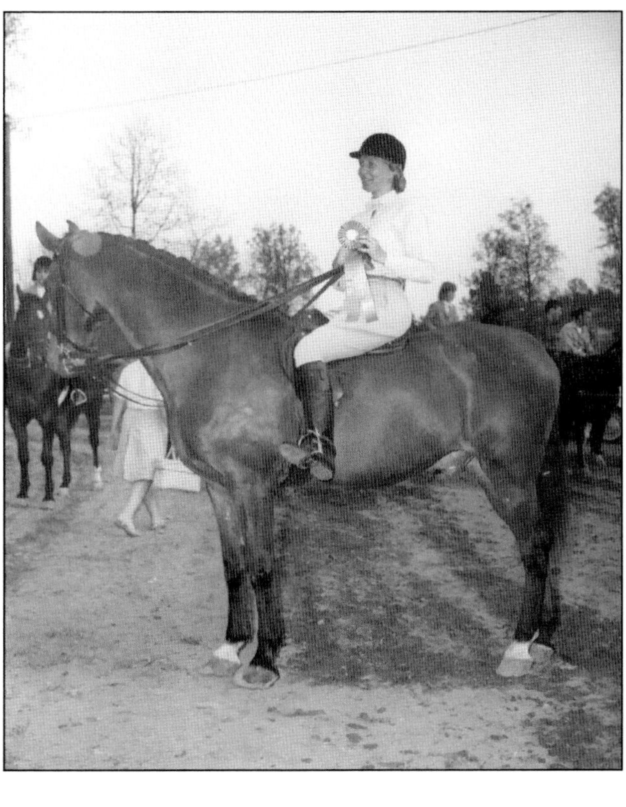

Martha Boren sits astride Tippy Tim, a bay she had ridden since she was a teenager. She captured the Open Pleasure Challenge Cup for the second time in 1964. (Courtesy of Martha Boren.)

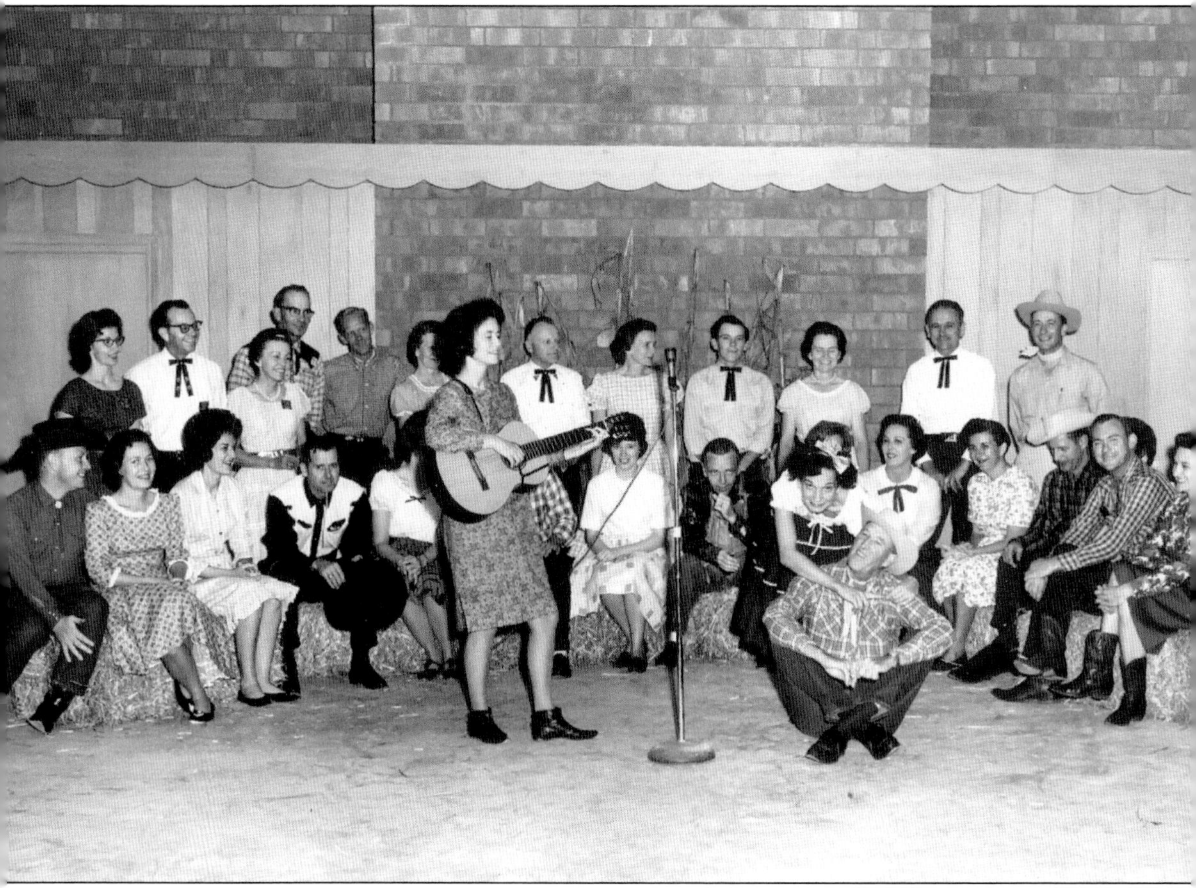

Around 1965 another community center fundraiser became a springtime tradition. It was the *Grand Ole Operetta*, a performance fashioned after the more famous Nashville show. This cast of local talent poses during a rehearsal inside the new building. Pictured are, from left to right, (in front) Sue Riley, Marian Pell, and Paul Sasser; (seated) Bill and Carmel Cheek, unidentified, Dick Anderson, two persons hidden, Jeannette Sasser, Fagg Nowlan, hidden person, Alleene Nall, Jane Pearce, Jack Hunt, and John and Frances Hall; (standing) Margie and Johnny Fields, Maureen and A.G. Toomes, Joe Gamble, Mable and Murphy Brown, Frances O'Conner, Ronald Stevens, Mary Lee and Richard Stevens, and Bill Barton. (Courtesy of Martha Boren.)

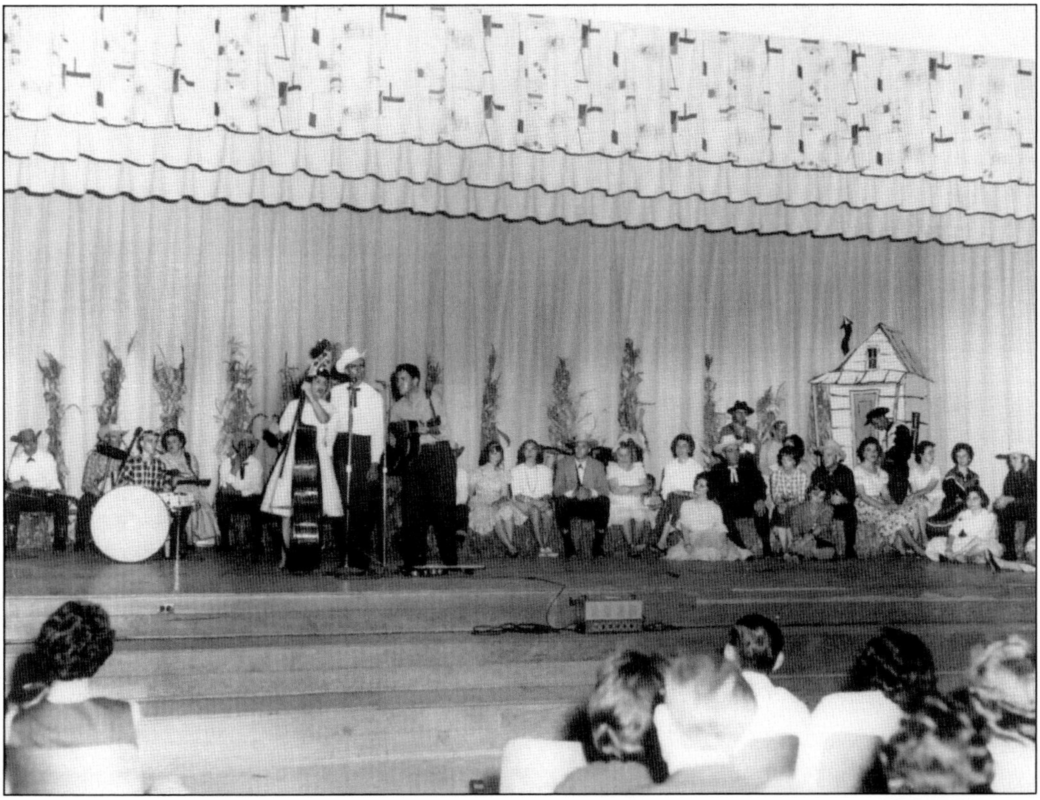

As the show's popularity grew, the production moved to the Southeast Guilford High School auditorium. Local radio celebrity Slim Martin is at the microphone with his wife, Wilma Arrington Martin, who is playing the bass. (Courtesy of Martha Boren.)

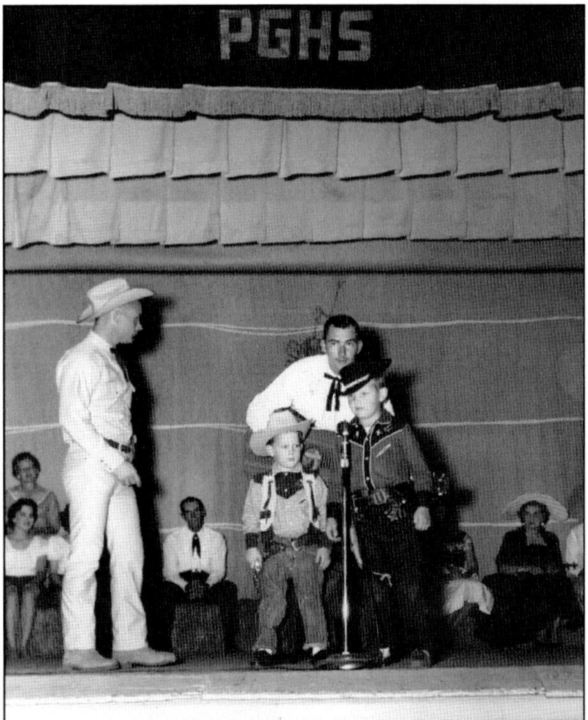

The young cowboys at the microphone are Gary Boren Jr. (left) and Ross Hunt, accompanied by Gilly Powell on guitar. Jim Boren Sr. is on the left. Hunt's mother, Sarah Kornegay Hunt, had the task of directing this eager group of amateurs. (Courtesy of Martha Boren.)

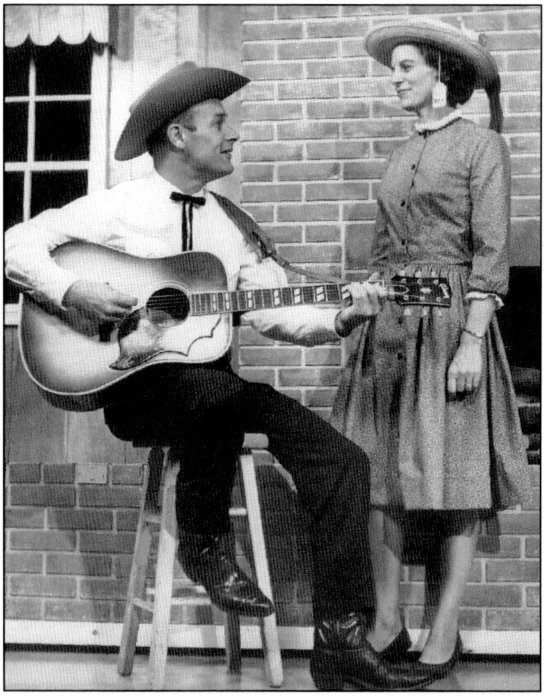

Jim Boren and Margaret Ross were among the local talent featured in the annual performance of the *Grand Ole Operetta*. In this photograph, he is the dashing cowboy guitar player and she is Maggie Pearl. (Courtesy of Martha Boren.)

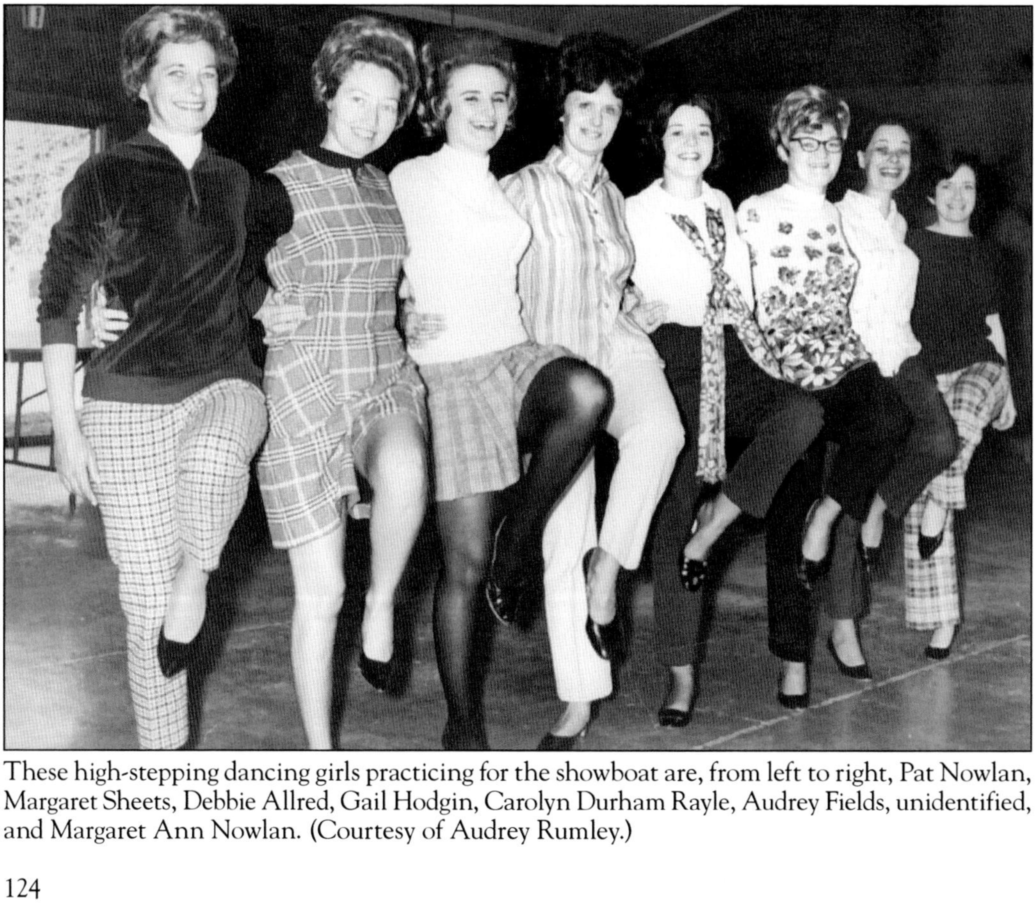

These high-stepping dancing girls practicing for the showboat are, from left to right, Pat Nowlan, Margaret Sheets, Debbie Allred, Gail Hodgin, Carolyn Durham Rayle, Audrey Fields, unidentified, and Margaret Ann Nowlan. (Courtesy of Audrey Rumley.)

Ismon Callicut, a master carpenter and builder, spent six years building the Grady and Robbie Dunn Siske house. It featured built-in furniture and radiant heat in the walls and floors. Dr. Siske is pictured mowing the acreage surrounding the ranch house built of Crab Orchard stone. (Courtesy of Phillip Way.)

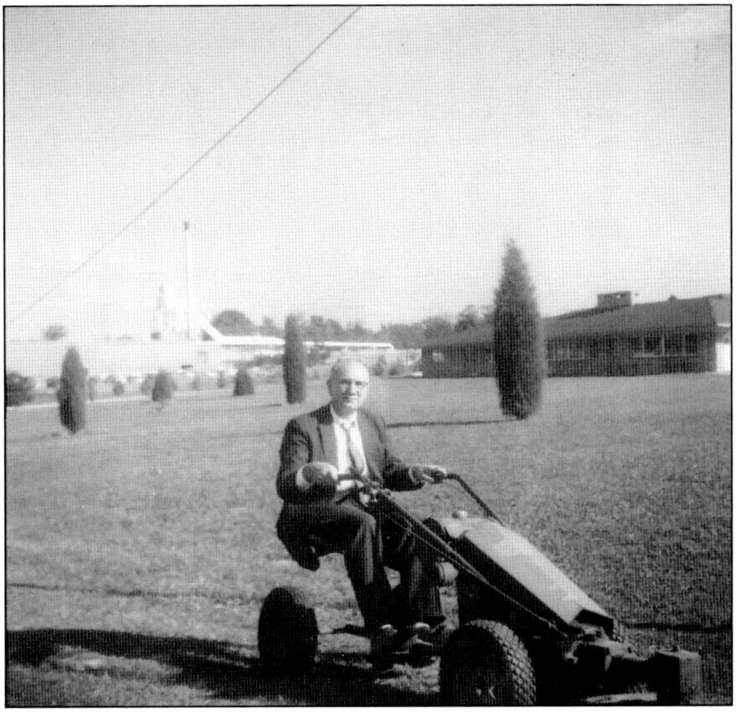

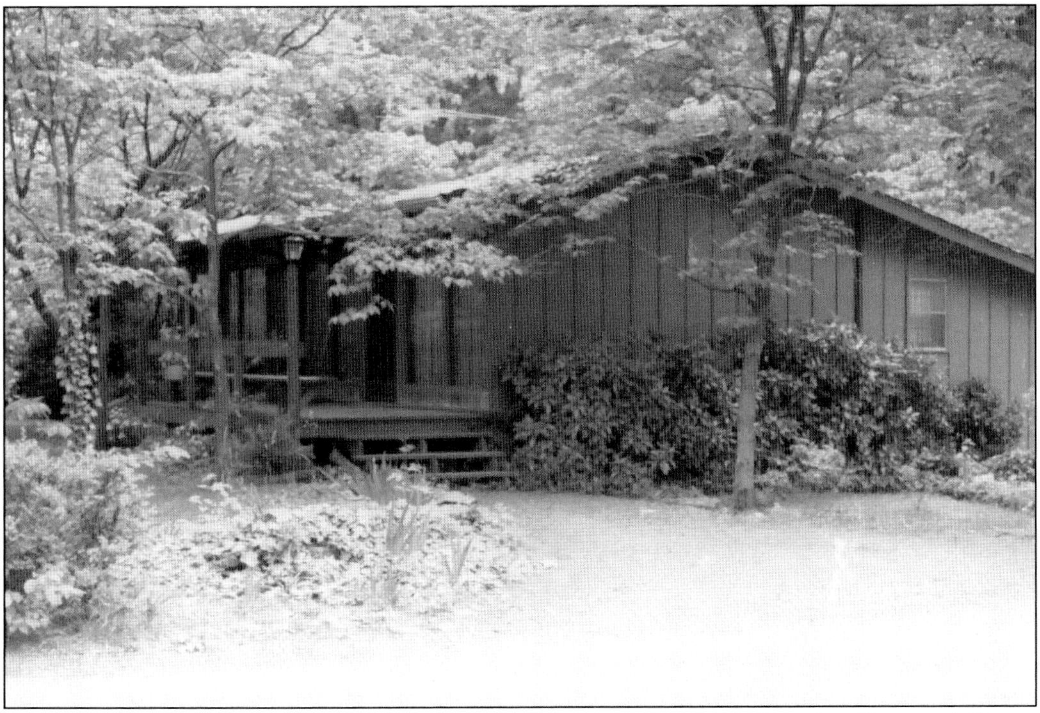

The house Lyle Dillon built in the 1960s with assistance from his father, Orville, was different from the typical ranch. It was a Sears house with a bank of windows across the front. There was at least one other Sears house in Pleasant Garden. It was built in 1923 by Lee and Etta Bowman Alexander. (Courtesy of Lyla White.)

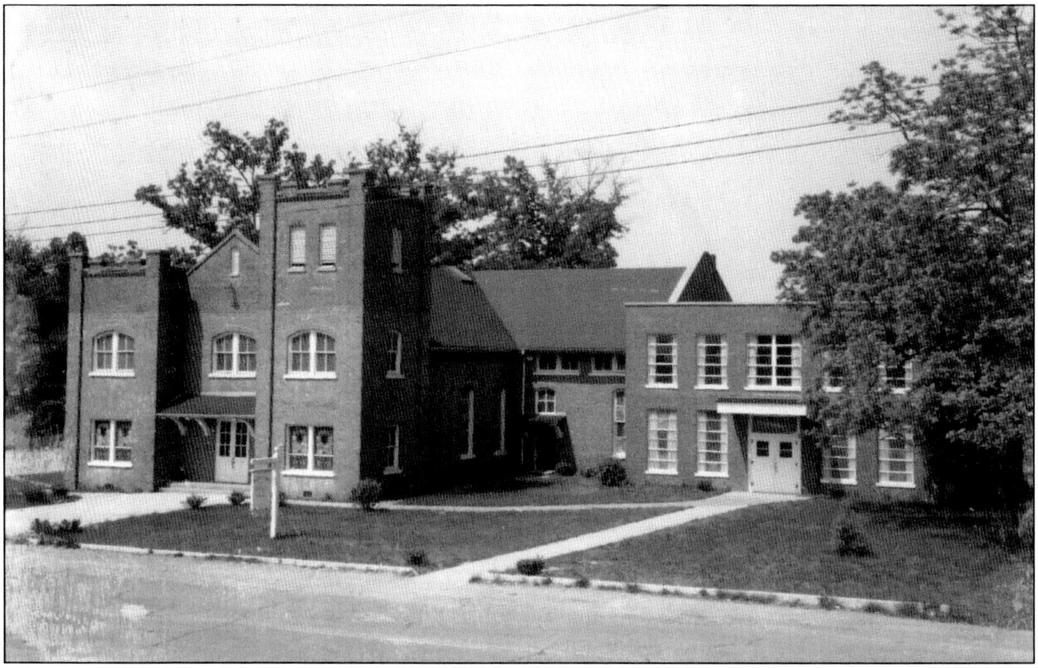

Pleasant Garden United Methodist Church is pictured here after the modern brick fellowship hall and classrooms were added in 1950. By 1963, plans were under way to build a new sanctuary to the right. When it was completed, the old sanctuary was removed. The fellowship hall remained for approximately 30 years.

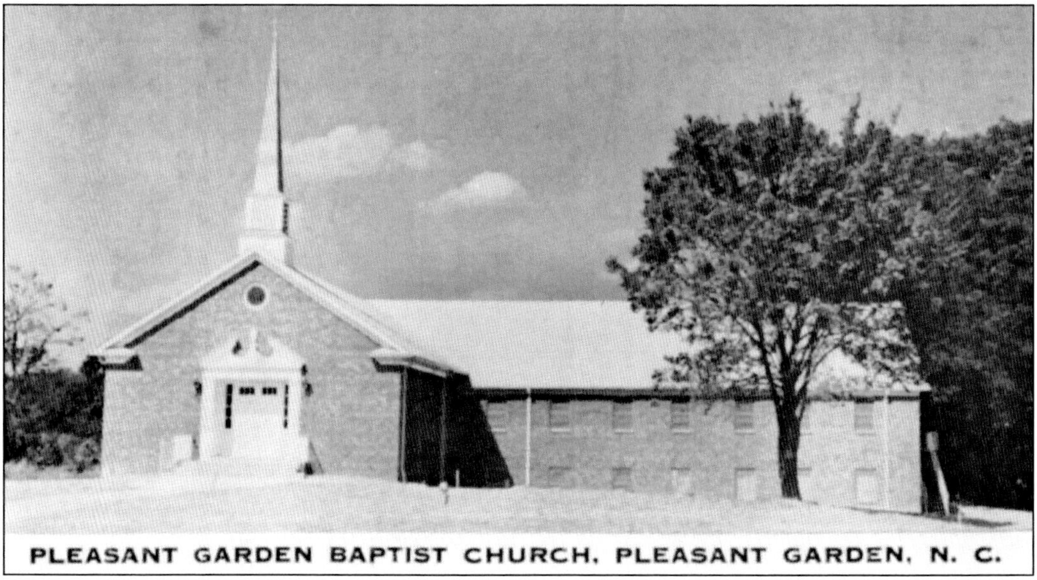

In the early 1930s, Pleasant Garden Baptist Church was organized with 17 members. The congregation bought the former Pleasant Garden Presbyterian Church from the Orange County Presbytery for $750 in 1938. Church membership doubled between 1955 and 1960 under the pastorate of Delano Suggs. When ground was broken for a new sanctuary and education wing across Neelley Road from the 1916 building, A.F. Dinsmore was chairman of the building committee. The $73,000 project was funded with church bonds. (Courtesy of Phillip Way.)

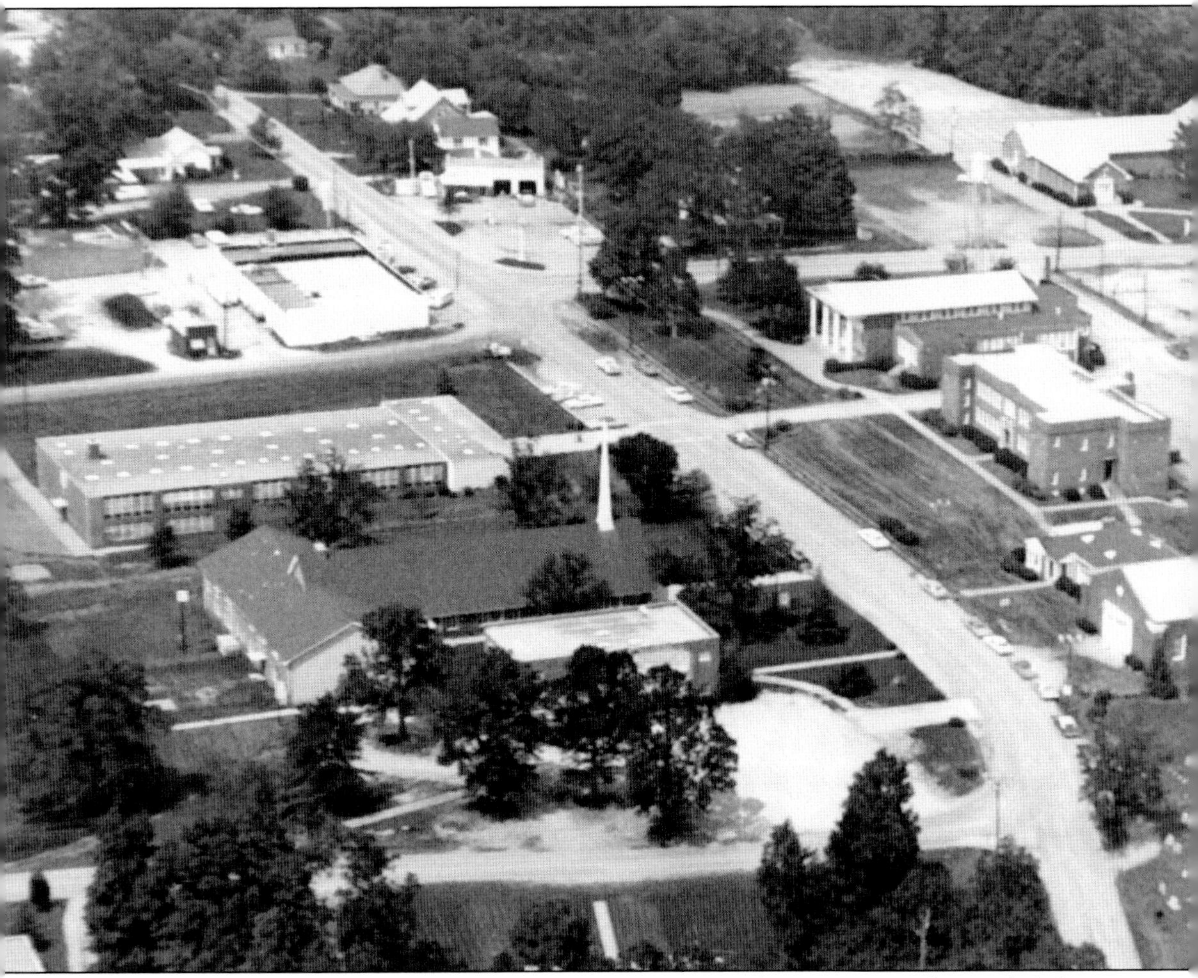

Phillip Way focused his camera on the heart of Pleasant Garden in 1969 and provided the viewer with a glimpse of how the town looked more than 50 years ago. Beginning at lower left is the new sanctuary of Pleasant Garden United Methodist Church; above it are the 1959 E.D. Idol Building, the supermarket, and the drugstore. To the right of the large Texaco is the 1960 Pleasant Garden Baptist Church. Three venerable Pleasant Garden High School buildings face Pleasant Garden Road. Once again, Jack Reddick was the pilot when this aerial image was taken. (Courtesy of Phillip Way.)